But What Is the Church *For*?

What Is the Mission of the Local Church?

Neil Darragh

WIPF & STOCK · Eugene, Oregon

BUT WHAT IS THE CHURCH *FOR*?
What Is the Mission of the Local Church?

Copyright © 2021 Neil Darragh. All rights reserved. Except for brief quotations in critical publications or reviews, no part of this book may be reproduced in any manner without prior written permission from the publisher. Write: Permissions, Wipf and Stock Publishers, 199 W. 8th Ave., Suite 3, Eugene, OR 97401.

Wipf & Stock
An Imprint of Wipf and Stock Publishers
199 W. 8th Ave., Suite 3
Eugene, OR 97401

www.wipfandstock.com

PAPERBACK ISBN: 978-1-6667-3291-7
HARDCOVER ISBN: 978-1-6667-2710-4
EBOOK ISBN: 978-1-6667-2711-1

11/15/21

Scripture quotations are from New Revised Standard Version Bible, copyright © 1989 National Council of the Churches of Christ in the United States of America. Used by permission. All rights reserved worldwide.

Contents

Part I: Perspectives | 1
    1. What Is the Church For? | 3
    2. Talking about Christianity in Public | 17
    3. The Realm of God | 28
    4. The Realm of God and Wellbeing | 41
    5. Contemporary Impact of the Realm of God | 52

Part II: Mission in Contemporary Society | 63
    6. Recent Mission Theologies | 65
    7. Dangerous Missions | 80
    8. Mission in a Secular Society | 89
    9. Secularization | 104

Part III: Mission in a Pluralist Society | 121
    10. Mission in a Pluralist Democracy | 123
    11. Strategies of Local Church Mission | 138
    12. A Local Theology of Mission | 152
    13. Self-Critique | 165
    14. The Next Step | 180

    Bibliography | 183

Part I

Perspectives

THIS BOOK SEEKS AN answer to the question: What is the church *for*? What is its purpose? What is its mission?

People become members of a Christian church and remain members of the church for a variety of reasons. For some, it is something integrated within their own traditional family life or their culture; it is already part of their identity. For others, membership in the church is a way of becoming closer to God, of maintaining contact with the divine, of becoming holier. For others it is the surest way to salvation, both in this world and especially in life after death. For others, it is a duty, something they are obliged to do by divine call or divine command. Others are attracted by the other people who belong to the church, by the way they relate to one another, or by their liturgy. Others are attracted by the church's teaching, its understanding of the world and of life's purpose.

These and, no doubt, many other motivations for belonging to the Christian church are personal ones. These are the things we get out of the church through our membership in it. These are what we might call the "benefits" of membership. Yet, while we might be grateful for these benefits, very few of us, I think, would regard these as an adequate statement of what the Christian church is *for*. If these personal benefits are all there is, it would make us simply "consumers" of holy "goodies." There is surely something more here, something more generous, life-giving, outgoing, and gracious than just our own spiritual wellbeing.

Nearly all Christians, I think, would agree with this. Certainly, nearly all missionaries, missiologists, and theologians would agree.

Part I: Perspectives

This book is a study in what would traditionally be called "missiology." As traditionally understood, missiology is concerned with the church's outreach beyond itself—the objectives and activities of the church *beyond* its benefits for those already its members. The church has benefits for its own members, of course, but it does not exist just for itself and its current members. It also has a purpose beyond itself, its *mission*.[1]

There is little debate today that what an investigator sees depends upon the standpoint of the investigator. Every investigation has a starting point that sets up a particular point of view on the subject of the investigation. An academic theologian's point of view is not likely to be that of an active missionary in the field; and an active missionary's point of view is not likely to be the same as that of the person who is the recipient of missionary activity. The choice of the starting point affects everything else that follows.

"Part I: Perspectives" of this book explains the starting point of this investigation. It also has a preliminary look at the language we use in talking and writing about mission. The traditional language that theologians commonly use among themselves doesn't quite work here because talking about "mission" is about the interface between church and society. Theological language that is commonly used in church and theological institutions needs to be adjusted so that it easily communicates outwards to the wider society and can itself absorb the wider society's communications inwards to the church. Moreover, there are some ideas, and the idea of "the realm of God" is one of these, which are central in this investigation and are best explained from the very start.

Part I, then, is intended to deal with these preliminary matters. Effectively, it sets out the approach to Christian mission adopted in this book.

---

1. Other terms such as "evangelization" or "outreach" are often used where I have used the term "mission." These terms are each a little different in meaning, but for most practical purposes and within the parameters of this book, they should be considered similar or at least overlapping. I do not normally use the term "evangelization" in this book except where quoting or paraphrasing someone else. This is partly because, within the Catholic Church, the term has come to mean almost everything, and so loses its capacity to pinpoint priorities. Partly, too, it is a neologism that is quite difficult to use both in local church discussions and in the public forum where, in my experience, it needs to be repeatedly explained. This is an issue of public communication which I address in the next chapter.

1

What Is the Church For?

THE PARTICULAR WAY WE approach mission, the *perspective* we adopt in the first place, is very important in any investigation into mission or church.[1]

The perspective on mission and church adopted in this book is best explained by calling attention to five distinct, but interrelated, strands in contemporary understandings of mission and church:

- God's mission,
- the missionary nature of the church,
- the distinction between the church and the realm of God,
- the question of *who* are missionaries, and
- the particular viewpoint of the *local* church.

This chapter proposes a point of view on each of these five strands.

God's Mission

The idea that the *church has a mission*, that is, that the church has a purpose, an outward objective to which church members are committed, is probably the most common understanding of the relationship between

1. At the beginning of this millennium, Indian Theologian Felix Wilfred called for a fresh approach to mission especially in the light of the challenges facing humanity and the possible role of religion. Wilfred, "A Vision for the New Century Role," 113. It seemed particularly important from an Indian perspective, and it is so also from my own perspective in Aotearoa New Zealand.

church and mission. It was the more common perspective among theologians and missiologists for several centuries up until the mid-twentieth century and it remains common among church members today.

The idea that the *mission has a church* is less common and is perhaps clearer when expanded to the following: *God has a mission in the world and the church is one of the means by which that mission is carried out.* In this sense, mission is God's action in the world and this mission then has a church (a community of believers) which is called to play an important role (we think) in that action. In this case, the priority is placed firmly on *mission*, that is, God's action in the world. The *church* comes subsequently and its nature results from the role it is expected to play in God's mission. The emphasis on God's mission within which the church has a part to play, rather than the idea that the church itself has a mission in the world in its own right, so to speak, was an important shift in mission thinking in the mid-twentieth century for both Protestants and Catholics.

In Protestant mission theology, this shift in emphasis is usually dated back to the International Missionary Council meeting in Willingen, West Germany, in 1952. It was this council that re-conceptualized mission as primarily the mission of God (*"missio Dei"*). This was a fundamental shift from an understanding of the church continuing the mission of Christ in the world (a Christology-based mission) to a Trinitarian-based understanding of God's mission in the world in which the church is called to participate.[2]

The concept of *"missio Dei"* is very common in mission theology today. Yet it has been given a variety of interpretations. The mission of the church could in fact become opposed to God's mission. This could be the case, for instance, if a church body decided to use mission illegitimately to further its own institutional interests or merely to bolster membership rolls.[3] Some interpretations of the "mission of God" laid emphasis on the sending of the Son by the Father without equal emphasis on the role of the Spirit, while Pentecostal mission theologies more commonly emphasized the role of the Spirit. In other interpretations, God's mission has been identified with God's action in *human history* but divorced from God's activity in the *wider creation*. Other interpretations, while understanding mission as fundamentally God's mission, have in fact made the

---

2. For an overview of this shift, see Van Gelder, "The Future of the Discipline of Missiology," 13. See also the earlier Hoffmeyer, "The Missional Trinity," 108–11.

3. Skreslet, *Comprehending Mission*, 31–35.

church the *sole agent* of it, while others by contrast have interpreted God's mission so broadly that it had little or *no reference to the church*.⁴

Perhaps the key point to note, as North American missiologist Charles Van Engen has observed, is that after its Fourth Assembly in Uppsala in 1968, "*missio Dei*" was used in the World Council of Churches' circles to emphasize that God is at work in the world anyway and the best the church can do is to join the movements of what God is doing in the world. This change from the classical idea of God working through the church to reach the world had profound and far-reaching effect on the mission theology of the people associated with the World Council of Churches.⁵

In Catholic mission theology, the Second Vatican Council (1962–65) similarly adopted the view that mission is first and foremost God's own work. God's Spirit calls people into service for mission. The church was born out of God's mission and it is in the light of that mission that the church has to be understood. Again, this mission is seen as Trinitarian; it proceeds from the Father through the Son and is carried forward by the Holy Spirit.⁶

In this book, my focus is on the part the church may play in the deeper and broader reality of *God's* (Trinitarian) mission in the world. This has a number of implications for our understanding of the church. These implications will occupy me more fully in the later chapters. In the meantime, we can note briefly just three of these implications.

One of these is that opting for this focus will lead us to give more importance to the church's *mission* than to the church itself. This means giving more attention and energy to what the church is doing in the world than to more self-focused issues within the church itself such as good community or good liturgy or good Christian education when these lack a clear outward focus towards God's actions in the wider world.

A second implication is that the *actual* church's mission—the one lived out in action more than simply talked about—might not always correspond with God's mission. The church therefore needs to continually

---

4. See for example the critical comments of Duraisingh, "From Church-Shaped Mission to Mission-Shaped Church," 14–15.

5. Van Engen, "Towards a Missiology of Transformation," 18. See also Kim, "Mission in the Twenty-First Century," 352–54. For critical commentary on the variety of interpretations of "missio Dei" see Heikkilä, "The World Council of Churches' Mission Statement," 78–88.

6. Second Vatican Council, *Dogmatic Constitution on the Church*; and Second Vatican Council, *Decree on the Missionary Activity of the Church*.

self-critique its missionary activities to ensure that they are in fact a participation in *God's* mission rather than some aberrant undertaking of fallible church enthusiasts.

A third implication is a warning. The idea that our missionary efforts are really those of God rather than of a church made up of human beings may lead too simply to the idea that whatever we are doing in good faith is God's work and God will give it success. It may thus support *self-promotional* and *self-reinforcing* mistakes and prejudices, provoking the kind of criticism of missionaries that has been expressed in post-colonial literature over the last few decades and too often validated in practice.[7]

The Missionary Nature of the Church

A second fundamental difference in perspective on mission and church lies in the difference between a church whose *very identity* is missionary and a church which sends out missionaries as *one of its several activities*. Common images of the church today such as "the body of Christ," "the family of God," the "temple of God," or as "communion" suggest a church already established in its own right which then sends some of its members out on mission. This is quite a different perspective from one that sees the church as constituted in the first place by is missionary activity.

The Second Vatican Council's *Decree on the Missionary Activity of the Church: Ad Gentes* (1965) is clear that "the pilgrim church is missionary by her very nature, since it is from the mission of the Son and the mission of the Holy Spirit that she draws her origin, in accordance with the decree of God the Father."[8] The idea of the missionary nature of the church is a strong theme, not just in the *Decree on the Missionary Activity of the Church*, but is pervasive throughout Council documents.[9]

---

7. Among others, see Scott, "Missions in Fiction," 121–25. Consider also the commentary in Price, "Popular Notions of the Missionary Task," 245–57. Similarly in films, Scott, "Missions and Film," 115–20.

8. Second Vatican Council, *Decree on the Missionary Activity of the Church*, #2. We should take note, however, of Stephen Bevans's observation that there is some ambiguity in the documents of the Second Vatican Council about the *location* of mission. The Second Vatican Council's *Decree on the Missionary Activity of the Church*, especially after chapter 1, seems still to have in its imagination the white "First World" missionary working in exotic lands and cultures. Bevans, "Revisiting Mission," 273–74.

9. The recurrence of this theme is detailed in Bevans, "Revisiting Mission," 283.

In the period between the Second Vatican Council and today, the belief in the missionary nature of the church has been repeated with further elaboration in major papal documents on mission, notably Pope Paul VI's *Evangelii Nuntiandi: Evangelization in the Modern World* (1975),[10] Pope John Paul II's *Redemptoris Missio: On the Permanent Validity of the Church's Missionary Mandate* (1991),[11] and especially in Pope Francis's *Evangelii Gaudium: The Joy of the Gospel* (2015)[12] with its appeal for an evangelizing church involving all church members that reaches out for the good of the whole society, rather than a church concerned for itself.[13]

In Orthodox theology, the document on mission of the Holy and Great Council of the Orthodox Church held in Kolymbari, Crete, in 2016 placed a major emphasis on mission, motivating Orthodox Christians to proclaim the faith and diaconally serve humanity.[14]

In recent decades, the idea of a "missional church" has engaged the thinking of Evangelical and Protestant theologians, perhaps more than that of Catholic theologians. The "missional church" became an important missionary emphasis in Britain through the "Gospel and Our Culture Programme" in the 1980s.[15] This idea later spread and developed in North America as the "missional church" conversation.[16] A missional church is

---

10. Paul VI, *Evangelii Nuntiandi*.

11. John Paul II, *Redemptoris Missio*.

12. Francis, *Evanglii Gaudium*. William P. Gregory summarizes the distinctive features of Pope Francis's teaching on mission in Gregory, "Pope Francis's Effort to Revitalize Catholic Mission," 7–19. And for a more personalized summary of Pope Francis's mission attitudes, see Motte, "Signs of a Future Transformation," 30–37.

13. Papal statements explicitly and substantially dealing with the church's mission date from Benedict XV's 1919 encyclical letter, *Maximum Illud* (1919) through to Francis's exhortation, *Evangelii Gaudium* (2013). The rationale for mission activity as presented in these papal statements is discussed in Patterson, "What Has Eschatology to Do with the Gospel?" 285–99. For a quick overview of changes in official Catholic approaches to mission as a result of both theological and demographic changes, see Connolly and Lucas, "A Theological Reflection on the *Missio Ad Gentes*," 411–20.

14. Holy and Great Council of the Orthodox Church, "The Mission of the Orthodox Church." For an interpretation of this document, see Voulgaraki-Pissina, "Reading the Document," 136–50.

15. Usually considered to have originated in the writings of Lesslie Newbigin, especially his *The Gospel in a Pluralist Society*. See the discussion of Newbigin's views on the witness of the local church and cultural engagement in Robinson, "Witness, the Church, and Faithful Cultural Engagement," 140–52. See also the testing of Newbigin's idea of the congregation as a hermeneutic of the gospel in Cronshaw and Taylor, "The Congregation in a Pluralist Society," 206–28.

16. For a history of the term "missional church," see Missional Church Network,

one that does not just send missionaries as one of its many activities but one whose very identity as a church is "missional."[17] A 2004 report of the Church of England's Mission and Public Affairs Council summarized the issue acutely when it said, "It is therefore of the essence (the DNA) of the church to be a missionary community. There is church because there is mission, not vice versa."[18] The term "missional," rather than simply a synonym for "missionary," was intended to shift the emphasis from the idea of the church in Europe and North America sending missionaries for the extension of Christianity around the world to the idea of a church facing the challenge of the conversion of their own European and North American post-Christendom culture.[19]

In this book, I adopt the perspective that the church is missionary by its very nature; that it is the missionary activity which creates the church rather than an already formed church which then engages in missionary activities. One of the important implications of this for a study of church and mission is that we would expect the missionary activities of a church to be substantial, clearly formulated, and a major influence on all other church activities, such as liturgy, community life, ministry structure, pastoral care, governance, education, and financial administration. Where this is not so, there are clear indications of a need for reform of the church itself.

The Distinction between the Church and the Realm of God

A third fundamental difference in perspective on mission and church lies in whether we identify the church with the realm of God or maintain a difference between them. In this study I shall use the term "realm of God" as a substitute for the more common "reign of God" or "kingdom of God" as an English translation of the Greek "*basileia tou theou*." There are reasons for and against such a translation. I shall consider these in the next chapter. For the meantime, when I use the term "realm of God," I do not intend anything substantially different (though the contemporary

---

"History of Missional Church."

17. For a summary and assessment of the idea of "missional" churches, see Richardson, "Emerging Missional Movements," 131.

18. Church of England's Mission and Public Affairs Council, "Mission-Shaped Church," 85.

19. Marshall, "A Missional Ecclesiology," 5–21.

implications and impact are different) from what many other writers intend by the English translation "reign of God" or "kingdom of God" or "kingdom of heaven."

If the "church" and the "realm of God" are regarded as virtually *identical*, then the missionary activity of the church needs to concentrate on bringing people into the church and making sure that this church resembles as closely as possible what Christ intended when he proclaimed the realm of God.[20] If, on the other hand, the realm of God as proclaimed by Christ is meant for *all* people and is much wider than the community of Christ's disciples who constitute the church, then the church is here to serve this coming realm of God for the benefit of all people whether or not they become members of the church.

This distinction between the "church" and the "reign of God which it serves" was developed following the Second Vatican Council in Pope Paul VI's exhortation *Evangelii Nuntiandi: Evangelization in the Modern World* (1975). Pope John Paul II's encyclical *Redemptoris Missio: On the Permanent Validity of the Church's Missionary Mandate* (1991) similarly maintains this distinction between the church and the reign of God but develops further the connection between them: the church is "seed, sign and instrument" of the Reign of God; the church's existence is not for itself, it exists for another reason, to be the sacrament of God's presence already revealed in Christ.[21] Pope Francis's *Evangelii Gaudium: The Joy of the Gospel* (2013) focuses on the term "evangelization" rather than the "kingdom of God" but states simply, "to evangelize is to make the kingdom of God present in our world."[22]

While this distinction and relationship between the church and the realm of God has been promoted by official church documents for some time, it is not commonly put into practice in local Catholic communities nor, it would appear, is it widely held by pastors in Catholic parishes. It is nevertheless commonly recognized by Catholic theologians. Thus, German theologian Walter Kasper, in his book on the nature of the Catholic

---

20. Some evangelical theologians regard the church and the kingdom as for all intents and purposes the same. North American evangelical Scot McKnight, for example, maintains that Christ came to build the church/kingdom, not to make the world a better place and not for the "common good." Nevertheless, he writes, a Christian does engage in public "good works" as a "spillover" from a loving Christian community of good deeds. McKnight, *Kingdom Conspiracy*, 206–08.

21. John Paul II, *Redemptoris Missio*, #2. See also Stephen Bevans's discussion of these documents in Bevans, "Mission as the Nature of the Church," 188–89.

22. Francis, *Evanglii Gaudium*, #176.

Church: "The goal of mission is only indirectly the Church and the spreading of the Church. Its purpose is first and foremost to proclaim the kingdom of God that has come with Jesus Christ and that is now breaking through in the Church through the Holy Spirit. It is about the petition in the Lord's Prayer: 'hallowed be your name, your kingdom come!'"[23]

The important implication of this distinction between the church and the realm of God is that the church's mission is no longer *primarily* about attracting people to become members of the church. It is *primarily* about working within society at large so that society itself becomes more like the realm of God for all people, not just for church members.[24] This requires a change of attitude among those church leaders who have previously understood their role as the pastoral care of church members and the conversion of nonbelievers. It requires rather an attitude that is focused on service to the realm of God in the world, a much larger reality than the church itself.[25]

In this book, I adopt the view that there is a relatively clear distinction between the church (community of believers) and the realm of God (kingdom of God, reign of God, kingdom of heaven) as we find it in the Gospels. The "church" is the community of the disciples of Christ. The "realm of God" is God's hope for the whole world—a much bigger reality than the church. The church is *for* the realm of God. This is its mission in the sense that its purpose is to participate actively in God's mission in the world.

Who Are Missionaries?

A fourth fundamental difference in perspective lies in the issue of whom we regard as "missionaries." For many centuries, mission activity was

---

23. Kasper, *The Catholic Church*, 292. Similarly, Ormerod, *Re-Visioning the Church*, 103.

24. By way of contrast, this appears to be a radically different approach from that of German missiologist Henning Wrogemann, who is clear that the goal of mission is not first and foremost to found churches, to bear witness in the field of social ethics, to achieve numerical growth, to propagate a *social gospel*, to establish a *missionary presence*, or to engage in *power encounters*. "Rather, mission has to do with *imparting a doxological impulse with a broad ecumenical impact, one that permeates the household of the entire creation (oikos).*" Wrogemann, *Intercultural Theology*, 381. Yet the issue here is that of "first and foremost," and once the implications of "doxological impulse" are spelt out the difference may not be so great.

25. Gerard Goldman presents a concise and accessible summary of what a kingdom-of-God centered church might look like in today's world in Goldman, "Church," 3–9.

strongly associated with *foreign* missions conducted by people designated specifically for this purpose, albeit with support from the missionaries' home churches or mission societies. These "missionaries" were regarded as distinct from the larger number of church members who participate in the church itself without special outreach except to the extent that they were all expected to be witnesses to Christ in their daily lives.

A characteristic of the more evangelical churches is that they do commonly regard all their members as missionaries. The "missional church" movement noted above called all their members to be missionary, often in the sense of calling people to be disciples of Christ but also in service of the realm of God in the wider society. The "basic Christian communities" of the Catholic Church, particularly in Latin America, are also "missionary," though not often called that, in the sense of working for social justice in the wider society. Yet this still leaves most of the members of the mainstream churches, those people we might call "ordinary parishioners," who do not see themselves as "ordinary missionaries." This is partly a question of language. Many church members see themselves as committed to social justice, i.e., serving the realm of God in the wider world, even though they may not see this as specifically a "mission," nor do they see themselves as "missionaries."[26]

Writing out of a North American Protestant tradition, Craig van Gelder identifies the idea that *every location is a mission location* (missions are not just in other countries or other cultures) as one of the critical changes in how North American Christians understand and participate in the mission of God in the world. In van Gelder's view, the most fundamental, and largely unattended, question for North American Christians is the relationship between the gospel and North American culture.[27]

A central theme of Pope Francis's exhortation, *Evangelii Gaudium: The Joy of the Gospel* (2013), is that "we are all missionary disciples."[28] The responsibility of working for the unfolding realm of God in the world is not first and foremost a special responsibility of specially delegated ministers, priests, vowed religious, or missionary societies. It is the vocation of all Christians.

---

26. Paul Lakeland was not alone in claiming early in this century that the "lay" vocation is responsible for working for a more fully human world and for commitment to the process of unfolding human freedom. Lakeland, *The Liberation of the Laity*. 184.

27. Van Gelder, "The Future of the Discipline of Missiology," 11, 15.

28. Francis, *Evanglii Gaudium*, esp. #111–34.

In this book, I adopt the perspective that all members of the church are in principle missionaries. The disciples of Christ and their communities are then "missionary" by baptismal commitment. Mission is not something that belongs to particular ministries or to those specially delegated for it.

An important implication of this perspective is that most missionaries in this sense are engaged in mission *in their own society*, i.e., most are not travelers to foreign countries or other cultures. Those who do travel to foreign countries are a minority who need special consideration, but our rethinking of mission and church needs to have a rekindled focus on the *majority* mission which takes place within the society in which a local church is itself embedded.

Perspective of the Local Church

A fifth fundamental difference in perspective derives from *whose* point of view the investigation is undertaken, and more specifically here, whether the point of view is that of a local church or of some group of people whose relationship to locality is unspecified.

The key feature of a "local church" or "local community," as I use these terms here, is that the community meets as a liturgical assembly with some frequency (weekly for example), and they have an agreed way (a social structure) of making common decisions and common policies. For the most part, as I envisage it, these will be parishes, ethnic communities, basic ecclesial communities, new emerging communities, "fresh expressions" of church, or communities of similar scale and relationship to place. North American parish priest and missiologist Robert S. Rivers, revitalizing an old but seldom practiced parish movement from "maintenance" to "mission," argues that the parish is where the vision and plan for evangelization become real.[29]

We could add to this that it is the local church too that can revitalize a neighborhood, and be itself revitalized, amidst the mass movements of migrants and refugees today.[30] A key feature of the "local" church is that it, in principle, includes any believer who lives within that locality. It is a theological equivalent of an "ecosystem," but an ecosystem which

---

29. Rivers, *From Maintenance to Mission*, 151.

30. For an example of mission initiatives in local churches in Toronto, see Nacpil, "The Church in the Twenty-First-Century Diaspora," 68–75.

in many cases today is constantly crossed by "biological corridors." It is composed not just of long-term residents but is frequently changed in its composition and style of living by travelers, migrants, refugees, and asylum seekers, all of whom can claim it as their own. The common modern phenomenon of migrancy is often experienced quite intensely within the life of local churches.[31]

Missiological writing sometimes does not specify its point of view or its standing point and this can, by default, appear to be some "objective" or universally valid viewpoint. The only universally valid viewpoint would be that of God. But this it certainly is not. A local church point of view is unlikely to have the same concerns or priorities as that of an international missionary society, a central denominational authority, a papal document, or an academic theologian. Moreover, the mission perspective of a local church in Southern Africa is different from that of Northern Europe; the mission perspective of a Pacific island is different from that of a local church in a valley in the mountains of New Guinea.

A local missiology, moreover, has a natural affinity with what North American missiologist B. Hunter Farrell calls an "activist missiology," which seeks to overcome the academy-practitioner divide because the local church mission is a collaborative space between research and practice.[32]

A deliberately local point of view helps correct a missiology that derives from a point of view not explicitly identified or one that is assumed to be universal. Catholic mission theology in particular, which often takes its cue from official church teaching, is prone to an exaggerated universalism.[33]

Catholics should stop defining themselves by episcopal oversight or papal rule, writes North American theologian Paul Lakeland, but focus attention on the quality of their own particular faith communities.[34] In a similar vein, North American Richard Gaillardetz has argued that only a

---

31. Missiological research has only recently begun to pay attention to the impact of migration on mission action. A helpful summary and discussion of this is in Haug, "Migration in Missiological Research," 279–93.

32. Farrell, "Re-Membering Missiology," 37–49.

33. In a recent volume overviewing Catholic mission in the last hundred years, it is notable how many chapters rely on papal encyclicals for their mission theology. See for example Bevans, *A Century of Catholic Mission*. In the same volume, Jim and Therese D'Orsa make a call not for lay missionaries but for more lay *missiologists*. Most Catholic missionaries are lay people, but most Catholic missiologists are clergy and religious. D'Orsa and D'Orsa, "Mission and Catholic Education," 239–46.

34. Lakeland, "Ecclesiology and the Use of Demography," 23–42.

theology of the church that asserts the simultaneity of the local and universal dimensions of the church can provide an adequate foundation for the full catholicity of the church and avoid the centralization of authority that has haunted Catholicism for most of the second millennium.[35]

Contrasting an overly globalizing view of mission and church, the (mainly Protestant) Council for World Mission has provided a description of what a local missional congregation or parish could look like. A "life-affirming" congregation

- lives a spirituality of engagement, which is reflected in its worship, and in the nurture and support of its members;
- is attuned to the communities in which it is set and is alert to the needs of the world, so that it is willing to stand alongside and speak out with those who are suffering or are marginalised;
- does not work alone, being in active partnership with other groups who share similar concerns;
- is a learning community, with its members taking seriously their re-reading of the Bible and their reflection on their experience, both as individuals and as a community.

All of the above lead the congregation to be "a community of transformation, manifesting the reign of God in its midst as lives are made new and justice is realised for those who have been denied fullness of life."[36]

Yet a local church perspective needs to retain also a clear awareness of its connections with the universal church—and all the grades in between. The church is a local community of believers and yet also the whole people of God. In this awareness of being both local and universal we identify with the early churches of the New Testament and the central core of Christian tradition.[37]

---

35. Gaillardetz, *Ecclesiology for a Global Church*. Similarly, Bevans, *Essays in Contextual Theology*, 130.

36. Woods, "CWM Perspective," 77–81.

37. R. Geoffrey Harris, in his examination of mission in the New Testament, argues that in the earliest documents of the New Testament, Paul's letters, there is a concept of the church as being both the local congregation of believers and yet also the whole people of God—or body of Christ—spread far and wide by God's mission. Harris, *Mission in the Gospels*, 185–87. John D. Zizioulos notes that in all ancient writers before Saint Augustine each local church is called "catholic," that is, the full and integral body of Christ. It is only through Augustine's seeking to combat the provincialism of the Donatists that the "catholic church" acquires the meaning not of the local Church but

In this book, I adopt the perspective that *the local church* can thrive only when it is aware of its own point of view in its own local context. Our formal theology of mission and church needs at the present time to attend to this underrated (among academic theologians, though not by local church members) point of view of the local church. This does not mean it should neglect the universal but simply that it is at the local level that the majority of missionaries actually operate. However much the local church may value its connections with the universal church it should not allow the universal to suppress the local.

An important implication of this perspective is that it is not the realm of God in general or the church in general that holds primacy of attention, but the interaction between the realm of God and church at a quite local level. This is where most (though clearly not all) missionary activity takes place, and this is where the majority of missionaries are located.

Conclusion

The goal of this chapter has been to set out the approach I take in this investigation into contemporary mission and church. It is a particular kind of approach, different from some others. Hopefully, this chapter will prevent false expectations in the reader. It also makes clear, I hope, that this is not the only possible approach to the subject of Christian mission.

I have set out this approach under five "perspectives." Each of these perspectives involves a fundamental choice about the best way to proceed. Put starkly, even if too simply, these choices are between:

- Does the mission belong primarily to God or primarily to the church?
- Does the mission create the church or does an already formed church then set out on mission?
- Does the church serve the larger reality of the realm of God or are these identical?
- Are all Christians missionaries from baptism or are missionaries specially designated?
- Should we approach mission from the point of view of the local church or is it rather the universal church that sets the agenda for mission activity?

---

of the church universal. Zizioulas, *The Eucharistic Communion and the World*, 101.

The perspectives I have adopted in this book are in each case the first of the choices listed above. To adopt the second alternative in any of these cases would produce a different book. It would be about a different mission and a different church.

2

Talking about Christianity in Public

THE PREVIOUS CHAPTER INTRODUCED the approach this book takes towards the investigation of mission and church. This present chapter is concerned with issues of *language*. What kind of language can we, or should we, use when we talk about God and Christianity?

Theologians have developed a specialist language to talk about the subject matter of their own discipline. Theology should not, however, be simply a matter of theologians talking to one another. It seems particularly inadequate if theological discussion about "mission" communicates with hardly anyone outside the circle of academic theologians and church professionals.

Teachers of theology in academic institutions wield a good deal of power over their students. Students are commonly required, for example, to learn a specialized theological language. Much of the study time of the first-year student of theology, as indeed in many other academic disciplines, may be spent learning the language of that discipline and showing that they can use it consistently. The theologian, whether academic or professional or pastoral, cannot be content with that requirement, especially where mission is a central theme of that theology. Theologians need to communicate to a wide range of people as immediately as possible without a requirement that other people first spend time learning a specialist language.

The issues involved in seeking a language suitable for investigating and communicating a theology of mission center around the issue of how *theological* language can also be *public* language. There is no single "public" language, but there are ways of talking theology that communicate as much as possible in a public forum that is much wider than tertiary institutions or church. This is the focus of this second chapter.

In their discussion of mission as "prophetic dialogue," North American missiologists Stephen Bevans and Roger Schroeder propose four images of the missionary in dialogue: the missionary as *treasure hunter*, as *guest*, as *stranger*, and as *someone entering into someone else's garden*.[1] Yet the missionary is not simply a listener with nothing to say. The missionary is also a prophet with a message. The images Bevans and Schroeder propose from this point of view are those of the missionary as *teacher*, as *storyteller*, and as *trail guide*.[2]

These images have the sense of someone entering into someone else's place. Historically the idea of "mission" has had this sense of going out somewhere else. Today the missionaries of the local church active in their own society are already in their own place. They do not go anywhere else. I shall adopt here the image of the missionary as "citizen theologian." This image has the sense of being already at home in the culture and the language of both the Christian church and the local society at the same time. I hope this image helps to keep before our minds the idea that the language we use about mission and church needs to be both theological and public as much as possible. A citizen theologian is someone who is committed both to being a responsible citizen concerned with the wellbeing of the whole of society as well as to thinking and speaking in Christian theological terms.

Such citizen theologians come from almost every walk of life. Their theological reflection has many faces, and the content of their theological reflections is commonly about personal, family, political, social, and environmental issues. Thus, they are "public" theologians in the tradition of Jesus who, as South African Scripture scholar Ernest van Eck argues, is portrayed in his parables as a social prophet concerned, for example, with issues of religious inclusivity and social injustice.[3] Australian theologian Robert Gascoigne says similarly that Christians themselves have a secular

---

1. Bevans and Schroeder, *Prophetic Dialogue*, 31.
2. Bevans and Schroeder, *Prophetic Dialogue*, 31, 48.
3. Van Eck, "A Prophet of Old," 1–10.

Talking about Christianity in Public 19

identity as well as an identity as members of the church: that is, they are citizens of secular societies and seek to contribute to those societies on the basis of their formation as Christians. The Christian community and its beliefs are part of the "background culture" of a liberal society, the basis on which those citizens who are Christians commit themselves to uphold fundamental democratic values.[4]

The use of the term "citizen" is not here confined to its usage in reference to a person's legal status as "citizen" or role in a system of representative government in a nation state. It includes reference to a wider identity and engagement in democratic politics in civil society, for example, or in international movements such as environmental activism.[5]

In this contemporary context, traditional "mission" theology begins to overlap, or perhaps even merge, with the more recent discipline of "public theology." Public theology, in British theologian Elaine Graham's terms, "upholds the public vocation of the church in a way which affirms its concern for the common good of society, and the individual calling of Christians to be faithful citizens as well as good disciples."[6] Public theology, in Graham's description of it, requires us to rethink the terms on which religious voices might contribute to debates about values in public life and faith-based activism and how they might help rejuvenate the practices of citizenship.[7] Public theologians place a premium on their commitment to dialogue with non-theological perspectives. They acknowledge the significance of the pluralist public realm, they value collaborative partnership in practical programs, and they recognize the

---

4. Gascoigne, *The Church and Secularity*, 100–102.

5. See Luke Bretherton on community organizing concerned with the construction of citizenship as an identity, a performance of democratic politics, and as a shared rationality. Bretherton, *Resurrecting Democracy*, 3–6.

6. Graham, *Between a Rock and a Hard Place*, 211–13. Mission theology and public theology do not often consult with each other. Public theology appeared as a distinct scholarly discipline in the early 2000s with major contributions from Scottish traditions of theology: Forrester, "Speak Truth to Power," 175–88; Storrar and Morton, *Public Theology for the 21st Century*. A major source of public theology today is the *International Journal of Public Theology*. See also Júlio Paulo Tavares Zabatiero on the role and responsibility of the theologian as "public intellectual": Zabatiero, "From the Sacristy to the Public Square," 56–69.

7. Graham, *Between a Rock and a Hard Place*, xxvii. The tasks of public theology addressed from a German viewpoint are examined in a recent collection of essays from the Berlin Institute of Public Theology in Meireis and Schieder, *Religion and Democracy*.

necessity to make their own deliberations accessible to those beyond their own boundaries.[8]

Public theology has long roots back through history into the very early Christian missions in the form of "apologetics" understood not just as defending the faith but in a proactive sense. English theologian Richard Conrad defines "apologetics" as "the whole business of *explaining* the Christian faith *attractively*, in a way that engages *respectfully* with people's insights and instincts, that welcomes *home* all that is valid in them, but also *challenges* them as appropriate."[9]

The Responsibility for the Translation

This book is essentially a theological one. It is written by a citizen theologian for citizen theologians and their churches. It assumes some knowledge of traditional theological language. Communicating the Christian message beyond the confines of theologians themselves involves translation of traditional theological concepts into something more like communicable *public* language.[10] If we recognize that the church is missionary then its theologians have a responsibility to articulate their theology as much as possible in a language that is publicly accessible. This is not always possible. Sometimes is it not even advisable because a more technical or professional language is still valuable, necessary even, in the more technical and critical discussions among theologians. It is usually necessary, for example, when examining the Christian traditions that serve as criteria for assessing the value of community projects or political stances (Are they good or bad? Is there a scriptural basis for supporting or opposing them? etc.). Nevertheless, there is still a responsibility on the

---

8. Graham, *Between a Rock and a Hard Place*, 180. For an example from Australia of how this might work, see Maddox, "Religion, Secularism, and the Promise of Public Theology," 82–100. Or from South Korea, Yun, "*Missio Dei Trinitatis* and *Missio Ecclesiae*," 225–39, and Yun, "The Points and Tasks of Public Theology," 64–87.

9. Conrad, "Moments and Themes in the History of Apologetics," 126.

10. Again, mission theology and public theology coincide here in their endeavours at translation. "The discipline [public theology] inhabits the boundary between the religious and the secular and its language undertakes an act of "translation" to communicate to a non-specialist audience. Furthermore, it is public because it believes it has a contribution to make to a wider audience beyond the boundaries of faith; and finally, because it takes seriously a responsibility to assist with the cultivation of civic discourse." Graham, *Between a Rock and a Hard Place*, 97.

theologian to speak as much as possible to people who are not explicitly and deliberately trained in theology.

Such translation is not a simplification or a reduction of academic theology to a lower level. It is an act of communication addressed to a wider public audience as distinct from a smaller academic audience. In either case it needs to be sophisticated and refined in order to communicate well with each of those different audiences. What then are the main features of such translation?

Attention to the Context

Attention to the context of any theological conversation is a first step in theological translation. A good deal of mission theology was written for or about foreign or cross-cultural missionaries trying to communicate with local people in a language which is a second language for the missionaries, a language in which the missionaries are not creatively fluent and in a culture with which they are not intimately familiar. For the foreign missionary during the period of European colonial expansion, a major task was often the translation from the European language of the missionary into a local non-European language. Today, a similar kind of language translation faces the now more numerous Asian missionaries in foreign, including European, cultures.

The citizen theologians with whom we deal in this book, however, do not normally suffer from such limitations. For the most part they deal with their own people in their own context even though that context is likely nowadays to be multi-cultural. Citizen theologians in their own culture have the rather different task of translating from a learned theological or church language into the various language contexts that make up the public forum in contemporary society. The task is much simpler if the theological language is already sensitive to the contemporary public languages.

Yet "public" language or language in the "public forum" (outside of a strictly church or academic theological context) is not singular and uniform. It contains some common vocabulary, such as that common in public news media. It also contains a large number of specialized languages familiar to particular sectors of society, such as the languages of scientific disciplines, community development language, the language of professional and public ethics, the language of human and civil rights, psychological and sociological language that has entered the public domain, and political language, as well as the language of popular religion. All of these may be distorted, or at least complicated, by the clever but often deceitful (and occasionally delightful) arts of "spin" and advertising.

The citizen theologian then is translating between a more strictly theological language and a public language suitable to a particular public conversation. This sounds complicated, but we should not allow ourselves to think that it is particularly difficult. Practical theologians, pastors, and religion teachers are doing it all the time. Similarly in disciplines other than theology, medical professionals, engineers, ethicists, psychologists, environmental scientists, and others are also constantly communicating with a public wider than their own academic disciplines.

Constant Awareness of the Public Requirements

The challenge here to a mission theology developed in tertiary-level educational institutions is that it be constantly aware of the public requirements of its language rather than just its academic respectability. No single theologian can hope to translate theological ideas into all the many public languages noted above. But local Christian communities are made up of citizen theologians who do have the language skills needed in one or several of these contexts. Some members of Christian communities are already specialists in these other (non-theological) languages. Can they translate across from the specialized language they hear and speak in church to the specialized languages they speak in other contexts especially where public wellbeing is at stake? One of the challenges to theologians then is to articulate more clearly the beliefs and commitments of theology into a public language that, in order to be understood, does not require a prior degree in theology nor even a prior church involvement.

Stated briefly, the challenge to theology is that it states explicitly what the impact of its understanding of God has in the world of personal, social, economic, and environmental wellbeing.

Many theologians can speak fluently about, for example, theological ideas such as the "reign of God" or "salvation" or "redemption," but do not know how this actually affects contemporary social, economic, or environmental decisions in their own society. In terms of the concrete realities that affect people's lives, what do we mean by the "reign of God," "salvation," or "redemption"? In these terms, the primary question in theology then becomes not so much "Do you believe in God?" or even

"What kind of God do you believe in?" but "What are the concrete impacts in our world of your understanding of God?"

The challenge then is to develop a public language that is theologically adequate yet is able to communicate its key commitments beyond the confines of its own members. This is a language that can contribute to a common vision or common objectives with other non-church sectors of society.

This is not a question of simply trying to make ourselves heard. The expression of Christian ideas in language and symbols of public language is a recognition of the value of public debate and the legitimacy of society's institutions and laws that result from it. The idea of natural law, for example, can be expressed in terms of human rights, and thus enter in, with respect, to society's debate on moral justice.[11]

The Risk

There is a risk here too. The attempt to reduce the amount of specialized academic language and widen the range of theological communication is often resisted by those who teach theology in educational institutions and by official church personnel. Partly this may be due to the competitive pressure on tertiary-level teachers to publish academic books and journal articles but little pressure to communicate publicly. There may also be pressure on church professionals to speak safe and official church language rather than the less guarded and frequently changing language of public communication. An extreme example of this is the 2010 official English translations of the Roman Missal, which employs Latinized English rather than English designed for immediate communication with a contemporary congregation, much less English tuned to a mission outreach into the wider society.

The issue of risk remains a real one even apart from outside pressures such as those noted above. How much risk is there that the original gospel message will simply be misunderstood as a result of translation into public languages? Will the church be deceived into gradually slipping into secular attitudes towards the world? Will the Christian beliefs be "watered down" to some lowest common denominator?[12]

---

11. Gascoigne, *The Church and Secularity*, 56.
12. Sociologist David Martin, recognizing the risks involved here, maintains nevertheless that ideas like liberty, equality, and fraternity, which are mottos of republican

This risk was taken by the early Christian churches when they translated the message of Jesus not just into the Greek language but into the various Hellenized cultures of their time. The translation into Latin and Roman culture took the same risk, and this has been repeated often as the Christian understanding of God has been translated into different temporal and local contexts. It is something that has to be done and it is something that is always risky.

Hence there is a need for constant interaction between theological language that examines the sources of Christianity in a specialized way and public language that communicates with a range of contemporary publics. This is a need for a contemporary effort in theological and public language that is conscious of risk and so is constantly self-critical even as it stretches outwards into wider contexts.

In the contemporary context of secular, pluralist democracies, civil institutions must be based on a shareable conception of the common good, rather than on the beliefs of any particular religion. If Christians seek to contribute to public political life, they must do so in ways that show a willingness to express the implications of their faith in publicly shareable terms.[13]

Three Kinds of Suspicion

There are at least three *kinds of suspicion* that accompany this continual task of translation and that are necessary for successful translation.

One is a suspicion that occurs *internally within the ranks of the citizen theologians*. This is the suspicion that comes from the experience of hearing theologians or church ministers talk theology in public when

---

principle and virtue, are secular translations of biblical texts, such as our oneness in Christ, the unity of humanity, and the way in which every human being is a king and a priest. Yet Christian language cannot be "emptied out" into the public realm without damage and compromise on all sides: Martin, *On Secularization*, 75. The task and the context of the citizen theologian is somewhat different from that of the sociologist, however. It is not an emptying out of his/her theological language in any general sense but a restricting of the conversation to what can be shared in the context of a common enterprise. There is much more that can be said theologically and that can also be shared in other contexts. The non-Christian parties to that conversation are similarly not saying everything that could be said. They are sharing their beliefs and commitments only to the extent that they are relevant to the common interests and can be mutually understood.

13. Gascoigne, *The Church and Secularity*, 63.

they don't seem (outside of their own church situations) to know what they are talking about. This is the experience of hearing words that play with words but don't have any clear impact on any current action or attitude. Is this just a word game that they play with one another about word consistency or building theoretical castles in clouds? This is a suspicion that is necessary to any missionary activity since theologians whose words are publicly meaningless (who are not "citizens" in any serious sense) are a danger to that mission.

A second kind of suspicion is one that *arises not from within the Christian community but from outside it,* from the non-church public who are in contact with or allied with the Christian community in some common task or project. This is the suspicion that arises when, for example, people who are not church members begin to wonder, "Why is this church or its ministers involved in this community project or this public issue? Is it a way of recruiting more people into their church? Is it to attract funding for their church, or is it a way of gaining political power for the church?" This kind of suspicion may be simply the suspicion of other non-governmental organizations (NGOs) or indeed government agencies, whose membership and source of funding is itself fragile and may be threatened by a more tightly organized church or the power of its ministers. It may also be based on some previous experience of church deceit in the public forum. In any case, such suspicion poses a serious question to the Christian church because it implies previous missionary activity that is perceived as dishonest. It challenges the church to be vigilant against any form of deceit in its outreach mission and to maintain a self-critical care about its mission intentions.

A third suspicion is one that needs to be *practiced by citizen theologians themselves in their attention to other sectors of society.* Since we need, as I have argued above, to be self-critical of our own specialized language and its sometime dysfunctions, we need also to note that other public languages, such as the language of public service or community development or environmental ethics, are also specialized languages that can fail to communicate in the common language of the general public or the local community. In the public forum, the language of government agencies and professional services may also appear esoteric, disabling, and even deceitful, a covering up of the real agenda. Citizen theologians, having come to the point where we are conscious that our own theological language may be disabling to those we intend to serve, need to be alert too to the disabling words of other (non-church) special interest agencies and services. We are not the only sinners in the field of miscommunication or disinformation.

The Temptation to Deceit

The temptation to deceit is one of the greatest threats in theological translation. We should consider here two levels of such deceit. One is relatively mild, the other more troubling.

The milder form we may describe as "promotional" language. A good deal of missionary language is promotional in the sense that it presents the church and Christianity in the best possible light with some loss of objectivity in doing so. In some ways this is a well understood literary form and so is only occasionally deceitful in that its audience recognizes it as simply promotional rather than accurate or factual. Citizen theologians may be familiar with it in sermons and homilies in church. We may need nevertheless to be alert to it, both in ourselves and others, and to guard against being entrapped by it in the public forum. This is especially so when other NGOs with whom we work are similarly engaged in promotional presentation. Their funding and their public reputation depend on convincing, and therefore sometimes inaccurate, self-presentation, which reports more than they have actually achieved and promises more than they can deliver.

A more troubling level of deceit occurs when the public language that presents a church's intentions does not correspond to their real intentions. In this case the translation is not simply a different way of communicating the same ideas to a different audience. Rather, it is an attempt to win public approval but conceal the real (internal) agenda. Sociologist Steve Bruce raises the issue of the "new Christian right" in America who, he maintains, have been effective in the public arena only when they have presented their case in secular terms. Hence "creationism" has to be presented as "creation science," apparently every bit as compatible with the scientific record as any evolutionary model of the origin of species and open to testing in the same way. Similarly, the case against abortion is made in terms of the inalienable rights of the individual. Divorce and homosexuality are damned as socially dysfunctional.[14] If Bruce's argument is correct, it illustrates a scenario in which the temptation to deception in the public forum is very strong. While we should not assume an intention

---

14. Bruce, *God Is Dead*, 20–21.

to deceive in any particular case, an argument in the publicly acceptable language of science, human rights, and social dysfunction that conceals the real biblical foundations of that argument is rightly and widely regarded as dishonest. A missionary zeal has here displaced a regard for truth, and this is a trap for the unwary (or dishonest) missionary.[15]

Conclusion

This chapter has been concerned with the capacity of our language to communicate a mission agenda. More specifically it has been concerned with the translation of traditional or academic theological language into more public language. The "missionaries" of the local church are, most effectively, the people I have called "citizen theologians." These are the people who can bridge the gap between what they hear and say in church and what they hear and say in the wider society because they themselves inhabit both the language of the church and also one or several of the other languages that make up contemporary society.

I have suggested here that we, especially those of us who have some pastoral, academic, or professional responsibility in theology, should regard ourselves as responsible for the translation between traditional (i.e., familiar in church) theological language and public discourse. I have suggested further that such translation requires from us constant attention to context, awareness of the public requirements of our language, recognition of the risk in making such translations, recognition of suspicions attached to such translation, and above all resistance to the temptation to deceive.

Among the concepts that are central to communication between theological and public languages is that of the "reign of God" or the "realm of God." Most explanations of the reign of God use biblical terms and first-century Mediterranean conditions to explain it. But how would we express it in contemporary public language?

---

15. On the dilemma faced by the new Christian Right in America when they maintain two distinct discourses, one for the faithful and the other for its public outreach, see also Graham, *Between a Rock and a Hard Place*, 164–66.

3

The Realm of God

IN THE THIRD OF the basic perspectives on mission I opted for in chapter 1, the church is *in service of* the realm of God. This is its mission in the sense that its purpose is to participate actively in God's mission in the world to bring about the realm of God. In our contemporary world, then, not just in the biblical world, what is this "realm of God"? What does it look like? What do we do to take part in it? Are we doing this simply by being members of the church and attracting others into the church? Doing good, loving others, and helping our neighbor are no doubt part of it. Yet the idea of the "realm of God" suggests a larger picture, something not just focused on individuals or even just communities of Christians.

Since the term "realm of God" rather than "kingdom" or "reign" of God may surprise or disturb some readers, I begin with a reflection on the use of that term. I move then towards articulating an initial working description of the realm of God that will serve as a basis for the investigation that continues in the following chapters.

Realm of God, Reign of God, Kingdom of God/Heaven

I use the term "realm of God" rather than the more traditional "reign of God" or "kingdom of God" (or "kingdom of heaven") as a contemporary English translation of the Greek *"he basileia tou theou."* There are arguments for and against any one of these terms as a satisfactory modern translation of the Greek. The English terms "reign" or "kingdom" are more commonly used in biblical translation, but from the point of view of a mission theology with a central interest in communication outwards to the wider society, these words have severe liabilities in that they carry strong sexist, royalist, patriarchal, and military associations.

We could argue that "reign," "kingdom," and "rule" are good translations of the Greek original (*basileia*) which also carries such associations. Yet in the contemporary world these terms carry histories of exploitation and autocracy that severely distort what we want to communicate here about God and God's relationship to humanity. This may not be a serious issue in conversations among theologians or among practicing Christians who are used to making translations in their heads, so to speak, from "ordinary" English to "religious" English where God is talked about as, but really isn't, like earthly kings and rulers historical or contemporary. It is an issue, however, in conversations with less alert Christians who really do think God acts like human kings and rulers. It is even more of a problem in public conversations outside church settings where our rather complex and in-house religious metaphors are either taken literally (and therefore dismissed) or simply regarded as anachronisms (and therefore interesting but irrelevant).

We could argue that God is more like a modern constitutional monarch than like the autocratic kings that New Testament Christians were used to. But then we have already moved a long way from the biblical idea and have considerably complicated the metaphor of kingship. We could also argue, as many do, that the kingdom/reign/rule of *God* is a *counter-*cultural idea. It stands for a kingdom of love and peace *as an alternative to* all the *other* kingdoms that we know about. Modern liberal democracies, however, also stand counter to such kingdoms and many were born in bloody revolt against such kingly rule. The counter-cultural metaphor loses its force for those who don't have kings and don't like kings in the first place—except perhaps in the severely constrained form of constitutional monarchs or national figureheads. The bottom line, though, is that in contemporary English these terms carry resonances that are far removed from the idea of the benevolent God central to Jesus' teaching.[1]

Some contemporary theologians have proposed the term "commonwealth of God" as a suitable English translation of the Greek "*basileia tou theou*." North American theologian Paul F. Knitter proposes it as a

---

1. For further discussion on the issue of a modern English translation in this context, see Sintado, *Social Ecology, Ecojustice, and the New Testament*, 135–45.

contemporary, non-patriarchal English translation.² Some contemporary citizen theologians may prefer this term. For my own part, while "commonwealth" is attractive from several points of view, including its origins in the idea of a "common good" and its use in the formation of several of the sovereign states that make up the US the waters here are too muddied by contemporary politics in such connections as the Commonwealth of Nations, British Commonwealth, Commonwealth of Independent States, Commonwealth of Dominica, Commonwealth of The Bahamas, Commonwealth of Australia, etc.³ It would complicate rather than clarify public discussion about the "kingdom of God" in the contexts with which I am familiar.

I have perhaps belabored this point a little too much here. In the end the whole discussion could be regarded as a minor point of language and most of the readers of this book can happily swap between "reign," "kingdom" and "realm" of God without too much difficulty—indeed I do this in this book when paraphrasing or quoting other writers. What this discussion serves to do, however, is to illustrate the difference between a theology that is mainly concerned about communicating its central concepts *within* the Christian community itself and one that, while concerned with remaining faithful to its origins, is also vitally concerned with communicating *outwards* to the wider society and therefore uses publicly accessible language as much as possible.

On balance, while I concede its defects, "realm" seems to me to be a better term in the context of an investigation into the church's participation in God's mission in the wider world. It provokes conversation that goes beyond repetition of familiar and in-group religious language. It avoids the implications of autocracy. It implies that we are talking about the "reality" of God's presence in our world rather than about ruling, even if benevolently, and obeying, even if willingly. North American missiologist Michael Barram captures this idea when he says of the Beatitudes in Matthew's and Luke's Gospels that they are not instructions or directives

---

2. Knitter, "The Transformation of Mission," 97. Similarly, John B. Cobb Jr. regards the "realm of God" as a better translation of the New Testament "*basileia theou*" than "reign of God" because it mixes connotations of God's rule with that of a sphere, not necessarily geographical, in which God rules. He concludes nevertheless that the best English translation may be "commonwealth" as a term that, besides not emphasizing the controlling power of a rule, further suggests that the realm may be organized for the common good. Cobb Jr., "Commonwealth and Empire," 144.

3. Not to mention the Puritan and brutal theology of the short-lived "Commonwealth" of England, 1649–60 CE.

for getting into the kingdom of God, but are "Jesus painting a picture, so to speak, of the way reality looks from God's perspective."[4]

While the terms we use are often important, the substance of what we mean by the "realm of God" remains our main concern. My main purpose, then, in this chapter is to investigate, even if briefly, the Christian origins of this concept with a view to its possible impact on the world of today.

New Testament: A Choice of Realms

In the New Testament writings, what are the characteristics of this realm of God that makes it distinct from any other realm? Jesus' preaching of the realm of God confronted people with a choice. People became disciples of Jesus Christ by making an act of faith, a choice and a commitment. This act of faith was not just in God in some broad sense, but in the *specific* realm of God that Jesus proclaimed and embodied. It required a deliberate choice of Jesus' realm of God rather than any of the other "realms" around them. Nearly everyone was already involved in one or several of these realms, often not by choice but by birth and family, or by politics, religion, or conquest. But what were these other realms and in what ways was the realm of God different from them?

One of the ways of clarifying what an idea means is by comparing and contrasting it with other similar or related ideas. Canadian religious studies scholar Mary Ann Beavis compares the New Testament "kingdom of God" with the *utopias of the Greco-Roman and Jewish world* of its time. She concludes that Jesus did proclaim a utopia, an ideal future, but did not subscribe to a theology of Jewish restoration. Rather he, and the movement to which he belonged, proclaimed the ancient myth of God as king of Israel and of the world, past, present, and future, in an *anti*political (though not *a*political) way. The contours or "constitution" of this kingdom can be found in the ministry and preaching of Jesus.[5]

In his study of the origins of Christianity, North American Scripture scholar Bart D. Erman maintains that if one word could encapsulate the common social, political, and personal ethic of the Roman Empire at the time of the first Christians, it would be "dominance." In a culture of dominance, those with power are expected to assert their will over those

---

4. Barram, *Missional Economics*, 47.
5. Beavis, *Jesus & Utopia*, 2–6, 83–104.

who are weaker. Virtually everyone, including the weak and marginalized, accepted and shared this common-sense, millennia-old view. With such an ideology one would not expect to find governmental welfare programs to assist weaker members of society, the poor, homeless, hungry, or oppressed. The Roman world did not have such things. Christians, however, advocated a different ideology. Leaders of the Christian church preached and urged an ethic of love and service. One person was not more important than another. All were on the same footing before God.[6]

South African Scripture scholar Ernest van Eck's *typology of three kingdoms* is another approach which helps to clarify the realms that captured people's lives or offered them alternative choices in the world of the New Testament. These were the kingdom of Rome, the kingdom of the Jerusalem temple, and the kingdom of God as proposed by Jesus. The *gospel of the kingdom of Rome* claimed that Rome was chosen by the gods to rule an empire without end, with sovereignty over sea and land and all its inhabitants and the "right" to domination, power, and violence with Caesar as main benefactor. The result of this ideology was the *pax Romana*, the Roman "peace" gained through violence. The *gospel of the temple elite* in Jerusalem, on the other hand, was based on the understanding of God as holy, expressed by creation as the divine order of the world. To replicate God's holiness was to separate the ritually and socially clean and unclean, a purity code that defined a society centered on the temple and its priests. Acting as God's appointed benefactors, the priestly elite preserved their power and privilege by always taking the side of Rome, accumulating wealth through tithes and offerings, and adding peasant land to their estates by investing in loans. The result of this ideology was "peace" gained through systemic violence by drawing boundaries to exclude the impure and social expendables.

By contrast, writes van Eck, the *gospel of the kingdom of God* proclaimed peace through justice. Mission and ethics went hand in hand. To be part of this mission required repentance (*metanoia*) from the gospels of Rome and the temple elite, and loyalty (*pistis*) towards God's kingdom. Enacting this mission was to stand up for justice and to show compassion towards the outsiders created by the gospels of Rome and the temple elite.[7]

With a similar intent of clarifying the New Testament message along with its impact today, Irish-American Scripture scholar John Dominic

---

6. Ehrman, *The Triumph of Christianity*, 5–6.

7. Van Eck, "Mission, Identity, and Ethics in Mark," 1–13. See also van Eck, "Interpreting the Parables of the Galilean Jesus," 310–21.

Crossan's cryptic typology sets out the broad choices as between *"Peace by justice"* (the Jesus program), *"Peace by victory"* (the Roman program), or *"Peace by death"* (the terrorist program). His answer to the issue of how to be a faithful Christian today in the midst of a violent American empire is in the radicality of God's nonviolence revealed in the revolutionary messages of Jesus and Paul: the nonviolent kingdom of God prophesied by Jesus and the equality advocated by Paul to the early Christian churches.[8]

I have chosen the above presentations of the "kingdom of God" not so much as an exercise in biblical theology, but because these writers clarify the choices the first Christians were faced with in becoming disciples of Jesus. More than that, each of these presentations is also related to the choices we now face in working for the realm of God today. The task of the church today is to understand how the choices made by the early church assist the contemporary church to discern the realm of God within the multitude of life choices in the multi-cultural and ever-changing world of today.

The Realm of God Today

One of the modern summaries of the meaning of the "kingdom of God" today that deliberately moves on from biblical terms and attempts to redefine it for the modern world is that of Walter Kasper. He summarizes the meaning of the "kingdom of God" as

> the kingdom of truth, justice, holiness, freedom, and peace. Witnessing to the one true God is therefore also about witnessing to God as the God of humanity and of each individual human person, as the God of love, justice, freedom, reconciliation, and peace. Without turning into a social gospel or even one of prosperity, mission thereby also serves peace, reconciliation, and justice in the world. It frees from being tied and destined by birth to a certain culture and religion. Mission helps to overcome tribalism and nationalism, overturns the idea of development being limited to purely economic and technological progress, and helps to integrate independently legitimate causes into a holistic and complete human development. Ultimately mission is in the service of the transformation of the world out of the spirit of the dawning kingdom of God.[9]

---

8. Crossan, *God and Empire*, esp. 240–41.
9. Kasper, *The Catholic Church*, 292–93.

The contemporary reader will note here how this description of the "reign of God" includes an attempt to deal with some characteristics of the contemporary world that were not apparent in the biblical accounts. Thus, issues about the "social gospel" and the gospel of "prosperity," the idea of "economic development" and "technological progress" and even the idea of a "holistic and complete human development" are only inchoately there, if at all, in the biblical accounts. They are our contemporary issues rather than issues for the biblical writers.

Such a definition of the "kingdom of God" is the kind of expression required of the modern systematic theologian but is perhaps too grand and all-encompassing to serve the local citizen theologian who will prefer something more concrete and sharply focused. Nevertheless, the concluding sentence holds to a line of thought and action that is critical for the citizen theologian: "Ultimately mission is in the service of the transformation of the world out of the spirit of the dawning kingdom of God." What is clear here is that the mission of the church is not just about my personal salvation, or about increasing the number of church members or even of those who recognize Jesus as savior. It is about the evolving realm of God, that is, the transformation of the world. Just what kind of "transformation" is intended here will occupy us through the remaining chapters of this book.

A part answer at a practical level to what such a transformation might look like today is proposed by North American theologian John B. Cobb Jr.: "We can ask: In what kind of society could people live in communities in which service to one another counted for more than wealth or power? In what kind of society could business be profitably conducted without placing profits above people and community? In what kind of society could the many smaller communities aim to support one another, rather than to compete with one another? In what kind of society could people renounce the use of force even in self-defense?"[10]

This is the kind of questioning which leads us beyond a biblical and traditional (in earlier times and places) understanding of the realm of God and further in the direction of saying what the realm of God would look like in our contemporary world. How would we recognize it if we came across it?

Yet there are two further dimensions of the realm of God that have not been taken into account so far in this chapter. They are particularly

---

10. Cobb Jr., "Commonwealth and Empire," 149.

important today and their absence would make this chapter seem out of date. (Nor are they included in Kasper's or Cobb's definitions above.) These are, firstly, that the realm of God is about *all God's creation*, not just about human beings, and secondly that reflection on the role of the *Holy Spirit* in this realm of God has become increasingly important in contemporary theology.

All Creatures in the Realm of God

The contemporary citizen theologian will have noticed by now that this consideration of the realm of God has so far been about the relationships of justice and peace in human society. Yet human beings do not exist in isolation from the rest of God's creation. For the New Testament writers, the non-human natural world was clearly part of God's creation and this most obviously at the "end-times" when large-scale cosmological and societal changes could be expected.

The New Testament and early church writers were conscious that they were a part, but only a part, of God's creation.[11] They were not particularly concerned about environmental issues in the sense that we are today when human use of other creatures has become so destructive. There was environmental destruction in their time, but it was localized. It had not reached the extent and intensity that has become so problematic for us today.

While the New Testament writers did not need to be particularly concerned about the vulnerability of God's creation—to them it seemed stable and awesome rather than vulnerable—the contemporary missiologist definitely does. Since the mid-twentieth century we have become much more aware of the immensity of "creation" and the cosmological triviality of the human species within it. At the same time, we have become aware that the biosphere that surrounds the very small planet that we inhabit is under threat of large-scale destruction as a result of human actions. In the twentieth century, the increase in the power of human technology and the growth of the population of human over-consumers on the Earth came to threaten life on the planet. Human overuse of

---

11. Ecumenical Patriarch Bartholomew, drawing on St. Anthony of Egypt (third century) and St. Maximus the Confessor (seventh century), reminds us of the early Eastern Christian tradition in which creation is a sacred book where we read the works of God. There is a liturgical or sacramental dimension to creation. Bartholomew, *On Earth as in Heaven*, 128.

resources and production of waste is now increasing to a point that is beyond the regenerative capacities of the Earth.

In this context, the natural world is no longer just a larger background to our concept of the realm of God. It has moved to a central place within it. For us, aware of the human potential to destroy the nature around us, ethical concern for the non-human beings of Earth has become an important part of how humans participate in the ongoing life of the realm of God.[12] Creation is part of God's mission and we have only just realized how much that part of creation that we inhabit, namely the planet Earth, is also part of our human mission.

In the 1990s, Brazilian theologian Leonardo Boff, one of the most prominent advocates of social justice and liberation, became widely known also as an advocate for an "integral ecology" founded on a new alliance between societies and nature. In Boff's view, such an ecology is the relationship that all bodies, animate and inanimate, natural and cultural, establish and maintain among themselves and with their surroundings. He poses the question: "How can we obtain a socio-economic system that will produce a decent sufficiency for all, within a development model worked out with nature and not against it, and in which the idea of the common good will also involve the common environmental good, that of the air, seas and rivers, living beings, the whole environmental landscape?"[13]

More recently, Pope Francis has taken up this theme of an "integral ecology" in his 2015 exhortation, *Laudato Si': On Care for our Common Home*. An "integral ecology" is one in which we recognize one complex crisis which is both social and environmental and which requires an economics in service of a more integrating vision. A particular feature of this exhortation is its insistence on the close connection between environmental issues and social issues. We cannot solve one kind without the other. A decline in the quality of human life and a decline in the quality of the natural world around us go together. What is needed today is what this exhortation calls an "integral ecology" which respects all the environmental, human, and social dimensions of the planet.[14]

---

12. Hence the increasing interest in recent theology in the spirituality of creation. Darragh, *Living in the Planet Earth*; Darragh, *At Home in the Earth*; Buxton and Habel, *The Nature of Things*; Nothwehr, "For the Salvation of the Cosmos," 68–81; Effa, "Spiritual Renewal and the Healing of Creation," 360–71; and Effa, "Celtic and Aboriginal Pathways," 54–62.

13. Boff and Elizondo, "Editorial: Ecology and Poverty," ix–xii.

14. Francis, *Laudato Si'*, #4.

Participation in the realm of God includes all the human and environmental concerns of today's world. Missiology then becomes "ecomissiology," which sets traditional theologies of mission and church in a broader context. This is an approach to mission that sees the mission of God in terms of all levels of reality, whether human or non-human, characterized by relationship and interdependence.[15] In British theologian Stuart Murray's summary, "Mission includes many elements: creation care, social action, community development, peace and justice advocacy, political involvement, cultural renewal and much else."[16]

Mission theology has thus become a central part of ecotheology and of a social ecology whose goal is wholeness, understood as a mutual interdependence, as the unity in diversity of all Earth beings.[17] Asian-American Pentecostal theologian Amos Yong points out that if the Spirit of God is also the Spirit of creation as well as the Spirit of mission, then Christian mission ought to be intentional about engaging with the environment.[18]

By the beginning of the twenty-first century, the realm of God could no longer be thought of simply as a realm where Christ reigns over the people of the world, but a reality which includes all Earth beings enlivened and indwelt by the Holy Spirit.

Realm of God and Holy Spirit

This leads us to a second major dimension of the realm of God that needs more attention today than it had in the past, namely, the role of the Spirit. The realm of God is a Trinitarian idea in that it is the action of the Trinity that creates and sustains this realm. There was a tendency until quite recently, however, particularly in the theology of the "Western" church,

---

15. Langmead, "Ecomissiology," 505–18. And further than that, Christology and missiology here interact. "Deep incarnation," where God becomes human, sharing the life conditions of the highest and the least in the process of incarnation, also becomes an important concept in missiology. Niemandt, "Missiology and Deep Incarnation," 246–61.

16. Murray, *Post-Christendom*, 253.

17. Sintado, *Social Ecology, Ecojustice, and the New Testament*, 159–60. Sintado bases his social ecology on a reading of the Gospel of Mark, the letter to the Romans, and the Book of Revelation, using the key tenets of social ecology and ecojustice as a basic hermeneutical framework.

18. Yong, "The *Missio Spiritus*," 131.

to associate the realm of God very strongly with the life and teaching of Jesus.[19] In that sense the realm of God could appear to be the action of the Father through the Son. Is there then a role of the Holy Spirit in all this?

Since the 1980s, a strengthening theology of the Holy Spirit called our attention to features of God's action in the world that were often lost in an unduly Christ-focused theology.[20] Attention to the role of the Spirit in this realm of God is not intended to separate the action of the Spirit from that of the Trinity, but it does call attention to some aspects of the realm of God that can be missed in a too-narrow Christ-centered focus. The concern about a narrow Christ-centered focus seems to have arisen mainly from the way in which Christology had been used to reinforce established ecclesiastical arrangements (priests as "other Christs" or representatives of Christ) and male-centeredness (the identification of "male" with Christ) or to reinforce human-centered theologies that ignored the rest of God's creation. Images of the church as the "body of Christ" or of a "cosmic Christ," if they become too dominant, could have the effect of pushing aside the more balancing images of the Holy Spirit. The Spirit is not a human image and is not incarnated in time or place. It "blows where it wills" and enlivens all creation.

It is the Spirit who plays the lead in Christ's life and mission as well as in the early Christian church. Jesus begins the announcement of his mission in the synagogue in Nazareth with the words of the prophet Isaiah, "The Spirit of the Lord is upon me" (Luke 4:18). The Acts of the Apostles is clearly a mission theology of the Spirit where, as Scripture scholar and missiologist vanThanh Nguyen points out, the Spirit is both the catalyst and the guiding force of the church's missionary enterprise. Nguyen lists the actions of the Spirit as constantly abiding, inaugurating, speaking, ordering, forbidding, redirecting, inciting actions, and comforting.[21] Similarly, for Australian Scripture scholar Francis J. Maloney

---

19. In contrast to this rather sweeping characterization of the "Western church" is the strong emphasis on the Spirit in the Pentecostal, charismatic, evangelical, and even more recently "renewalist" theologies. Some of this, and the relationships between these theologies of the Spirit, is captured in Lord, "Spirit-Driven Gospel Communities of Transformation," 168–92.

20. Boff, *Ecology and Liberation*, 49. This along with a number of other prominent theologians in the 1980s and 1990s, e.g., Johnson, *Women, Earth, and Creator Spirit*; Wallace, *Fragments of the Spirit*; and, more recently, Kim, *Joining in with the Spirit*.

21. vanThanh Nguyen, "Missionary Churches in Acts," 135–45. Similarly, R. Geoffrey Harris notes that in Luke's theology the Holy Spirit is seen as the initiator and inspiration behind all the phases of mission activity: Harris, *Mission in the Gospels*, 135.

(following Pope Francis), the Spirit is the "protagonist" of mission in the Acts of the Apostles in the sense that the book is a history of the Spirit-directed witness to Jesus by the founding apostles, especially Peter and Paul. The messenger, Jesus (the central figure in the Gospels), has become the subject of a message of what must happen for God's design to be fulfilled (Acts 1:8).[22] Theologian and Anglican priest Alison Morgan points to the New Testament witness to the role of the Spirit in bringing renewal of life to the newly called people of God—new life, new birth, new creation, new hope, a new self, new tongues, new gifts, new teaching, a new people, a new commandment, good news.[23]

Our biblical images of the Spirit encourage a theology of mission where the realm of God and the action of the Trinity is before, after, and beyond, as well as within the actions of the church. The world is the sphere of the Spirit's work *beyond* the church where, as English theologian Samuel Wells notes, Christian disciples are humbled by acts of charity the church could seldom encompass, surprised by good will that puts the church to shame, and challenged by examples of integrity, courage, kindness, and wisdom the church badly needs.[24]

A Contemporary Working Description

To progress the investigation undertaken in this book, we need now a contemporary articulation of this fundamentally biblical idea of the realm of God, a translation that is not just a translation from one language to another, but also a translation from a biblical sociology and cosmology to a contemporary one. This requires a working description that is not overly complex or lengthy but that functions as a normative reference for our public attitudes and actions. In my own engagements in the public forum, I have used the following description of the "realm of God" as a guideline for decision among the competing objectives and stances:[25]

---

22. Moloney, "Mission in the Acts of the Apostles," 400–410.

23. Morgan, "What Does the Gift of the Spirit Mean for the Shape of the Church?" 152.

24. Wells, *Incarnational Mission*, 17.

25. When I say I have used this description in my own engagements in public forums I do not mean that I recited this at people. I mean that I used this description in my own mind for clarifying my own attitudes towards public issues as well as in more private discussions with Christian citizen theologians.

> The realm of God is what the world would be like if it were in accordance with the will of a benevolent God; an image of a process, based in the present but also projected into the future, of ideal relationships among human beings within the vitality of the planet Earth.

This description is broad. It lacks specifics. Yet it serves as a first stage in our search to identify the realm of God in our contemporary world. (I should note perhaps that the Christian understanding of God is always God as Trinity—my comments above on the Holy Spirit have not been forgotten in this description but are implicit within it.)

Conclusion

The concept of the "realm of God" is a central one in a perspective that sees this realm of God as the objective of mission activity. This chapter has looked at New Testament interpretations of the realm of God with a view to understanding what is involved in an option for the realm of God as distinct from other competing realms.

The working description of the realm of God as proposed above is preliminary. It may even seem banal after the rather complex lead-up to it. It clarifies, nevertheless, that this realm is animated by a benevolent Triune God, is evolving, and relates us to all the beings and processes that make up the planet Earth. Important too is that this description is in language that is comprehensible (not necessarily agreeable) in the public forum rather than just in church or theological circles. Yet this description of the realm of God still lacks specifics. Importantly for us, it does not yet say what this "realm" is really like at ground level. We need to move to a more specific level before this description can be a guideline for our involvement in society. This will be the work of the next chapter.

4

The Realm of God and Wellbeing

THE PREVIOUS CHAPTER WAS concerned with the meaning of the "realm of God." I proposed there a working description of the realm of God that moves us from biblical language to more contemporary language. Thus, *the realm of God is what the world would be like if it were in accordance with the will of a benevolent God; an image of a process, based in the present but also projected into the future, of ideal relationships among human beings within the vitality of the planet Earth.*

Lest it seem too vague for our purpose in investigating the mission of the church, let me note some important broad parameters that are established in this description.

    a. It makes it clear that the realm we are talking about belongs to God. We are not dealing here with an atheistic or even agnostic humanism. We are small players in a larger process, and part of our action is a constant search to understand and tune ourselves in to the dream, the will, the hope, the intention of God for us and our world, the movements of the Spirit ahead of us. This God is benevolent rather than malevolent or simply whimsical towards human beings. Our involvement in our world is therefore worthwhile because we can cooperate for good. It is a world that is ultimately coherent, however difficult to understand, and allows us to become involved in rational processes rather than just random, whimsical events with no cohesion or rationale. "God" is a word that is difficult in secular societies, but even there it is recognized that many individuals are guided by their own private understanding of "God" and that this is entirely legitimate provided it is not used as an imposition on those who have a different understanding of "God" or no god.

b. This realm is in process; it is evolving; it is underway but not yet achieved. It points and works towards an ideal state of existence. It does not say at this point what these "ideal relationships" actually look like, because that is something we will need to work on further. Part of our mission in the world consists in working out what the closest approximation of that ideal might be in our particular place and our particular time. This is not an established utopia which must be achieved at all costs. The ideal itself is evolving in our understanding of it. Thus, it is better described as "eutopia" (activity that seeks a better world) rather than a "utopia" (an unattainable ideal).[1]

c. It is not just about human beings in isolation from the rest of creation, but is concerned with human beings within the planet Earth. It involves us religiously and ethically within the planet Earth and particularly in how we relate to and deal with the non-human beings and processes that make up this planet.

In brief, this description of the realm of God tells us at least that a) it belongs to a benevolent God, b) it is a process with a changing embodiment in time and place, and c) it engages us religiously and ethically in relationships within the planet Earth.

When citizen theologians engage in the wider society, they are stimulated by the hope of contributing to the evolving realm of God. The realm of God supplies Christians with a central vision from which particular hopes and objectives are derived. Other organizations and individuals in a pluralist society also have their own hopes and objectives that similarly drive their own engagement. Some of these we may find to be destructive or self-serving. But many are constructive and altruistic. Which of these other organizations should Christians cooperate with, negotiate with, resist, or simply remain neutral towards?

I have often been asked by non-Christian citizens to explain and account for my own vision of society as a Christian. What is the Christian vision exactly and does it correspond with other visions for a good society? More importantly, perhaps, as Christian citizens we need to be able to account *to ourselves* for that vision. What seemed to be clear within a

---

1. Beavis, *Jesus & Utopia*, 2–3.

church context or within Christian theology may crumble or evaporate when it encounters and is challenged by different and sometimes contrary visions for a good society.

Is there some common, non-biblical language that Christian citizens can use to explain this vision? Are there other visions and other words in contemporary society that serve as contemporary translations of the biblical vision of the realm of God? Do some of the objectives of non-Christian individuals and organizations correspond with those of Christians working for the realm of God even if those non-Christian objectives are expressed in different terms?

Rethinking God's Mission in the World Today

In the mid-twentieth century, the focus of mission studies turned from what had been the church's standard missionary agenda, the conversion of non-Christian peoples, towards a study of mission in a pluralist world of many religions and secular ideologies. Theologians began to look for new ways of expressing their understanding of God's mission in the world. One of the early modern ideas put forward as a guiding principle for rethinking this mission was the biblical idea of *shalom*. As proposed by the Dutch missiologist Johannes Hoekendijk, *shalom* was understood as meaning peace, integrity, community, harmony, and justice. This described the objective of the church's work in the present day that connected back to Jesus and his mission as well as to the promises of the Old Testament.[2] While *shalom* was a deep and inspiring concept within the Judeo-Christian tradition,[3] it was again, like the concept of the "kingdom of God," not the kind of language that communicated easily in the public forum of a contemporary pluralist society.

More recently, the World Council of Churches's document "Together towards Life: Mission and Evangelism in Changing Landscapes" used the concept of *"fullness of life"* from John's Gospel to describe the purpose of God's mission. "We affirm that the purpose of God's mission is fullness of life (John 10:10) and that this is the criterion for discernment in

---

2. See Skreslet's comments on Hoekendijk's role in missiology in Skreslet, *Comprehending Mission*, 75.

3. One of the conclusions of the group reports from the mission conference Edinburgh 2010 was entitled "Wholeness and *Shalom* as the Goal of Mission." Kim and Anderson, *Edinburgh 2010: Mission Today and Tomorrow*, 170.

mission."[4] Fullness of life is here understood particularly in terms of liberation of the oppressed peoples, the healing and reconciliation of broken communities and the restoration of the whole creation.[5]

"*Flourishing,*" or more expansively, "full human flourishing," is another image that captures in modern terms the sense of God's mission in the world today. In Australian theologian Neil Ormerod's words, "Whatever the detailed results of modern biblical criticism, we must surely see the kingdom as a symbol of total human flourishing, a symbol of life as God originally intended and continues to intend it, freed from the distortions of sin and evil."[6] In theological language, the image of "flourishing" overcomes some of the negative implications of traditional mission images such as salvation, redemption, and atonement. In a more philosophical mode, Lithuanian philosophers Andrius Bielskis and Egidijus Mardosas argue for "human flourishing" which consists of "people becoming independent practical reasoners, able to use their rational powers for the pursuit of a meaningful life."[7] It is also a word sometimes used in the public forum outside of church circles.

Yet the idea of "flourishing," while biblically founded and full of positive encouragement, may also carry liabilities in the public forum. In my own experience, the idea of "flourishing" implies perhaps too idealistic or romantic a vision for citizen theologians living with the constantly frustrated hopes of people living in deprivation. It seems too far away from the reality of survival that confronts hopes for a better society. It may be nevertheless that there are situations where "flourishing" does indeed communicate a convincing sense of the realm of God and citizen theologians may prefer it in their own contexts.[8]

However uneasy we may feel about contemporary concepts or images as equivalents of biblical ones, the task of finding such concepts is not optional for mission engagement with the wider world. We do still need to find words that have currency in the public forum and that are not just repetitions of ancient biblical words. Simply to repeat biblical

---

4. World Council of Churches, "Together towards Life."

5. World Council of Churches, "Together towards Life," #102.

6. Ormerod, *Re-Visioning the Church*, 104.

7. Bielskis and Mardosas, "Human Flourishing," 185–201. Here they follow MacIntyre's reformulation of the Aristotelian-Thomist tradition.

8. A commitment to human flourishing is often, for example, a key value in assessing research in practical theology. See Bennett et al., *Invitation to Research in Practical Theology*.

or traditional words that have become part of the church's in-group language is to admit that we do not know what these words mean in real contemporary life. In that case we admit that there is no such person as a citizen theologian, for that kind of theologian has no idea what it is to be a citizen.

The Christian missionary in the role of citizen theologian will already hear in public discourse a number of words and concepts that are appealing as ways of expressing the essence of the realm of God. As well as the term "flourishing," there are also words like "wellbeing," "resilience," and "sustainability"[9] that are used commonly enough in public discourse to talk about a vision for a good society.

The Concept of Wellbeing

I propose to focus here on the concept of "wellbeing" as one that is widely used in public discourse. If we can give careful consideration to the concept of "wellbeing" as a sufficient, even if not perfect, contemporary translation of the biblical concept of the "realm of God," it should not be too hard to give similar consideration to other, similar public images where desirable. We may need to be alert here too to the fact that there are fashions in public discourse just as there are in theology. A word or concept that serves us as a translation in one time and place may not serve so well in a different time and place. I propose, nevertheless, to pursue an investigation into the concept of "wellbeing" as an entry into public discussion of what an embodiment of the realm of God might look like in many contemporary situations, while admitting that it might not be suitable for every time and every place.[10]

---

9. Ernst M. Conradie suggests that "sustainability" may be regarded as a secularized expression of "providence" in that it expresses faith in the God whose creative, nurturing, redemptive, and innovative love sustains the whole earth, moment by moment. Similarly, "salvation" can be understood as comprehensive wellbeing. Conradie, "Climate Justice, Food Security . . . and God," 119–25, esp. footnote 31.

10. The concept of "wellbeing" has already entered into official Vatican language where "wellbeing," understood as the "fullness of the good, which has its origin and consummation in God and is fully revealed in Jesus Christ" and in which "lies the ultimate goal of every ecclesial activity." Such wellbeing "flourishes as an anticipation of the kingdom of God, which the church is called to proclaim and establish in every sphere of human enterprise, and is the special fruit of that charity which, as the bright path of ecclesial action, is expressed even in the social, civil, and political realms." Congregation for the Doctrine of the Faith and Dicastery For Promoting Integral Human

A 2015 document of the Organisation for Economic Co-operation and Development (OECD) provides an example of a public and international use of the concept of "wellbeing." "How's Life? 2015: Measuring Wellbeing" describes what it considers the essential ingredients that shape people's wellbeing in OECD and partner countries. It includes measures of both material wellbeing (such as income, jobs, and housing) and the broader quality of people's lives (such as their health, education, work-life balance, environment, social connections, civic engagement, subjective wellbeing, and safety). This third (2015) edition of "How's Life?" adds some new ways of understanding wellbeing. It includes a focus on child wellbeing and the risks for children in non-affluent families; it introduces new measures to capture some of the natural, human, social, and economic resources that play a role in supporting wellbeing over time; it suggests that "doing good," that is, volunteer work, brings a variety of other wellbeing benefits to both volunteers and to society at large; and it shows that where people live can shape their opportunities for living well.[11]

In its engagement in society, a local church encounters community development projects, community services organizations, and government agencies which see themselves as having a mission to provide services outside the boundaries of their own organization for the wellbeing of society. An example of this from my experience is a community development project in which I was involved that saw its mission as to transform its local community to be a place "where people thrive and prosper for generations, a place with a strong and vibrant community spirit, valued for its natural beauty and history." This was its definition of "wellbeing" incorporated into its own vision statement.

Is such a concept of "wellbeing" the same as, or nearly the same as, or overlapping with the concept of the "realm of God"? Whether it is or not is of importance to the local Christian church because this determines the degree to which local Christians will *cooperate* with, *negotiate* with, *resist*, or simply remain *neutral* towards the efforts of other organizations in promoting such wellbeing. There can hardly ever be complete agreement between community ideas of wellbeing and the Christian idea of

---

Development, "Considerations for an Ethical Discernment," #2.

11. OECD, "How's Life?" Such documents build upon the Universal Declaration of Human Rights, adopted by the United Nations General Assembly in 1948, and the two treaties that try to ensure governments enforce these rights: the International Covenant on Civil and Political Rights and the International Covenant on Economic, Social, and Cultural Rights.

the realm of God, because community organizations in a secular society will normally have "no-go" areas that protect its pluralism. Discussion about God or gods, ideas of a supernatural, notions of divine intervention, life after death, or faith commitments to a savior, for example, cannot normally be on the agenda. To require complete agreement would be a return to a state of Christendom where society and church are the same and everyone else is marginalized. The issue is not whether there is complete agreement, but whether there is *enough* agreement to allow cooperation about a particular social vision and projects.

Until quite recently the most common applications of the idea of "wellbeing" were to *human* wellbeing rather than to the life of all Earth beings. We could note that the understanding of wellbeing as set out above from the OECD is focused primarily on human beings, with a secondary reference to "environment" insofar as this affects human beings. The theologian, operating from a God-centered rather than a purely human-centered perspective, will be concerned as well with the wellbeing of all God's creation including the non-human beings of the planet Earth (Earth-centered). One of the earliest calls for theology's attention to the close link between the economy of the poor and the ecology of the planet was from Ecumenical Patriarch Bartholomew, who saw the web of life as a sacred gift from God such that we must serve our neighbor and preserve our world with both humility and generosity, in a perspective of frugality and solidarity alike.[12]

For the theologian, as for the ecologist, human beings are not the only consideration in matters of wellbeing. Nevertheless, not all Earth beings can be treated equally. The life cycles of the Earth include decay and predation so that the wellbeing of every Earth being is not the same—wellbeing makes sense only within the cycles of life and death. The term "resilience" is one commonly used in ecological discourse and the citizen theologian will always need to have this concept in mind in discussion and engagement about wellbeing. The issues of "resilience thinking," understood here as addressing the dynamics and development of complex social–ecological systems,[13] are very wide, and we will need to return to them later. In the meantime, we can note simply that the citizen theologian will always have a focused eye on the effect of human actions on the natural and built environments as well as on human persons.

12. Bartholomew, *On Earth as in Heaven*, 323.
13. Folke, "Resilience Thinking."

The key point for us at this stage in our investigation is whether a local church can see commitments to the wellbeing of society and of the Earth around them as equivalent to its own commitment to the realm of God. Michael Barram describes the Bible as seeking to transform our moral imaginations so that we serve a God who will make abundance, generosity, cooperation, sustainability, compassion, mercy, love, and justice become realities.[14]

Some at least of the non-church and non-religious organizations in society have a vision and objectives that amount to a non-theological description of a better society. Such future ideals often have specific physical, social, economic, and environmental outcomes. Some of them have long time frames that will not necessarily occur within the lifetimes of the current participants. In this sense such projects may correspond at least in part with the theological concept of the realm of God and may be a concrete expression of it in contemporary terms.

A commitment to "wellbeing" as such is *intentional* language. Intentions are not the same as the actual reality of what really happens. To talk of the "realm of God" is also intentional language. It implies, as far as we are concerned, an *intended* embodiment in particular times and places where it may become, or fail to become, a reality. Yet even at the somewhat ephemeral level of "intentions," one of the tasks of the citizen theologian and the local church is the discernment of whether such "wellbeing" corresponds or fails to correspond with the theological "intention" that we call the unfolding and evolving, the already-but-not-yet, realm of God. If so, the language of "wellbeing" becomes a means of communication between the local church and other communities or organizations that make up a pluralist society.

Sin as Deprivation

No Christian theologian can ignore the influence of sin in our world. The citizen theologian does not engage in society at large with naive optimism as if people were always loving and kind. Like the concept of the realm of God, the concept of sin similarly needs to be translated (even if only partially) into contemporary language so that we can deal with it in real, contemporary terms rather than confining it within biblical history

---

14. Barram, *Missional Economics*, 244–45.

or historical theology. Part of the citizen theologian's mission is to be alert to and seek to overcome sin in contemporary society.

There are places, times, and dimensions of our world which are "deprived" of the realm of God. The task of the citizen theologian is not just to discern the *presence* of the realm of God but also its *absence*, and, even more importantly, its *privation*. This "privation" theme is like a shadow following along beside us throughout this search for the public impact of our participation in the realm of God. Privation is more than a simple absence. It should not be understood as simply a fact of evolution in the sense that an evolving or already-but-not-yet realm of God implies a goal not yet reached and therefore at any point in time still lacks something hoped for. Rather than simply a fact of evolution, the term "privation" refers not just to an absence of something but to something that *should* be there but in fact is not.[15]

In contemporary terms we are perhaps best to call this "*deprivation.*" Deprivation is a lack of something which a person or group of persons should have but in fact do not have. "Deprivation" is a concept used in the public forum that has many (not all) of the characteristics that the theologian can recognize as "social sin" or "structural sin." It acknowledges that people may suffer from disablement or handicaps from which we agree they should not suffer; this disablement was not inevitable (fate, evolution, the will of God) but is a result of some prior fault or omission mainly by people other than the sufferers. Moreover, there is something that can be done to relieve and prevent that suffering.

A state of "social" sin is not necessarily the result of the personal sins of the individual or group of individuals affected. It may be the result of *other* people's sins whether as direct action or as lack of responsible action. The concept of deprivation is one that is used in the public forum in regard, for example, to neighborhood disintegration revealed in a lack of basic facilities, ethnic or class discrimination, and breakdowns in children's development and education. The citizen theologian can recognize here a concept very close in its practical applications to the theological concept of social sin or "original" sin. In making this recognition the citizen theologian's attitude and action towards dealing with deprivation is in many aspects the same as dealing with social sin.

---

15. The view that evil has no positive nature, but is the loss of good, is supported most influentially in theological tradition by Augustine of Hippo (*The City of God* XI.9) and Thomas Aquinas (*Summa Theologiae* I.49).

The citizen theologian's reflection and involvement in the realm of God includes a concern for sin, not as a reality parallel to the realm of God, but as a deprivation of the realm of God and its ongoing evolution. In the public forum where the citizen theologian's commitment to the realm of God is carried out, the concern for society's wellbeing also always addresses the deprivation of the realm of God, a deprivation of wellbeing.

Challenges to Theology

These interactions between traditional theological concepts and the concepts in contemporary discourse about the public good raise challenges for theology itself. Are there really equivalents between talk about "flourishing," "wellbeing," "resilience," "sustainability," and more internal church-familiar concepts like the "realm of God" or "sin"? Have we lost too much when we engage with others in the public forum where we abandon traditional theological or biblical language and use the common public language?

The questions are real ones and such translation across languages needs to be done with care. It is difficult and risky to translate theological concepts into public language, such as the language of wellbeing. Here our traditional theology and church language is challenged to affirm or deny that the stated objectives of public and civil organizations amount to descriptions in public rather than theological language of the realm of God as realized in a particular place and time.

The citizen theologian is challenged to find answers to such questions as:

a. Just what are the characteristics of the reign of God in our time and place as it evolves in partial fulfillment before the "end"?

b. Can we describe the characteristics of the realm of God in terms of specific contemporary outcomes not just in biblical terms? Is theology able to do this or at least to recognize it when someone else describes it?

Theologians normally ascribe the causality here to God. In pluralist societies, legislation and projects for public wellbeing or community development that do not have a distinctly religious foundation normally can neither affirm nor deny divine causality. Is the realm of God describable in a way that has concrete on-the-ground objectives which are not formulated in terms of divine causality? It is on this basis that a local church and its members can cooperate with, negotiate with, ignore, withdraw from, or oppose actions taken purportedly for the wellbeing of the society.

Conclusion

The challenge to citizen theologians, to mission theology, and to local churches is to articulate their Christian vision of the realm of God in terms that communicate within the public forum. For it is in the public forum rather than just within the Christian community itself that their mission activity takes place.

The concepts of "wellbeing" and "deprivation" lead us beyond repetitions of biblical terms in our mission engagement with the wider society. While exact translations may not be possible and some of us may even be uneasy about leaving biblical and traditional theological terms in the background of our public conversations, such terms take us down the track to articulating publicly not so much the "meaning" of the realm of God but its *impact* in our societies.

5

Contemporary Impact of the Realm of God

WHAT IS THE REALM of God when understood from the point of view of its impact in contemporary society? This is a central mission question because its answer determines what the missionary, the citizen theologian, actually does. This requires an understanding of the realm of God not so much in biblical, abstract, or systematic terms but in terms that are "actionable." What does a commitment to the realm of God require of us in terms of attitude and behavior? "Not everyone who says to me, 'Lord, Lord', will enter the kingdom of heaven, but only one who does the will of my Father in heaven" (Matt 7:21). Rather than asking what the realm of God *means*, we ask, What is the *public impact* of making a commitment to such a realm?

That a commitment to the realm of God involves us in personal holiness and an active involvement in the church community itself is not at issue in this investigation into Christian mission. These things are usually (though not always) taken for granted and are not commonly in dispute in theology. The issue for us here is whether it also, and *primarily*, commits us to working for a better world.

We can expand this question of "public impact" by formulating the key question guiding the investigation at this point as:

Does commitment to the realm of God call Christians to an engagement in the social, environmental, and economic issues of society?

In conversations in the public forum (outside of faith-based groups), theological or church language often makes communication difficult. Yet in such public conversations we can usually understand, though not necessarily agree with, one another when our intentions and objectives are expressed in terms of the social, environmental, and economic results we hope for. This kind of translation from theological to public language is necessary if our purpose is to serve the wider realm of God rather than simply require other people to learn the particular language of the church's own internal theology in order to understand us.

From Theological Concepts to Public Stances

I propose to invoke here a distinction between what I shall term "*theological concepts*" and more down-to-earth "*public stances*" as a way of dealing with the issue of translating between theological and public languages.[1]

Theological debates often take an oppositional or competitive form where one interpretation of a theological concept denies or delimits the validity of another. So, for example, the argument that the realm of God is here and now and this is what we need to focus on "competes" with the argument that our present life is a vale of tears but we can look forward to the realm of God that will come after our own death or at the end of time. There is also a "both-and" position which proposes that the realm of God is partly now but fully in the future. In theology, such debates are commonly argued as true or false interpretations of the gospel message. They are argued on the basis of Scripture and from Christian tradition.

Yet this is not the end of the matter. Theological debates often resolve at a more concrete level into *public stances* that are important in society. Let me illustrate this. In a pluralist society, local churches and citizen theologians concerned for the good of society are likely to be involved, along with people of no explicit faith commitment, in community development projects or social and environmental policy decisions. These projects or policies require decisions about whether some proposed action needs to be taken here and now, should focus rather

---

1. While not quite the same, there is a similarity here between my concern to move from theological concepts to public stances and Jonathan Burnside's concern to move from biblical law to practical action for justice in our contemporary world and his insistence that religious beliefs should not be excluded in principle and cannot be excluded in practice from a liberal democracy. Burnside, "Words of Wisdom, Words of Prophecy," 560–76.

on long-term goals, or should allow the situation simply to resolve itself by fate, the market, natural attrition, or future catastrophe. The people involved in these public policy negotiations will have a variety of foundations for supporting one strategy rather than another.

For the Christian citizen theologian this foundation is their understanding of the realm of God. But what difference does this make to the stances they take in community projects? In my experience in these circumstances, Christians with a commitment to the realm of God as "partly now but fully in the future" will commonly adopt a longer-term view than those public officials whose involvement is limited by their employment contract or term of office; such Christians are also likely to have a stronger commitment to the project than people with just personal or business interests in it. On the other hand, Christians who see the realm of God as essentially after death (heaven) will see little urgency in any social action. And Christians who identify the realm of God with the church itself will want to see some particular benefit for the church out of the project. Each of these views on the realm of God has a different impact on Christian engagement in society.

My point here is that while *theological concepts* (like the "realm of God") are often unintelligible or unacceptable in public language, the *public stances* implied in those concepts, once stated as political or ethical choices, become intelligible to almost everyone. While the theological concepts may not communicate publicly, the statement of the public stances implied in them makes clear both to the citizen theologian and to their fellow citizens where they can cooperate, where they are prepared to negotiate, and where they are in opposition or simply indifferent. Discussion about the "realm of God" itself may have a quite limited audience, but discussion of its "impact" can have a much wider public.

The Public Impact of the Realm of God

For our purposes in this investigation, I propose to use five "particularizing" questions which I have found to be the most productive in teasing out the implications of the realm of God for its public impact: What is it? Where is it? When is it? Who brings it about? Who belongs to it?

In the previous chapter, "The Realm of God and Wellbeing," I proposed that, among others, the idea of "wellbeing" is at least partially a way of describing *what* the realm of God is in the contemporary world. The various descriptions and options for how "wellbeing" is implemented in contemporary society are public discussions into which the citizen theologian can enter, informed and guided by theological understandings of the realm of God. *What* the realm of God is in the contemporary world remains a key, perhaps *the* key missiological question. The previous chapter on "wellbeing" was the beginning of an answer to that question.

Yet we need to go further than the question of *What?* We can discover more about the impact of the realm of God by investigating four other dimensions of the realm of God, namely its:

- *location* (Where is it?),
- *timing* (When is it?),
- *agency* (Who brings it about?), and
- *membership* (Who belongs to it?).

Location: Where Is It?

Is the realm of God within our present experience of life or does it refer rather to a "spiritual" existence beyond and other than our "sensory" experience? If it is about "this" world, is it purely internal to the Christian individual and community or is it located in the wider world around us?

Theological debates about where the realm of God is located put several broad choices to the local church about its public stances. A local church that sees the realm of God as located in a *spiritual realm beyond death* need have no concern for the wider society except to prepare people for a "happy" death through which they can enter into that realm. A local church that puts emphasis on the realm of God as *internal to the individual person* or as *internal to the church itself* is likely to have minimal engagement in the issues of the surrounding society. Or, more commonly in my experience, it is likely to accord quite low priority to the issues of the wider society even though it may be sympathetic to them. The priorities of its organization and its ministers are more personal, pastoral, and oriented towards the life of the church community itself than directed outwards to the wider society. Mission, in other words, is minimized.

A local church that puts emphasis on the realm of God as located in the *wider society* (and keeping in mind that church members themselves are part of that society), on the other hand, will have strong motivation to work for the wellbeing of that society rather than just for the church community itself or the personal salvation of their own members. Similarly, a local church which limits the realm of God to human society but does not include the *planet Earth* in that realm will have little sense of responsibility for the human relationships with the non-human beings and processes of Earth. The church's understanding of where the realm of God is located will have a direct impact on its public stances towards the wider world.

Timing: When Is It?

Future unpredictable intervention from outside or continuing transformation from within?

That the realm of God is already present in the life and actions of Jesus Christ himself and will be fulfilled in the future is not often in dispute in Christian theology. Debates are concerned rather with the question: Will this future realm be a supreme intervention by God at some unpredictable time that bears little relationship to any human actions or is it a continuing transformation into the future of the world as we currently know it?

Christian theology is about change, "*metanoia*," a change of heart. Christians do not regard the current world as perfect, requiring no improvement. But is this change a transformation occurring over a period of time and in which contemporary Christians play a part? Or should our attitude rather be one of waiting for that future time when God will intervene to bring about that change.[2]

At the level of public stances, attitudes towards timing are important because results may not be immediately forthcoming and often cannot be expected within the lifetime of this generation. People and organizations involved in social transformation may be under pressure for quick results in order to maintain public interest (and funding) or for the sake of their own careers. People whose involvement is more theologically or ideologically motivated can take a longer-term view that extends even beyond their own lifetimes.

---

2. By way of example, Gary D. Badcock illustrates this latter position when he concludes his book on the church with the statement that the renewal of the church, though a goal toward which we can surely work and concerning which we can think, is ultimately something for which we must pray and wait. Badcock, *The House Where God Lives*, 337.

A theological position that the timing of the realm of God will be an *abrupt intervention by God at the end of time* discourages engagement in the present realities of social, environmental, and economic issues. Rather, in this case, the church's mission to society should be to convert people to faith in Christ so that as many as possible may be ready for that intervention of God. Action for social change will have little or no effect on this coming. Engagement in structural change is therefore not necessary, though compassionate care for those currently suffering might well be part of that readiness.

On the other hand, a theological position that regards the timing of the realm of God as a *continuing transformation into the future* encourages Christians to engage creatively in current social and environmental issues. It supports a public stance for action that is both immediate and extended into the long term. It supports continuing action even in a struggle through seemingly impossible odds and at great personal cost. Yet it also demands continual self-criticism, for the realm of God is not to be confused with personal obsessions. The long-term view may extend well beyond the lives of the current generation.

Christian participation in the realm of God as continuing transformation into the future is thus conscious of the timing and time-conditional strategies. In English theologian Luke Bretherton's terms, it is a "democratic politics" that involves living with the reality that a) there will inevitably be unforeseen consequences; b) "we" are part of the problem; c) we cannot step "outside" to a different space and time but must generate change from "within"; and (d) that with different people in a different place, another way of proceeding might be more appropriate.[3]

These different theological understandings of the realm of God have strong and long-term impacts on the public stances of the local church and its citizen theologians.

Agency: Who Brings It About?

Who are the agents of this realm?

That God is the primary Agent of this realm is not normally in dispute in theology. What is more in dispute is a) whether God alone brings about this realm or whether there are also human agents who contribute to its realization; and if there are such human agents, b) are they

---

3. Bretherton, *Resurrecting Democracy*, 286–87.

Christians only or are there others who can be such agents, and c) can some people bring it about *for* others?

a. The theological position that God *alone* is the Agent of this realm usually includes a belief that human beings are fundamentally corrupt and therefore cannot be faithful agents of God. Contrary to this is the position which holds that God's grace can overcome this corruption of sin so that humans can be agents, though limited, in bringing about this realm of God. The debate between a "fall-redemption" theology which emphasizes human corruption and divine rescue on the one hand (illustrated in the popular hymn "Amazing Grace") and on the other hand a "creation" theology which emphasizes the continuing creative activity of God in people and in creation[4] illustrates respectively a more negative and a more positive evaluation of human agency in contributing to the evolving realm of God. This kind of debate will seem quite esoteric in many local churches today and quite unintelligible in the public forum. Yet the translation of these differing theological positions into public stances has a full-bodied impact on a local church's mission.

At the level of public stances, the position that God alone is the Agent of the realm of God resolves down to a public stance that Christians and churches have *no role* to play in society. This is a "non-involvement" stance. (This may be mitigated, though, if the church itself and its morality is under threat and the church then seeks to defend itself against threats to its own existence or interests.)

We should note that there is an equivalent "non-involvement" stance by *non-church organizations*—essentially a laissez-faire, hands-off, "it's not our business" stance to issues in society. Such positions in this public debate are based on ideologies or philosophies that are *equivalent to* theological positions. Instead of "God" there is fate, the free market, self-interest, "I'm not my brother's keeper," etc., which provide a motivation or rationale.

b. A second kind of theological debate about human agency is whether Christians rather than anyone else are the *only* true agents of this realm of God. That is to say, at the human level of agency, can people who are not Christian and not members of the Christian church be

---

4. A strand of theology that has flourished recently in the many publications in ecotheology, but which also has a long tradition back through Karl Rahner, Thomas Aquinas, Maximus the Confessor, Athanasius, and Irenaeus.

agents of the realm of God? In case this seems an unlikely debate today, we could recall the arguments that took place not so long ago during the Second Vatican Council (1962–65) about whether the natural potentialities of the human person and human society could serve in any significant way as preparation for the working of God's grace in the world.[5]

The theological position that only Christians can be agents of the realm of God resolves down to the public stance that in matters of wellbeing, Christians should set up their own organizations (e.g., welfare organizations, social service groups, lobbyists, political parties) to bring about a better society—in some cases parallel to non-church organizations with similar objectives. Christian mission here does not see any true value in non-Christian attempts for promoting wellbeing.

Again here, there is an equivalent *(non-church) public stance* in which some group or organization claims a monopoly on public services which, in their view, they alone are qualified to deliver. At the level of public impact, the debates about agency are shared by church and non-church organizations. A concern for the wider society combined with a view that no one else is competent to do this is common enough in both church and non-church organizations. In some cases, the argument is valid in the face of incompetent or self-interested entries into matters of public concern. In other cases, these groups are simply protecting their own territory against competition.

By contrast there is a theological position that *many people and organizations* in society, along with Christian churches, can play a positive part for the wellbeing of society. In this case, at the level of public stances, a church would be looking for other charitable and public agencies which it could support and with which it could

---

5. Richard Gaillardetz calls attention to this debate leading up to the final version of the *Constitution on the Church in the Modern World: Gaudium et Spes* (1965). There were, on the one hand, bishops and their theologians who were willing to grant the limited, but still positive, natural potentialities of the human person and human society (regarded as a more "Thomistic" anthropology). On the other hand, there were other influential figures who did not believe that events transpiring in the natural order could serve in any significant way as a preparation for the working of God's grace in the world (regarded as a more "Augustinian" anthropology). Gaillardetz concludes that, while including both these tendencies, the document's dominant tone is better reflected in the Council's confident assertion that "the achievements of the human race are a sign of God's greatness and the fulfillment of his mysterious design." (*Pastoral Constitution*, 32). Gaillardetz, *Ecclesiology for a Global Church*, 52.

cooperate for common objectives. Given too that the church is aware that the Holy Spirit is active in the world independently of the church, the local church will be looking for such initiatives of the Spirit outside of the church itself. There are historical examples of where Christian churches have recognized and adopted such initiatives of the Spirit in the wider world: religious freedom, human rights, democracy, the moral equality of all people, and the evil of slavery. For many local churches the key issue here is to decide just how high (or low) a priority should be given to such cooperation.

Again here, there are equivalent *(non-church) public stances* which see wide cooperation for common objectives as desirable and often necessary. The realm of God is not the motivation or rationale in this case. The rationale is rather some other principle such as a belief in "cooperation," a recognition that it is supported by public opinion, social scientific evidence, or government policy.

c. A third kind of theological debate concerns whether some people can bring about or at least enhance the realm of God *for others*. Christian missionaries who travelled to foreign countries or operated in other cultures have traditionally done so on the basis of this theological position.

In doing this, foreign missionaries in other countries have sometimes been accused of adopting a public stance in an arrogant rather than a helpful and humble way. Yet arrogance under the guise of helpfulness is not confined to Christian missionaries. Non-church organizations can be similarly accused. The desire of outsiders to help the "deprived" in ways that the outsiders know best is often adopted by public agencies, non-governmental organizations, as well as churches. What is the role, for example, of a government agency or a church in helping people in conditions of deprivation? What role should the deprived people themselves have in determining *their own* futures? Local organizations find themselves constantly arguing that the people affected need to have a say in how a project supposedly for their wellbeing is conceived and implemented, while outside experts and power brokers are constantly doing just the opposite. The problem of arrogance is not confined to Christian missionaries. Hence too the frequent arguments and anger from people suffering from some form of deprivation that they have had no part in deciding the solution, yet they are the ones who know most about it and will suffer most from failed attempts at solutions.

Membership: Who Belongs to It?

Who are the people who belong to this realm of God?

Are those who participate in the realm of God the same as those who are Christian? Is it broader or narrower than those who are Christian? Are there some people who are excluded?

There are a number of key theological debates here. Is the realm of God larger than the church or are they identical in membership? If identical, then mission action consists in bringing as many people into the church as possible. In this case, the objective of mission activity is conversion to the church or at least to faith in Christ rather than engagement in attempts to create a better society. If, however, the realm of God is much larger than the Christian church, and includes all people, then a commitment of churches to participate in the realm of God translates into public action for the wellbeing of the whole society. Further again than that, if the realm of God includes all of God's creation, then a commitment to the realm of God translates into a commitment that human behavior contributes to the wellbeing (resilience) of the other beings and processes of the Earth.

In this book I have adopted the basic perspective that the church's mission is in service to this realm of God. This entire discussion about public stances derives from this understanding of the mission of the church.

Conclusion

A local church and its members who are concerned with the society around them and attempt to create a better society are continually making judgements about the kind and style of their engagement. These judgements are about concrete actions at particular times and places, and require an understanding of the contemporary impact of the realm of God that is considerably more specific and contemporary than any discussion about its biblical or traditional origins. We can render the broad concept of "wellbeing" more specific by considering how the dimensions of location, timing, agency, and membership commit us to engagement in our time and our place.

Part of this engagement is about finding a public language that allows citizen theologians to communicate with other citizens of good will. Traditional *theological concepts* can almost always, or at least very often, be expressed in terms of their implied *public stances*, for better or for worse, on contemporary wellbeing. This communication enables local churches to make decisions about cooperation, negotiation, or resistance to the actions of other organizations in a pluralist society.

Once we have achieved some, even if not complete, clarity about *what* the realm of God looks like in terms of its public impact, and about *where* it is, *when* it is, who are its *agents*, and who are its *members*, we are in a position to investigate what the local church's mission in that realm of God can usefully be. This leads us to an investigation that seeks to clarify what is meant by "mission." Part II of this book enters into that investigation.

Part II

Mission in Contemporary Society

PART I OF THIS book set out some basic perspectives on mission and church. In the first chapter, I named five starting points for this investigation:

- the mission belongs primarily to God, in whose mission the church seeks to participate;
- it is the mission that creates the church rather than the other way round;
- the church is not identical with, but rather in service of, the evolving realm of God;
- all Christians are missionaries from baptism;
- the point of view of the local church is important and needs addressing.

Taken together, these five perspectives constitute a deliberate option for one kind of mission theology rather than others.

The second chapter of Part I was concerned with how a local church and its "citizen theologians" communicate with the wider society. Citizen theologians inhabit both the Christian theological world (the language we hear in church and in conversations with other Christians) and some of the many language worlds of the wider society. Chapters 3, 4, and 5 focused on the concept of the "realm of God": its origins in the New Testament, its interpretation today as "wellbeing," and its contemporary impact.

These considerations are important yet preliminary to the central task of this investigation into mission and church. "Part II: Mission in Contemporary Society" is concerned then with the central question: What is the church *for*? What is its *mission*?

A basic perspective adopted throughout this book is that the church participates in God's mission. Given that perspective, what is the mission of the Christian church within that larger mission of God?

6

Recent Mission Theologies

MISSIONARIES, THAT IS, ALL active Christians, are sometimes unaware of the theology that underlies and gives coherence to their mission activities. Their mission theology may be inherited from previous missionaries or simply taken for granted in the church to which these contemporary missionaries belong. One of the tasks of local churches, and of missiology as a theological discipline, is to identify and critique the variety of mission theologies that are already influencing the thought and action (or inaction) of a local church. Some of these theologies, whether merely implicit or clearly explicit, may be inappropriate for that local church or, as has sometimes been recognized in hindsight once it is laid out before us, simply wrong. (I discuss some examples of mission gone wrong in the following chapter.)

The purpose of this chapter, then, is to arrive at a satisfactory description (not quite a definition) of "mission." It should be satisfactory at least to the extent that it allows us to continue this investigation with a common understanding of what we are talking about.

The Variety and Convergence of Mission Theologies

In his 1991 overview of the history and theology of mission, *Transforming Mission: Paradigm Shifts in Theology of Mission*, South African missiologist David J. Bosch identified a number of different approaches to mission which were dominant in successive periods of Christian history:

the missionary paradigm of the *Eastern Church*, the paradigm of the *medieval Roman Catholic Church*, and of the paradigm of the *Protestant Reformation*. Each of these established a distinct and competitive style of mission activity, and each of these is still operative today.

Bosch found it much more difficult, however, to identify a single dominant paradigm in the period following the eighteenth-century European "Age of Enlightenment." After that period, mission theologies became much more varied. By the 1990s, there was a whole variety of models of mission among which Bosch identifies mission as the church-with-others, mission as "*missio Dei*" (mission of God), mission as mediating salvation, mission as the quest for justice, mission as evangelism, mission as contextualization, mission as liberation, mission as inculturation, mission as common witness, mission as ministry by the whole people of God, mission as witness to people of other living faiths, mission as theology, and mission as action in hope.[1]

By the 1990s, there was also a turn in mainstream mission theology from a focus on "foreign" missions to a focus on "Western culture," that is, to a focus on countries formerly regarded as already "Christian," i.e., not needing "missionaries." The churches of these mainly North Atlantic countries were used to seeing themselves as "sending" rather than "receiving" missionaries. In a later book specifically concerned with mission to Western culture, Bosch proposed the following as ingredients of mission to "Western" culture: it must have an *ecological* dimension, be *countercultural*, be *ecumenical*, be *contextual*, and be primarily a ministry of the *laity* flowing from a *local, worshipping community*.[2] Many of these ingredients had been unknown or seemed unimportant to a previous generation of Christian missionaries.

In Catholic mission theology, this attention to "Western" culture was stimulated by Pope John Paul II's 1991 encyclical on mission[3] which encouraged, in addition to "foreign" missions, a "new evangelization" that focused back into countries that had formerly been considered already Christian.[4] In Latin America, the project of an "integral evangelization"

---

1. Bosch, *Transforming Mission*, Part III.

2. Bosch, *Believing in the Future*.

3. John Paul II, *Redemptoris Missio*. For further distinctions and clarifications on "evangelization," see Congregation for the Doctrine of the Faith, "Doctrinal Note 'On Some Aspects of Evangelization.'"

4. John F. Gorski gives a helpful description of such terms as "mission," "evangelization," "new evangelization," "mission activity," and "pastoral activity" in Catholic

was advocated by Catholic theologians such as Brazilian Leonardo Boff for whom to evangelize meant "to bear testimony to a vision of respect and acceptance of all cultures on account of God and the divine worth within cultures."[5]

Missiologist Charles Van Engen, working out of a North American Protestant tradition, helps us gain a sense of the variety of mission theologies over the last few decades that distinguish contemporary mission thinking from its predecessors. He identified five successive paradigm shifts in contemporary missiology:

1. exploration of mission thinking focused on discovering new cultures, new people, and new languages outside Western Europe;
b. expansion of mission agencies and denominations to include theological and missiological richness of the new civilizations and cultures they encountered;
c. enculturation during a time of decolonization and the rise of the nation-states around the globe that spawned an emphasis on national churches determining their own structures, leadership, priorities, and destinies;
d. the "Exodus" paradigm (with its foundation story in the Hebrew liberation from slavery in Egypt), in which the search for liberation in various contexts around the world called for a liberating engagement of the socioeconomic and political realities of nation-states;
e. the "Exile" paradigm (with its foundation story in the Jewish exile in Babylon), in which Christian persons, groups of people, churches, and mission agencies engage one another and their contexts as pilgrims in a foreign land in the midst of the largest mass migration of people in the history of the earth.[6] This involves Christian mission "from everywhere to everywhere by everyone to everyone" around the globe.[7]

---

theology. These terms indicate important shifts in mission thinking which, though now largely of historical importance, continue to recur in contemporary discussion. Gorski, "From 'Mission' to 'Evangelization,'" 31–44.

5. Boff, *Good News to the Poor*, 5. The concept of "new evangelization" has gone through many stages. For a brief summary of its history see Leavitt, *The Truth Will Make You Free*, esp. 26–37.

6. Here I have used Paul Hertig's succinct presentation of Van Engen's paradigms in Hertig, "Introduction," xxxi.

7. Van Engen, "Conclusion," 289–96.

The twenty-first century has seen both a variety of theologies of mission as well as attempts to find some coherence in this variety.[8] In an endeavor to bring some coherence into the variety of mission theologies, Stephen Bevans and Roger Schroeder discerned three major theologies of mission articulated in the last half of the twentieth century:

- mission as participation in the mission of the Triune God ("*missio Dei*"),
- mission as liberating service of the Reign of God, and
- mission as proclamation of Jesus Christ as universal savior.

To these Bevans and Schroeder added:

- "prophetic dialogue" as a synthesis of the above three major theologies and as a comprehensive theology of mission.

In this "prophetic dialogue" model, mission must be *dialogical* in reflecting God's Trinitarian nature, appreciating the dignity of humanity, and learning from culture. But it must also be *prophetic* in speaking for justice and peace, and in proclaiming the Lordship of Christ even while acknowledging the truths in other religions. Bevans and Schroeder propose that "prophetic dialogue" can serve as an overarching umbrella for an understanding of the various elements in the practice of mission (witness and proclamation; liturgy, prayer, and contemplation; justice, peace, and the integrity of creation; inter-religious dialogue; inculturation; and reconciliation).[9]

The Edinburgh 2010 Conference was a major missionary gathering this century which included Protestant, Orthodox, and Catholic participants. The papers written in preparation for that conference illustrate the considerable changes in mission theology over the hundred years between the mainly Protestant Edinburgh 1910 Conference and the

---

8. A good sense of the shifts in mission theology over the last hundred years or so, from a variety of geographical and denomination perspectives, is conveyed in Wild-Wood and Rajkumar, *Foundations for Mission*.

9. Bevans and Schroeder, *Prophetic Dialogue*, esp. 2–3. See also their earlier *Constants in Context*, esp. 348–98. The whole issue of *Missiology: An International Review* 41.1 (January 2013) is focused on prophetic dialogue. Some missiologists regard "prophetic dialogue" as a "smallest common denominator" catchphrase for mission theology and prefer more cautious or more abstract definitions. See, for example, Wrogemann, *Intercultural Theology*, 384, 377–408. Wrogemann's book is focused on mission as "oikoumenical doxology."

more widely ecumenical Edinburgh 2010 Conference.[10] The endeavor to find an overall, coherent, and ecumenical focus in mission theology is also illustrated in the Edinburgh 2010 Conference's "common call" which includes a carefully articulated description of the mission of the church:

"We believe the church, as a sign and symbol of the reign of God, is called to witness to Christ today by sharing in God's mission of love through the transforming power of the Holy Spirit."[11]

Because it is a consensus statement from an ecumenical conference, this common call glides over the points of difference among conference participants, but it does establish some of the major points of a contemporary Christian mission theology:

- the distinction between the reign of God and the church as its sign and symbol,
- the witness to Christ,
- God's mission of love, and
- the transforming role of the Holy Spirit.

The Local Church as Agent of Mission

The above notes on the variety of mission theologies have shown, I hope, that there have been many answers in the past to the question, What is the church's mission?[12] Some of these are overlapping, but some are simply incompatible in terms of a contemporary local church's mission policy. Yet there is also a sense of commonality or coherence among many of these varied theologies. We need to identify them and examine them because many of them, even if not recognized, are lurking somewhere in the minds and attitudes of our own local churches and our own citizen theologians. Only a few of these will be priorities for our own contemporary local churches. From here on, then, having recognized the wide range of existing mission theologies, my aim is to be more focused.

---

10. Kerr and Ross, *Edinburgh 2010: Mission Then and Now*.
11. Kim and Anderson, *Edinburgh 2010: Mission Today and Tomorrow*, 1–2.
12. For readers interested in pursuing the differences and similarities in recent mission theologies, Craig Ott puts five different perspectives (Roman Catholic, mainline Protestant, Latina evangelical, Orthodox, and North American evangelical) in conversation with one another. Ott, *The Mission of the Church*.

I seek now to identify *priorities* in the *local church*'s outreach into the wider society.

Most of the mission theologies I have noted above are *general* models in the sense that they are seen to be applicable to many different kinds of mission *agents*: the mission of the Catholic Church as a whole, for example, or of a mission society founded for foreign missions, the Orthodox churches in general, a religious order/congregation/institute founded for mission work, or the "evangelical" movement as a whole. My perspective in this book is that of *local churches* as agents of mission rather than any of these larger-scale organizations that more commonly attract the attention of missiology.

The key feature of a "local church" or "local community," as I use these terms here (and as introduced in chapter 1), is that the members meet as a liturgical assembly with some frequency (weekly, for example) or that their several Sunday assemblies have a common "home" (a parish church, for example), and they have an agreed way (a social structure) of making common decisions and common policies. For the most part, as I envisage it, these will be parishes, ethnic communities, basic ecclesial communities, new emerging communities, "fresh expressions" of church, or communities of similar scale. These are often, but are not necessarily, "parishes" in a traditional, structural sense. Some of them may be much more informal, like the "fresh expressions" of church called for by the Church of England's 2004 report "Mission-Shaped Church"[13] or Anglican missiologist Michael Moynagh's small ecclesial communities going to the edge of society,[14] or Latin American basic ecclesial communities. This is the way I use the term in this investigation. It should not be too hard, I think, for local churches who prefer a different definition of themselves to adjust my reflections to accord with their own identity as local agents of mission.

In the local churches with which I am familiar, there are two critical points of decision-making that affect, in a quite fundamental way, the mission activity of that local church and its citizen theologians. These are

a. whether priority is placed on *service to the realm of God* or on *conversion to Christianity*, and

---

13. Church of England's Mission and Public Affairs Council, "Mission-Shaped Church."

14. Moynagh, *Church in Life*.

b. whether mission is seen primarily as *being "sent out"* into the world or as *"response to"* the Spirit already in the world.

These are not exclusive alternatives. Yet they do present us with a choice of *priorities*. The choices we make here will result in big differences in our mission activities and they will result in very different kinds of church.

Service to the Realm of God or Conversion to Christianity?

Is mission to be understood primarily as *service to the realm* of God especially in terms of peace, justice, and ecological sustainability, or is it to be understood primarily as *conversion to Christianity*?

This question asks about our *primary* orientation towards mission activity—"primary" because it is rarely just exclusively one or the other.[15] Nevertheless, a priority option for service to the realm of God on the one hand or conversion to Christianity on the other will determine almost everything else we do about our outward mission into the wider world beyond the church. This is perhaps the most basic question we can ask about the missionary activity of a local church in countries that can be regarded as liberal democracies where churches can operate with relative freedom. (Note that churches which suffer persecution or are seriously restricted by the state will have other priorities which require quite a different discussion.)[16]

This basic difference in orientation has been argued out in evangelical churches, especially in North America, around the difference between what are often now called the "missional" and "attractional" orientations

---

15. Yet many statements of the purpose of the church will simply put these two purposes together without prioritizing. This is often seen as a "holistic" approach and in some cases required by a cultural context. See, for example, Nkansah-Obrempong, "Africa's Contextual Realities," 280–94.

16. Consider, for example, the complex discussion about freedom of religion and belief in modern day Turkey in Kitanovic and Bogiannou, *Advancing Freedom of Religion or Belief for All*. Or more intensely, consider the Arabic political theology of Andrea Z. Stephanous of the Coptic Evangelical Organization for Social Services, Egypt, which promotes dynamic citizenship as a base for coexistence and an institutional role for the church in predominantly Muslim countries. Stephanous, "Towards an Arabic Political Theology," 216–21. These have quite a different tone from the mission theology I am promoting here.

to mission activity. These are not always mutually exclusive but do indicate strong differences in emphasis. North American evangelist Rick Richardson describes "missional" churches as those that seek to model an alternative kingdom community oriented toward service and mission; these churches see themselves as the incarnation-like extension of Jesus' ministry, values, and presence into the world. "Attractional" churches, by contrast, tend to think of people as consumers where pastors provide the religious goods, services, and experiences that congregants can consume. Richardson is mounting an argument here for the value of a "missional" rather than an "attractional" church.[17] These descriptions of "missional" and "attractional" perhaps represent the extremes of the two orientations. Nevertheless, even in more moderate versions, the difference between a local church that is focused outwards towards action in the world and one that is focused on attracting people into the church where they can obtain religious services is a fundamental difference in mission orientation.[18]

By contrast to the idea of a "missional" church, a clear proposal for the "attractional" orientation is that of American New Testament scholar Graham Twelftree. From his analysis of Luke's Gospel and maintaining that this is valid also in other New Testament texts, Twelftree argues that the purpose of the church is the mission of proclaiming and demonstrating the good news of God's salvation in Jesus so that others can be saved and join the caring, joyful community of believers preparing for the return of Jesus.[19]

There are intermediate positions between the above two clear-cut options. "Missional" church, for example, is sometimes understood as "church *planting*." The 2004 Church of England report "Mission-Shaped Church," an influential and fruitful official church document on mission, defines church planting as "the process by which a seed of the life and message of Jesus embodied by a community of Christians is immersed for mission reasons in a particular cultural or geographic context."[20] In

---

17. Richardson, "Emerging Missional Movements," 131.

18. Another way of putting this is to say that a "missional church" sees itself as the presence of Jesus among his people, called out as a spiritual family, to pursue his mission on this planet. See Cole and Helfer, *Church Transfusion*, 15. On the difference between a "consumer church" and a "barefoot church," see also Hatmaker, *Barefoot Church*.

19. Twelftree, *People of the Spirit*, 217. See also the discussion of church as an event whose purpose is primarily the edification of believers through the proclamation of God's word instead of mission in Silberman, "Un-Missional Church?" 61–76.

20. Church of England's Mission and Public Affairs Council, "Mission-Shaped

this proposition, the objective of church planting is *primarily* about creating new and attractive kinds of church communities even though it is ultimately intended to benefit the society as a whole.[21]

The tension between a "missional" and an "attractional" orientation to the wider world exists not only in evangelical and Anglican theologies. It is particularly evident at a practical level in local Catholic churches when conversations and policies named as "mission" turn out to be, in fact, about the *Rite of Christian Initiation of Adults*, that is, bringing people into the church, or about how to attract already baptized but no longer practicing Catholics back into regular church attendance. There is an "attractional" dimension in all mission policies and practices. Pope Francis's missiology, for example, while clearly focused on ecological and social justice commitments, also contains a strong missiology of attraction rooted in an "attractive message" of God's mercy and tenderness embodied in an "attractive community."[22] Indeed, a primacy element of mission is "witness," living out what we believe. Yet the idea of trying to be "attractive" as primary purpose can be narcissistic or too self-focused or simply self-delusion.

The basic premise of the investigation I undertake here is that our primary concern as missionaries is how we can participate in and be contributors to the evolving realm of God in the world. The purpose of the church is to discern and participate in the coming about of that realm. Paul F. Knitter put this succinctly when he described the mission of the church as "dialogue with others in service of God's kingdom for the poor and marginalized. In such mission-as-dialogue, conversion remains a goal, but is primarily (not exclusively) conversion to the service of God's kingdom."[23]

This mission includes the actively pursued hope that many other people will also become members of the church, but for all sorts of reasons they may not. Whether they do or not, active engagement in bringing

---

Church," 32.

21. The difference between the "attractional" orientation and a "missional" one is sometimes used in a rather different sense where the attractional orientation measures success by attendance and income, whereas the missional orientation measures success by the number of people in mission and the number of self-replicating congregations produced. See Brown, "Missional Ecclesiology in the Book of Acts," 65–88. Here the primary orientation in both cases, whether called "attractional" or "missional," is conversion to Christianity more than service to the realm of God. There is nevertheless an outward mission to found new congregations.

22. See Bevans, "Pope Francis's Missiology of Attraction," 20–28.

23. Knitter, "Mission and Dialogue," 200.

about God's realm (or God's "reign" or God's "will" or God's "hope" or God's "blessing") for the whole world is still the church's primary mission.[24]

Sent Out or Responding to the Spirit

There is another understanding of mission that is often embedded in the consciousness of the local church, and which needs some critical attention. This is the idea that "mission" is primarily about being "sent out."

The sense of being "sent out" is particularly strong if the "Great Commission" in Matthew 28:19 (Jesus' final command, "Go therefore and make disciples of all nations . . .") is seen as the basis for the mission of the church. South Indian Theologian Christopher Duraisingh observes that this "commission" has often been distorted and has led to the idea that mission is "out there" somewhere. It has further led to missions that attempt to colonize and "civilize" other people. He proposes, as a corrective, that we should recover the understanding of mission seen in Acts 1:8, in which the risen Jesus promises his disciples that they "will receive power when the Holy Spirit has come" upon them, so that they may be his witnesses "to the ends of the earth." Here mission is a spontaneous outcome of receiving the Spirit. The Spirit always goes ahead of us. The church's mission is primarily a witness shaped by first discerning the Spirit who is already at work.[25] Scripture scholar James D. G. Dunn makes the point that in earliest Christianity, mission was not conceived as taking the Spirit into new territory so much as following where the Spirit was leading the way.[26]

The realm of God is the power of the Spirit among and around us calling us to discern and respond to that presence. There is a critical difference in orientation between being "sent out" to somewhere where the God is *not yet* and participating in God's mission where the Spirit is *already*

---

24. One of the places where the priorities become particularly acute is in the public debate about public funding for faith-based schools and the teaching of religious education. There is a tension here between inclusivity and Christian distinctiveness. English theologian and educationalist Howard Worsley seeks a solution here by relating the concept of *"missio Dei"* to "church schools (as places of inclusive mission)," "religious literacy," and "prophetic dialogue." Worsley, "Mission as Public Theology," 171–82.

25. Duraisingh, "From Church-Shaped Mission to Mission-Shaped Church," 11.

26. Dunn, "Is There Evidence for Fresh Expressions of Church in the New Testament?" 58.

there ahead of us.[27] The mission of the local church, then, is to point to and cooperate with God's already immanent and transforming presence.[28]

The idea of mission as primarily responding to the Spirit already alive in the wider world is in tune with, even if not exactly the same as, the idea that the church participates in the evolving realm of God already present but not yet complete in the world around us. This evolving realm of God is the power of the Spirit active not only within but also beyond and ahead of the church. The Holy Spirit to which we respond is the Spirit of Christ, not some other spirit. We discern the presence of, and respond to, that Spirit by recognizing where the realm of God, already underway in the life and mission of Jesus Christ, is now discernible in the world which we inhabit.

One of the clear implications of this sense of responding to the presence of the Spirit in the wider world is that Christians, as missionaries, need to avoid the temptation to act as if the church itself somehow held the franchise or the copyright, so to speak, for Christ's continuing mission. God's mission is larger than the church and has more agents than the church members. The Holy Spirit is active more widely and more unpredictably than just in the church. Where, however, the idea of mission as being "sent" somewhere else is embedded in the consciousness of the local church, and it often is, it may be difficult to shift towards the idea of mission as a response to the Spirit already present outside of the Christian community. Again, this does not mean that no one need ever be sent out on mission; it means, rather, that being "sent" is just one dimension of the central mission of the church to discern the evolving realm of God in the world and respond to the Holy Spirit in that world.

A second practical implication of this sense of responding to the Spirit in the world is what Indian theologian Felix Wilfred calls "reverse universality." In its early days Christianity recognized the community of humanity by allowing the translation of its sacred book into all languages and by sending out missionaries to the entire world. But this is a unilateral universality. For Christianity to be more completely universal requires a *multilateral* universality. This calls for the reading and interpretation of its message by diverse people through their conceptions of the destiny of

---

27. The collection of essays in the volume edited by Jane Williams, *The Holy Spirit in the World Today*, faced the question, Is the Holy Spirit to be found in the world? Its answer is "yes."

28. See Bevans, "God inside Out," 102–9. See also Searle, *Theology after Christendom*.

the human family. If the outgoing universality is from God, so too is the incoming universality for which Christianity needs to make room. The incoming universality is the movement by which the Christian faith is appropriated by humanity as its own.[29]

What Then Is the Mission of the Local Church?

In spite of differing definitions, the idea of "mission" has always included some notion of Christians "going outwards" beyond the world of Christians and into the wider world of non-Christians (where the Holy Spirit may have already preceded us). Yet that "wider world" is not homogeneous. Today we are commonly aware of sociologically identified marks of human diversity such as time and place, religion, culture, class, age, gender, and nationality.

In addition to these marks of diversity, the world of belief and unbelief is also shaded and colored in ways that immediately impact on any Christian venture "outwards" into that wider world. In a reminder particularly relevant to churches in "secular" societies, English theologian Samuel Wells points out that people who are not Christians are so for a variety of reasons and they perceive the church and God with a variety of attitudes. He discusses six kinds of "unbelievers." The first kind is the *lapsed*: those who were once disciples, in many cases happily so, and are no longer. A second kind are the *seekers*. Wells notes that for disciples, being with seekers is often a refreshing reminder of the wonder of God. A third kind is perhaps the most subtle—those of *no professed faith*. A fourth kind is those of *other faiths*. A fifth kind are the least subtle kind, those who are *hostile*. The sixth kind is the *neighbor*. And Wells warns here that, for Christian disciples, being with the neighbor may lead to the anxiety of being overwhelmed by the needs of others, an anxiety that might make disciples draw back from mission and confine their vision to ministry.[30]

Can we then articulate what is meant by the "mission of the church" from a local church viewpoint?

The orientation adopted in this book is that mission is best understood as primarily, though not exclusively, about service to the realm of God already partially and dynamically present in the world around us.

---

29. Wilfred, "Christianity and Religious Cosmopolitanism," 115.
30. Wells, *Incarnational Mission*, 18–20.

Through this activity, the church further hopes to attract other people into the Christian community. In this case, and without attempting anything so precise as a definition, the mission of the church includes the following key elements

 a. the activity of a local church and its members,
 b. directed outwards to the wider world,
 c. in response to the Holy Spirit,
 d. with a primary objective of service to the realm of God, and
 e. a secondary objective of attracting new people into its community life and action.

This listing of key elements of local church mission serves the purpose of moving us forward to the next stage in this investigation rather than establishing a definition that binds us forever. It is in many ways unsatisfactory, but it does indicate where some choices have been made among the variety of mission theologies. We can perhaps clarify where these choices have been made by expressing this in terms of what the alternatives could have been, i.e., what mission, as here defined, is *not*, or rather is *not primarily*:

 a. Mission is viewed here as primarily an activity of the *local church* rather than the universal church, a national church, a mission society, or an academic discussion of missiology in general. Identifying the "agent" of the mission is important because mission activity and its objectives may differ according to *who* carries out that activity. Writings on mission sometimes stumble or mislead because they do not identify which kind of mission agency they are referring to.

 b. Mission is an activity *directed outwards* into the wider world with its varied mixture of belief and unbelief rather than primarily to internal church matters such as community life, ministry, education, development, administration, or liturgy. This direction outside the church itself is important because once the idea of "mission" has become popular (as it has today), everything tends to be labelled "mission." "Mission" then comes to mean everything and nothing in particular. Our language about mission loses its cutting edge and becomes pointless unless it refers to some particular church activities and objectives as distinct from others. So, counting the Sunday collection or visiting sick parishioners are "church" activities—internal to the church community itself. They are not themselves "mission" actions (in my use of the term "mission"), even though they may support mission or lead to mission.

c. Mission is a response to a discernment of the *Holy Spirit already present in the world* rather than primarily an activity that goes to places where that Spirit was formerly absent. This discernment is important because it makes clear that the Holy Spirit is present and active in the wider world, not confined to the church itself. The church does not normally initiate or control the mission. The church does not hold the franchise on God's mission. The mission exists before and sometimes in spite of the church.

d. Mission is an activity undertaken primarily *in service to the evolving realm of God* rather than primarily for the purpose of seeking converts to the church. This is important because it sets service to the evolving realm of God as the primary objective of mission action.

e. Mission has an active hope nevertheless that other people will be *attracted to becoming disciples* of Christ and take part in this mission. This is important because it sets attracting new disciples as a necessary but secondary objective of the church's mission.

However partial this description may be, it gives us a sufficient orientation to allow us to move on to more refined reflections on mission in the next chapters.

Conclusion

This chapter has made a preliminary attempt to address the question, What is the mission of the church? It has called the attention of local churches to where they stand among a number of possible, though not all desirable, mission attitudes which direct, often unconsciously, their missionary activities or their lack of such activity.

A local church's decision for its own priorities among these mission theologies still leaves open some important questions about the way our local church interacts with other people and organizations within the wider society. What is the church's attitude to that wider and quite complex society?

Before we deal with that question, however, we may need to do some internal housekeeping, that is, to look at the ways in which missions can, and historically have already, gone wrong. Are there dangers in undertaking mission activity at all?

7

Dangerous Missions

MISSION THEOLOGIES SHOW A range of orientations towards the wider world. It does make a difference whether a local church opts for a mission policy that is primarily about converting people to Christianity or primarily about serving the still-unfolding realm of God. It also makes a difference whether a local church sees itself as in "dialogue" with the world, or as taking a strongly "prophetic" stance towards the world, or as being in "prophetic dialogue" with the world. It makes a difference too whether a local church regards itself as sent to carry the message of Christ out into a non-Christian world or whether it regards its mission as including also a response to the Spirit already out there.

The mission theologies considered in the previous chapter are still quite "high-level" orientations of the church to the wider world. They provide directions and encouragement for mission engagement in that wider world. They are normally expressed in "intentional" language. That is, they express the church's future goals rather than describe its track record. They express a working hope for participation in the life of the Trinity, or the salvation of the world, or the liberation of all people, or for prophetic dialogue with the world. Intentions are not always realized. The real results are not always the intended ones. The church's mission can, and often does, fail. Mission activities may, in fact, be dangerous to both missionaries and to the intended recipients of that mission. This chapter attempts to deal with this negative side of mission activity.[1]

1. This chapter draws on ideas from a previously published article: Darragh, "Hazardous Missions and Shifting Frameworks," 271–80.

Criticisms of Mission Activity

Mission activity may be dangerous. "Dangerous" implies more than a simple failure to achieve mission goals. It raises the specter that mission activity may actually be harmful to missionaries or to mission recipients. One of the greatest mission hazards is the one already noted in chapter 1, "What Is the Church *For*?" This is the belief that the church's mission, because it is done in the name of God or with good intentions to carry out the will of God, must in fact be part of God's mission. But missionaries, like anyone else, are capable of bad theology, of misunderstanding or misconstruing the mission of God. A major reason for putting our mission theologies under scrutiny is to correct for misunderstandings of the mission of God and therefore also of the church's attempts to participate in that mission but with unintended side effects.[2]

Traditionally, missionaries have been conscious of dangers for the *missionaries themselves* especially when the mission involved travel to foreign lands or cultures—the risks of travel, sickness and disease, and the hostility or indifference of the people to whom the missionaries were sent. Mission activity may also, however, be dangerous to the intended *recipients of that mission*, not just to individual persons but also to their cultures and their societies. In recent decades Christian missions have come under serious criticism, some of it well-founded, from both within and outside the Christian churches. Australian multi-faith mediator Brian J. Adams sums up the contemporary criticisms of mission activity under three forms:

a. the post-colonial critique of the use of missionaries to facilitate physical and structural violence and abet colonial expansion and control of the colonized;

b. the postmodern perspective where all views and claims on truth are equally valid so that the rational ground on which much of mission is founded is weak at best, if not outright immoral;

c. the multi-cultural arena, where many manifestations of mission are seen as repugnant attacks on another's identity or values and, thus, should not be part of a society in which respect between groups prevails.[3]

---

2. See for example, Price, "Popular Notions of the Missionary Task," 245–57; Ross, *A Vision Betrayed*; Rynkiewich, "The World in My Parish," 301–21. Scott, "Missions and Film," 115–20; Scott, "Missions in Fiction," 121–25.

3. Adams, "Mission and Interreligious Dialogue," 307.

Some of these criticisms of mission activity apply particularly to cross-cultural and foreign missions associated with colonialism. Criticism may be minimized when the mission activity takes place within the missionaries' own society and own culture, as is typically the case with local church engagement in their own wider society. Mission within the missionary's own culture can be free from many of the liabilities of cross-cultural or foreign missions. Missionaries within their own culture can, for example, be expected to know the language, civil protocols, family systems, spirituality, and history of the people they serve. In short, they begin at the point that cross-cultural missionaries can achieve only after many years of study and experience and often simply fail to achieve at all. Missionaries in their own culture and society do not normally require the extensive financial support required by expatriates and their message is less likely therefore to include a legitimation of wealth.

Yet even within our own cultures, most of us have experienced the aggressive intrusions of people who want to "do good" for us, welcome or unwelcome. Such well-meaning but unwelcome "doing good" is not peculiar to religious missions. It also features in the activities of welfare agencies, community development projects, and radical politics, most of which have good intentions for the wellbeing of others.

Any local church needs to be alert to, rather than defensive about, any such criticism circulating in the wider society and take it into account in its own mission policies. Well-founded criticisms identify dangers in the church mission activity. Three areas in particular deserve our attention: a) the assessment of *deprivation* in the intended *recipients* of the mission, b) the identification of the *benefits* which the *missionaries* are thought to take with them, and c) the setting of *qualities* required of missionaries.

What Is Wrong with the Intended Recipients of the Mission?

To engage in mission activities assumes that the people for whom the mission is intended lack something which the missionaries can bring to them. *What then is wrong with or lacking in the recipients of mission that they should be the focus of missionary activity?*

It seems arrogant to ask what is "wrong" with or "lacking" in other people. Yet a "prophetic" approach of mission does just this. It is more acceptable perhaps to say I have something to "share" with you, yet this may simply disguise an intent to tell you something you don't know but I think you should know. A "share with you" approach is at least a softer approach than missionary "preaching" and implies a willingness to dialogue or withdraw if the approach is unwelcome. But it may also conceal the real agenda and in that sense be deceptive. The key point here is that a missionary is not engaging in missionary activity merely to "learn" or to "listen." The missionary engages in mission not as a non-directive counselling program or as a learning experience but with a message to impart for the good of the recipients. The intention to impart a message makes sense only if the missionary recognizes some lack or wrongness in the recipient. Missionaries who cannot identify this should not be there at all.

Prophetic-dialogue is the model of mission proposed by Bevans and Schroeder as a synthesis of the three theologies of mission that they discern in recent missiology.[4] The three earlier models of mission are a) mission as proclamation of *Jesus Christ as universal savior*; b) mission as participation in the mission of the *Triune God (missio Dei)*; and c) mission as *liberating service* of the Reign of God. If prophetic-dialogue helps us to *synthesize* the models of mission, the distinct characteristics of those three earlier models provide us with a way to *analyze* in a more differentiated way what missionaries have seen as wrong or lacking in the recipients of mission. I propose to do some of this analysis here, and I shall refer to these three models respectively as the "salvationist," "trinitarian," and "liberationist" models of mission theology.[5]

In a "salvationist" mission theology the question of "lack" or wrongness is not often asked. This is presumably because the answer is thought to be clear already. The recipients of the mission have not recognized Christ as savior or are not members of the Christian church. This lack deprives them of salvation. Similarly, the "lack" is relatively clear in a "trinitarian" mission theology where the lack is the people's unawareness of the life of the Trinity. In these cases, the question of what is lacking in the recipients of mission is already answered—a lack of faith in Christ or a lack of awareness of the life of the Trinity. A "liberationist" mission theology is more likely to see this "lack" as a state of victimization embedded in the structures of society causing suffering to some but not all

---

4. Bevans and Schroeder, *Constants in Context*, 35–37.

5. I am guided here by Stephen Spencer, who uses this typological framework to examine the mission theology of his own local church. Spencer, "Missional Identity of a Parish Church," 84–99.

members of the society. The missionary brings a "conscientization" that brings awareness of exploitation and of a Christian God who supports their struggle for liberation.

If we move on to Bevans and Schroeder's more synthetic model of prophetic dialogue, a mission theology as "dialogue" indicates an intent to avoid intrusive or abusive confrontations with other people; yet mission as "prophetic" is a deliberate intent to confront and eradicate the evil in people and society. Mission as "prophetic dialogue" seeks to balance a willingness to listen with the knowledge nevertheless that a lack or wrongness in the dialogue partner will be identified in the course of dialogue.

When mission is understood as primarily "service to the realm of God," the missionary already believes that the realm of God is evolving and not yet complete. "Something lacking" is inherent in the very notion of the realm of God still in progress. More than that, the missionary is also aware that the process of the realm of God can be interrupted by evil. In a mission of service to the realm of God, the fact of *something* lacking in the world is already clear. Traditionally, this lack, this deprivation, could be identified as, for example, the inhumane practices or a lack of "civilization" in paganism; and more recently as atheistic materialism, denial of human rights, oppression, poverty, or even a culture of "spiritual boredom" and "aggressive secularism."[6] The missionary needs to be able to identify *what* exactly is lacking. It is this identification that will focus the mission activity. It is also this identification that justifies the mission activity. Missionary activity is not needed unless there is some advantageous result that does not already exist in the society.

Any mission activity in service of the realm of God assumes, then, that there is some deprivation in the recipient of mission that the missionary can fill, or help to fill, or enable the recipients to fulfil themselves. The "lack" in the recipients is here more difficult to identify than in the case of "salvationist," "Trinitarian," or "liberationist" mission theologies since it requires identification of some deprivation in the wellbeing (which includes wellbeing into and beyond death) of the society.

Mission intentions may be delusional, dangerously self-interested, or even fanatical. Mission activity is an intent to influence other people. It can be misguided. Hence the need to articulate exactly what is thought to be lacking or wrong in the recipients of the mission rather than simply assume that being a missionary is a good thing or that *our* mission is

---

6. Weigel, *Evangelical Catholicism*.

surely also *God's* mission. The mission objectives need to be up-front and clearly stated so that they are open to critique by both the missionaries and the people they seek to influence.

What Are the Benefits Missionaries Bring?

The converse side of the question of what is "wrong" or "lacking" in the *recipients* of mission is the question of what "benefits" the *missionaries* bring with them to right that wrong or fill that lack or counter that evil. Even if there is indeed something wrong or lacking in the recipients, this does not establish that *these* missionaries are the ones *capable* of remedying the bad situation. They may make it worse, and help may be better sought elsewhere. *What are the benefits that missionaries are supposed to bring to the recipients of their mission, and do these benefits also come with a package of harmful side effects?*

It has often been supposed that entry into the Christian church or conversion to Christ is in itself beneficial to the person converted. This offer of conversion is the "benefit" that the missionary brings. Such benefit is not nearly so obvious when the mission is understood as service to the realm of God. What increase in wellbeing and what kind of wellbeing does this mission activity actually bring to these people and to this society? Is it contributing, for example, to peace and harmony in that society? To holiness? To happiness? To justice? To the elimination of violence, or sexism, or racism? To better care of, or more empowerment to, the vulnerable?

If the conversion of people to the Christian church is seen as in itself a service to the realm of God, then this can be so only if the church itself is "good" and "holy." If the church itself fails in matters of social justice or in its commitments to an integral ecology of wellbeing, its mission activity comes with a package of harmful side effects or perhaps fails entirely in its mission outreach. One of the harmful side effects (unintended) of many missions during the period of European expansion, for example, was the endorsement of a gospel of wealth often evident in the lifestyles of European missionaries.[7]

In the contemporary world of mission, parish mission partnerships have become a major mode of international mission, especially in the US Catholic Church. The benefits and potential hazards of these partnerships

---

7. Bonk, *Missions and Money*; Bonk, "Mission and the Problem of Affluence," 295–309.

are beginning to receive some critical attention from missiologists. When these partnerships include "works of mercy" from the Global North to the Global South, there can be issues of dependency and paternalism. Authentic solidarity and respect for the dignity of the human person are not easily achieved in cross-cultural missions. North American missiologist Michael Haasl concludes from his own research that in such parish mission partnerships heeding the voices from the South is at least as fundamental as the work of mercy itself.[8]

Missionaries can ensure their mission is indeed part of the mission of God if they know a) just what benefits they are able to contribute to the realm of God in their local contemporary society and b) how they can avoid or compensate for any harmful side effects that accompany their mission. A church that itself practices forms of sexism, classism, racism,[9] lack of transparency in its decision-making, clericalism, or injustice, or colludes with violence, brings with it severely harmful side effects along with, no doubt, some benefits to society. Implied here is that a reform of the current church may be required so that the local church and its missionaries can be adequate to their task as participants and contributors to the evolving realm of God.

Qualities Required of Missionaries

What are the qualities required of missionaries so that their activities are beneficial rather than harmful to the recipients of their mission?

The previous two questions above are objective ones in the sense that they are about things that missionaries should know, be aware of, in their mission policies and actions. This third question is more subjective in that it asks about the personal qualities of the missionaries themselves. What are the personal, cultural, lifestyle, and technical qualities required for mission?

A local church, seeking to ensure that its mission is indeed a participation in the mission of God and not some inadequate or aberrant departure from it, needs to be sure that the people who act as missionaries are personally qualified, that is to say, are genuine witnesses to Christ and his message. Missionary organizations and explicitly missionary churches

---

8. Haasl, "Catholic Parish Mission Partnerships," 407–27.

9. Lewis, "The Dynamics and Dismantling of White Missionary Privilege," 37–45.

have perhaps paid more attention to this question than to the previous two in that they have usually provided training for potential missionaries and had some selection process for discerning who should or should not be sponsored as a missionary.[10]

For local churches with a mission in the local society, the issue of the selection of missionaries is difficult to manage. On the principle that all baptized Christians are missionaries, most of the missionaries are simply church members going about their ordinary affairs, witnessing to Christ in their actions and in their conversations. Yet when church members engage with other members of society in action for the wellbeing of society, the question of who *represents* a local Christian church becomes important. It is important because Christians acting with a mandate from their church, as distinct from private individuals acting on their own initiative, can rally support and influence for a cause or project. They are accountable to their local church. Other members of society can provide feedback and criticism to that local church. That church's reputation, the confidence other members of society have in its integrity, its resilience, its self-discipline, and its ability to adapt to new circumstances and new information enhance its capacity to achieve common objectives.

Local churches often do not have specific criteria for selection of their mission representatives but can learn from the missionary organizations that have already paid explicit attention to this. The key proposal I want to make here is that local churches give attention to selection and capacity-building for missionaries within their own community who are able to engage with other members of society for their common wellbeing.[11] This can be done in a quite formal way similar to that in which many contemporary organizations have a transparent process for selection and performance reviews of their personnel. A primary requirement though is that a local church be agreed on its own mission theology. It is this requirement that the previous chapter began to address, and which will occupy the following chapters in this book.

---

10. Lee, "Training Cross-Cultural Missionaries from the Asian Context," 111–30; Gittins, *Ministry at the Margins*; Whiteman, "Integral Training Today for Cross-Cultural Mission"; Silberman, "Imitation in Cross-Cultural Leadership Development," 240–50; Hibbert and Hibbert, "Defining Culturally Appropriate Leadership," 240–51; Curtis, "Missiological Missteps," 56–66.

11. See also Michael Haasl on the need for training in the case of international parish partnership missions. Haasl, "Catholic Parish Mission Partnerships," 407–27.

Conclusion

The key point of this chapter is the recognition that not all mission activity is in fact a participation in the mission of God. Missionaries are still faulted human beings. Their mission activities may be harmful rather than beneficial to the realm of God and to the wellbeing of the recipients of their mission.

As an addition to the previous chapter's option for a theology of mission as primarily (but not entirely) about service to the realm of God, this chapter has been a call to self-criticism. It has pointed to the dangers that frequently accompany mission activity. Recognition of these dangers has pointed towards a need for an assessment, not just an assumption, of the existing deprivation in the society, a need to be clear about the specific benefits that these particular missionaries bring to that society, and a need to establish the qualities required in missionaries.

These reflections on mission theologies and the dangers that may accompany mission activities have been fed largely by historical experiences of Christian mission. Warned by the dangers of history, the contemporary local church treads carefully in new kinds of contemporary society, aware that its own mission takes place within somewhat different frameworks. Most important here for local churches is the perspective they adopt towards the wider society in which they are embedded.

8

Mission in a Secular Society

THE MISSION OF THE church as I have described it in chapter 6, "Recent Mission Theologies," is, primarily, the activity of the church that is directed outwards to the wider society in service of the realm of God. What the church actually does in carrying out this mission will differ according to how the church assesses that wider society. Is that wider society antagonistic to the mission so that Christians go out there like sheep among wolves (Matt 10:16)? Or can they rather expect a welcome and hospitality? Can they expect an enthusiastic reception of their message? Or can they expect simple indifference?

The churches of the New Testament show a variety of attitudes to the wider society. In Matthew's account of Jesus' instructions in sending out the first disciples, they can expect a welcome in some cases. There they are to respond with a blessing. In other cases, they can expect rejection, and there the disciples are to respond (in that dramatic and memorable gesture) by shaking the dust of that town from their feet as they leave (Matt 10:7–15). The letters of Peter encourage a practical adaptation to the society of their time, while the book of Revelation responds to a world violently antagonistic to the Christian disciples. The books of the Gospels are concerned with carrying Jesus' message about the realm of God out into the wider world. In John's Gospel in particular, as British theologian R. Geoffrey Harris notes, the attitude to "the world" is deeply ambivalent. The world can be a place where faith is awakened, and also the place where faith is threatened or distorted, the place where life is created, and where life can be prematurely extinguished.[1]

We can expect that the way contemporary local churches engage with the societies of today is likely to be different from the way the New Testament churches engaged with the Jewish, then Hellenist-Roman cultures at that time. We can expect a difference in the ways in which a contemporary church might carry out its mission in a modern Islamic nation, in a modern Pacific Island nation that regards itself as a Christian state, or in a nation that regards itself as a liberal pluralist democracy. Or again, a church under persecution from the state will have a different attitude towards society from that of a church established as the national religion.

Contemporary Democracies

The kind of societies which are the concern of this book are contemporary pluralist democracies. These are the kinds of societies where freedom of religion is accepted at least in principle by the state, where there is religious and cultural diversity, and where there is a belief in some defined form of separation between church and state. Although there are debates about the meaning of "democracy," we can adopt for our purposes The International Institute for Democracy and Electoral Assistance's (IDEA) definition of democracy as "popular control over public decision-making and decision-makers, and political equality between citizens in the exercise of that control." The IDEA's measures of democracy are based on five main dimensions or "attributes": representative government, fundamental rights, checks on government, impartial administration, and participatory engagement.[2]

Within contemporary democracies, churches may nevertheless adopt a number of different attitudes towards their society. Even within the United States of America, for example, missiologists propose differing basic attitudes towards their own society. Gary D. Badcock's preferred mission model for the contemporary church derives from the evangelization of the Hellenistic-Roman world that followed the first age of Jewish Christianity. In this model, the two relevant and positive features are a) the successful and sustained attempt made by the early church *to reconcile*

---

1. Harris, *Mission in the Gospels*, 175.

2. International Institute for Democracy and Electoral Assistance, "The Global State of Democracy 2019," 2.

the best in the intellectual traditions of Hellenism with the new faith, and b) the *organization of the life of the church* that emerged based largely on prevailing patterns in Roman legal and administrative practice.[3]

By contrast, Richard Horsley sees a parallel between the first-century Roman Empire and the twenty-first-century American empire, both of which he sees as standing in opposition to the kingdom of God. This requires that a contemporary local church adopt an *attitude of radical opposition to the current power arrangements of society*.[4] A similarly strong opposition to the "first borderless empire—the United States of America" is maintained by the writers of the volume *The American Empire and the Commonwealth of God*. They are opposed to the emergence of a global *Pax Americana* on political, economic, and ecological grounds, but also on religious-spiritual-moral grounds.[5]

Intermediate between these quite contrary positions are the *more personalized and less political interpretations of the kingdom of God*, such as that of Elliott C. Maloney, which encourage Christians to live a good Christian life within the wider society, conscious of the need to remedy social injustices, to care for the whole human family, especially those dehumanized by hunger and ignorance, but leaving the larger political issues to God's final intervention.[6]

Inculturation and Liberation

Two themes that run through contemporary understandings of the relationship of the church to the wider society, especially in Catholic theology, are those of "inculturation" and "liberation." There is a considerable body of theological writing that advocates *inculturation* of the gospel into existing cultures. Filipino theologian José M. de Mesa defines inculturation as "the in-depth re-appropriation and re-expression, as well as the fresh rethinking and reformulation of the gospel in each human culture in a manner that is dialogically affirming and prophetic."[7] Particularly

---

3. Badcock, *The House Where God Lives*.
4. Horsley, *Jesus and Empire*.
5. Griffin, *The American Empire and the Commonwealth of God)*.
6. Maloney, *Jesus' Urgent Message for Today*.
7. Mesa, "Mission and Inculturation," 224. The foundations of this concept and the word "inculturation" itself in official Catholic theology lie in Pope Paul VI: Paul VI, *Evangelii Nuntiandi*.

important today, in the context of mass migrations of people around the world, is inculturation of the Christian gospel in indigenous cultures and the reinvigoration of both that can result.[8]

There is also a considerable body of theology that advocates *liberation* from society's existing power structures when these cause and maintain social injustices.[9]

Any local church, then, asks itself the question: Is our society founded on qualities that can be seen to embody the realm of God in this time and place so that the Christian gospel can find a home here and be inculturated into the customs and values of the society even while seeking to critique and transform other features of that society? Or, is our society basically inimical to the Christian gospel so that a primary goal of Christian mission will be one of seeking the liberation of people from existing customs and power structures even while learning from positive aspects of that society?

The orientation of mission activity as inculturation *in* or as liberation *from* is very different. Yet that is not to say that inculturation and liberation are opposites in practice. They are not mutually exclusive because democratic societies are not uniform or monolithic. A Christian stance towards society will normally include both these threads but with careful discernment of where one or the other is required.

Every local church and its citizen theologians, whether deliberately or by default, are engaged in discerning between the structures, values, and customs of their society which attract inculturation and those from which liberation is required. They are continually faced with decisions about *cooperation with* or *opposition to* the beliefs, structures, and customs that make up that wider society. In between these, and perhaps most important, is the opportunity for *negotiation* where both parties

---

8. In my own country of Aotearoa New Zealand, the integration of Christianity and the indigenous Maori religion/culture has recently become a focus of Christian theology. See Tate, *He Puna Iti I Te Ao Marama*; Marsden, *The Woven Universe*. And in the South Pacific more generally, see Darragh, "Pacific Island Theology," 624–26.

9. In its Latin American form, see, among many others, Sobrino and Ellacuria, *Systematic Theology*; Boff and Boff, *Introducing Liberation Theology*. The historical and continuing impact of Latin American liberation theology on the Catholic Church is summarized in Luciani, "Medellín Fifty Years Later," 566–89. Or we could refer here to "liberative" theologies so as to include a wider range than just Latin American theologies: De La Torre, *Introducing Liberative Theologies*. In any case, liberation theologies take many different forms today in their resistance to oppressive globalization: Rieger, "Empire, Deep Solidarity, and the Future of Liberation Theology," 354–64.

(the church and the relevant segments or associations of the wider society) may be able to change to their mutual benefit.

A recent example of where Christian discernment about engagement in social structures needs to take place is the current ethics of investment and divestment of funds. Individuals and churches who have responsibility for funds face decisions about the ethical investment or divestment (withdrawal of existing investments) of those funds. This is an ethical mission decision about what contributes to and what diminishes the evolving realm of God. The decision here is about whether companies or industries or banks in which investment is made meet or do not meet ethical standards. In New Zealand Quaker Robert Howell's analysis, this discernment means setting standards for "exclusions," "inclusions," and "engagement." *"Exclusions"* (do not invest, divest if already invested) apply to organizations involved in industries such as armaments and weapons systems, nuclear power, gambling, tobacco, animal exploitation and experimentation, significant environment abuses, high carbon emissions, and gas, oil, and coal extraction and production companies. On the other hand, *"inclusions"* (ethical reasons to invest) where preference will be given, apply to organizations involved in industries like environmentally sustainable goods and services, clean technologies, renewable energies, green business, progressive employment practices, local community activities, public goods such as public transport, sustainable housing, and low carbon emissions. Between "exclusions" and "inclusions" there is a category of *"engagement"* with organizations or companies seen to be willing to change; that is, negotiation rather than simple exclusion may still be an ethical option.[10]

This careful, informed, and energetic combination of cooperation, opposition, and negotiation also operates in the area of ecotheology. We live with terrifying examples of environmental destruction in many societies today. Yet there are also many examples of success where cooperation

---

10. Howell, *Investing in People and the Planet*. Among several shareholder advocacy groups, the Interfaith Center on Corporate Responsibility in the US has as its mission to build through the lens of faith a more just and sustainable world by integrating social values into corporate and investor actions. The Catholic Impact Investing Collaborative (CIIC), founded in 2014, has as its mission to share stories, build relationships, and connect Catholic Impact Investors. In the UK, the Ecumenical Council for Corporate Responsibility is a church-based investor coalition and membership organisation working for economic justice, human rights, and environmental sustainability. Similarly in Australasia, though not faith-based, the Australasian Centre for Corporate Responsibility.

and negotiation, especially with legislators, has brought success. In his aptly named book *The Optimistic Environmentalist*, Canadian lawyer David R. Boyd chronicles a number of successes in the past fifty years where environmental problems have been solved and substantial progress is ongoing on others: endangered species pulled back from the precipice of extinction; thousands of new parks protecting billions of hectares of land and water; the salvation of the ozone layer, vital to life on Earth; the exponential growth of renewable energy powered by wind, water, and sun; the race to be the greenest city in the world; remarkable strides in cleaning up the air we breathe and the water we drink; the banning of dozens of the world's most toxic chemicals; and a circular economy where waste is a thing of the past. Many of these successes are the result of legislation where environmentalists have lobbied their lawmakers to legislate against destructive human behavior.[11] From the point of view of local churches and citizen theologians these successes provide encouragement to cooperate, oppose, or negotiate with the efforts of other organizations and groups for the wellbeing of Earth and its inhabitants.

I use these two examples of ethical investment and environmental action because these are areas of mission seldom discussed in historical missiology and only recently attended to in local churches. Such movements for social justice and ecological responsibility provide opportunities for the *inculturation* of the gospel. And this occurs in the same society in which the structural evils call for a theology and action for *liberation* from those supporting structures. Moreover, the successes of people's engagement in that same society give encouragement to attempts at *negotiation* towards a better society.

Historically, a mission policy of *inculturation* has most commonly been a theological response to societal conditions of *colonization* supported by an institutional church policy of *central control*. A mission policy of *liberation* has most commonly been a theological response to societal conditions of *structural injustice* supported by an institutional church practice of *cooperation* with existing power structures. In contemporary democratic societies, a key decision for local churches is their theological response to their own *secular society*. Local churches may still be ambivalent or undecided about their support for or opposition to the structures and values of a secular society. It is this "secular" feature of contemporary society that needs some attention today.

---

11. Boyd, *The Optimistic Environmentalist*.

From Christendom to Secular Society

"Christendom," as described recently by British theologian Joshua T. Searle, is "a social order in which, regardless of individual belief, Christian language, rites, moral teachings, and personnel were part of the taken-for-granted environment."[12]

The breakup of Christendom in sixteenth-century Europe which followed the Protestant Reformation resulted in religious wars and persecutions. The idea of a "secular" society seems to have originated as a pragmatic solution to these conflicts.[13] A secular society involves, in its simplest form, a separation, or at least a functioning distinction, between church and state such that the church should not interfere in political matters which are the proper concern of the state, and the state should not impose or privilege any particular religion. It was an option for the coexistence of different religions rather than the privileging of one religion and the persecution of others in the same state.[14]

With the spread of democratic societies in Europe in the late eighteenth and nineteenth centuries, the idea of a secular society became more important and more fundamental than just a pragmatic solution to conflict. Basic to a secular society is the principle of religious freedom— people should have the freedom to believe and practice the religion of their choice, or no religion at all, without state coercion or discrimination. Yet there are several different ways of institutionalizing this distinction between church and state. The United States of America (no privileged status to any single religious tradition) and France (prohibition of any manifestation of religion in public) are perhaps the most prominent examples of two different ways of institutionalizing this distinction in liberal democracies today. There are, nevertheless, several other ways of

---

12. Searle, *Theology after Christendom*, xvi. Or, as described by Peter C. Phan, it is "the politico-religious order promoted by medieval popes (particularly from Gregory VII to Boniface VIII) who championed a world in which Christian teachings and church law would imbue every aspect of human life and in which they could exercise an absolute and supreme power over every human being, including political rulers." Phan, "A New Christianity, but What Kind?" 201–18.

13. Levey, "Secularism and Religion in a Multicultural Age," 4.

14. Theologians now sometimes use the term "*post*-Christendom" to refer to "the culture that emerges as the Christian faith loses coherence within a society that has been definitively shaped by the Christian story and as the institutions that have been developed to express Christian convictions decline in influence." Murray, *Post-Christendom*, 19.

managing this distinction such as retaining an established church but protecting the religious freedom of other faith communities (England, Greece, and Denmark), retaining some official ties to a particular faith (the Catholic concordats in Spain, Portugal, and Italy), and honoring religious neutrality by supporting or accommodating many religions (Germany, Sweden, and India).[15] Currently, relations between the state and religious groupings, including Muslim, are being institutionalized in a variety of complex ways in the post-communist Baltic states.[16]

What Kind of Secularism?

The variety of ways in which secular states have been institutionalized in practice suggests different versions of the idea of secularism itself.

The term "secularism" itself can sometimes be difficult for Christians. This may be simply an historical leftover since in the past the established churches often supported the idea of Christendom. More significantly, perhaps, the term "secularism" can have a range of meanings from commitment to a humanist materialist rationalism to a rather more modest and tolerant principle of religious freedom and a separation of religion and state.

Political theologian Ian Tregenza observes that, in the prevailing political discourse, the term "secular" demarcates a neutral public sphere governed by institutions and forms of reasoning that are thought to be non-controversial and at least potentially available to all. "Religion" on the other hand is seen to belong to a realm of "private" belief resting on forms of understanding ("revelation") or authority (Scripture, tradition) that are beyond the scope of public reason. The secular has come to be identified with the "real," the "natural," or the "rational," while religion is by definition the "unreal," the "supernatural" ("invented") or the "non/irrational."[17] If the "secular" is understood in this way, it clearly has many benefits for society, while "religion" is a liability.

The generally supposed benefits of secularism are summarized by British sociologist S. Sayyid as: a) it creates the conditions for scientific and technological progress by removing the claims of religious authorities to control the production of knowledge; b) it is necessary to ensure

---

15. Levey, "Secularism and Religion in a Multicultural Age," 4.
16. Elbasani, "Governing Islam in Plural Societies," 4–18.
17. Tregenza, "Secularism, Myth, and History," 173.

peace and harmony to prevent religious passions from getting out of hand, and it does this by confining religion to the private, not the public, sphere; and c) it is the precondition for the exercise of democracy based ultimately on the idea of the "sovereignty of the people" rather than on the idea of a sovereign God or priesthood.[18]

These are the *supposed* benefits of the more aggressive form of secularism which sees religion as anti-scientific, irrational, and undemocratic. Not everyone agrees that secularism is indeed beneficial in the above ways. It is probably this form of secularism with its seemingly forced choice between the secular and the religious that has provoked objections from religious leaders. They see secularism as the cause of an erosion of faith and of Christian values in society.[19]

In church circles, the argument against "secularism" is sometimes proposed in a way that suggests we need to oppose it (rather than cooperate or negotiate with it). Yet there are relatively few Christians in democratic societies today who want a return to the kind of Christendom of the European Middle Ages. The idea of a secular society with its principles of religious freedom and the separation of church and state is widely accepted by Christians.[20] Are there then different kinds of secularism?

Philosophers Jocelyn Maclure and Charles Taylor propose a distinction between a "republican" and a "liberal-pluralist" model of secularism.[21] Both these models show respect for the moral equality of citizens and freedom of conscience. The *republican model*, however, favors the emancipation of individuals and the growth of a common civic identity, which requires marginalizing religious affiliations and forcing them into the private sphere. The *liberal-pluralist model*, by contrast, sees secularism

---

18. Sayyid, "Contemporary Politics of Secularism," 188.

19. Yet the distance between Christian and secular ideas may not be as great as is commonly believed. See Martin, *On Secularization*, 75.

20. But to the contrary, note Pope Pius X's opposition to religious freedom and the separation of church and state in his 1906 encyclical *Vehementer Nos*.

21. Some commentators make a distinction between a "hard" and a "soft" secularism. *Hard* secularism refers to the situation where the state refuses to grant religious expression any form of official status within the wider society. *Soft* secularism, on the other hand, emphasizes peaceful coexistence and political order in multi-cultural and multi-religious societies based on human or constitutional rights rather than on religious beliefs. Such secularism supports state neutrality towards the different religions within the society so that no particular religion can dominate. See Olav Hovdelien's interpretation of Charles Taylor's earlier typology of secularism: Hovdelien, "In Favour of Secularism, Correctly Understood," 234–47.

as a mode of governance whose function is to find the optimal balance between respect for the moral equality of all citizens and respect for freedom of conscience.[22] This latter "liberal-pluralist" model of secularism may also be called "open" secularism.[23]

This "open" form of secularism requires continuous negotiation and debate about the boundaries between the responsibilities of religious and state institutions. There is no strict, unchangeable boundary between state institutions and private or civil or religious institutions. At the same time, the good functioning of a multi-religious and multi-cultural nation requires that we be able to maintain a coherent and consistent distinction between, on the one hand, the responsibilities of the state and, on the other hand, the legitimate activities of individual citizens, families, businesses, and civil associations, including religious ones.

Public and Private Spheres

In the traditional heart of secularism is a distinction between the "public" sphere and the "private" sphere. As it has been commonly understood, the public sphere is the sphere of citizens and national constitutions. It is the proper sphere of the state, not of religion. The private sphere is the place where the state should not interfere. It is a sphere of religious preferences but also of many other individual preferences as well as free associations, cultural practices, businesses, and family life. Yet in practice, the boundary between these spheres is constantly being negotiated within a nation. What is "public" and what is "private" is understood differently in different nations and undergoes continual negotiation over time. Secularism pure and simple does not exist in the real world. All actual practices of secularism consist of institutional compromises, and institutional reconfigurations vary according to the historic place of religion in each country.[24]

The "public" sphere, in other words, should not be thought of as a product of objective reason (scientific and rational) but is made up of a

---

22. Maclure and Taylor, *Secularism and Freedom of Conscience*, 34. See also a review of this book by Michael P. Krom, "Secularism and Freedom of Conscience," 387–90.

23. Maclure and Taylor, *Secularism and Freedom of Conscience*, 58.

24. Modood, "Muslims, Religious Equality, and Secularism," 178–81.

variety of national histories, local cultures, and new migrations.[25] The public sphere is populated by deep commitments or "causes,"[26] many of which are not normally called "religious" but which call upon people's loyalty beyond their own personal benefit. Moreover, the state itself may enter the public sphere not as neutral and rational but as itself a center of "ultimate concern," demanding loyalty from its citizens as a kind of civil religion.[27]

The boundaries between church and state that were so important in overcoming Christendom and in achieving a secular society need continuous negotiation. British theologian Luke Bretherton remarks that, historically, there has always been such negotiation. At the macro level in Europe, for example, with the exception of France, churches have been incorporated into the state through a variety of forms of establishment. At the micro level, in supposedly secular institutions such as prisons, the military, and hospitals, chaplains have continued to have an established and often prominent role. Yet today we are going through a period when these previous settlements are having to be renegotiated.[28]

The state in fact often intrudes into what has been considered the "private" sphere. The use of physical force as legitimate coercion (by police or other law enforcers), for example, is the work of the state. The state intrudes in the "private" sphere by acting as a monitor over the private sphere, especially in maintaining peace and containing violence. The state, while acknowledging and promoting religious freedom and freedom of speech, may also legitimately put boundaries around that freedom—that religions may not, for example, promote hatred or violence. Family life also falls within the "private" sphere, yet the state may intrude in family life in cases, for example, of neglect or child abuse and may often provide and control the education of children. In the reverse direction, though,

---

25. We can see this evolving today in Arolda Elbasani's analysis of the complexities in post-communist Baltic countries, where new democratic aspirations required institutionalizing a more equal playing field for their respective religious communities. The evolving institutional choices to incorporate these communities has vacillated between the democratic urge for religious freedoms and equality on the one hand and the role of founding traditions and heritage of majority privileges on the other. Elbasani, "Governing Islam in Plural Societies," 4–18.

26. These provide positions of unassailable authority—whether from God, reason, or common sense—in order to accuse opponents of violating fundamental law. On the constructive use of prophetic rhetoric in the American context, see Kaveny, *Prophecy without Contempt*.

27. Hartney, "States of Ultimacy and the Cult of the Dead Soldier," 214–70.

28. Bretherton, *Christianity and Contemporary Politics*, 14.

churches and other civil organizations continue to monitor, and sometimes object to, the "legitimacy" of such state intrusion.[29]

For our purposes, the key point here is that a local church, along with other non-governmental organizations, has its own responsibility for both maintaining and negotiating the boundaries between the public and private spheres. This includes acknowledging the historic secular principle that the state should not privilege any particular religion.

The project of open secularism rescues citizens from the dictates both of absolute monarchs and of arrogant ecclesiastics. It promotes democracy and freedom to choose any particular religion or no religion.[30] In this atmosphere, a local church can still speak and act critically and engage in principled debate with other social institutions and associations. It can cooperate with, negotiate with, or oppose diverse religious, philosophical, and political standpoints within the public sphere. Moreover, the churches (along with other social organizations) can themselves gain from the opportunities in the public sphere to refine their own thinking by reflection and critical argument.[31]

Mission in a Secular Society

What then should be a local church's attitude towards its own secular society in the light of recent debates about secularism and the public and private spheres of society?

Important, firstly, is the acknowledgement that the mission of a Christian church, with its focus on the evolving realm of God, is committed to the principles of freedom of conscience and tolerance of differences in society. In that sense a Christian church is committed to an "open" secularism. Christian mission and secularism are not opponents

---

29. These relationships and the negotiations that accompany them are played out in different ways in different national contexts. Fourie and Meyer-Magister give a comparative example of how the churches in Germany and South Africa structure their public engagement in Fourie and Meyer-Magister, "Contextuality and Intercontextuality in Public Theology," 36–63.

30. Second Vatican Council, *Declaration on Religious Freedom*.

31. Calhoun, "Afterword: Religion's Many Powers," 118–35. For more of the philosophical underpinnings of a critical engagement of a Christian church in the public sphere see Yazell, "Radical Orthodoxy, Political Ecclesiologies, and the Secular State," 155–64.

unless "secularism" is understood as anti-religious materialism or as a state-imposed, exclusive ideology.

Religious liberty is one among several human rights that constitute part of the common ground of contemporary democracies.[32] The church, even more perhaps than the state, is committed to maintaining the common ground (common humanity, common good, public good) that is required for a peaceful and just society.

Contemporary debate about secularism has passed beyond its origins in issues of religion and state. It now has to deal with all the moral and spiritual diversity that exists within a nation. The democratic secular state should treat with equal respect not just the religious diversity within its borders but all the moral and spiritual diversity that is compatible with living together in peace.

In this expanded form, open secularism is a necessary feature of diverse societies in the sense that it seeks to secure freedom of conscience and the moral equality of its citizens. Yet the state is not completely neutral here. There are constitutive values, such as human dignity, basic human rights, and popular sovereignty, that provide liberal, democratic systems with their foundations and aims.[33]

The church's mission, then, in a secular pluralist society today is not an attack or defense against an enemy of Christianity, but an entry into a common project, in the sense of an attempt to form a common life. In that common project, the church respects the secular character of the state, and this recognition also frees the church from the temptation of wielding temporal power.[34]

The contemporary challenge is how to balance the functional neutrality and pluralism of the public realm with respect for cultural and religious diversity.[35]

Charles Taylor's proposal for a way forward (for all citizens, not just for Christians) in this debate is to acknowledge that "secularism" is an essential feature of religiously diverse societies. It is a complex requirement aiming to secure freedom of both belief and unbelief as well as equality between citizens. A good starting point for rethinking this whole issue, he proposes, is the trilogy of "liberty, equality, fraternity." We may

---

32. Trigg, *Religion in Public Life*, 230–31.
33. Maclure and Taylor, *Secularism and Freedom of Conscience*, 11.
34. Gascoigne, *The Church and Secularity*, 61–62.
35. Graham, *Between a Rock and a Hard Place*, 18.

translate these today as meaning: a) no one must be forced in the domain of religion or basic belief; b) there must be equality (no privileged status) between people of different faiths or basic beliefs; c) all spiritual families must be included in the ongoing process of determining what the society is about (its political identity), and how it is going to realize these goals (the exact regime and its privileges).[36]

Thus a central task of Christian mission is, while maintaining its own specific Christian identity, to cooperate with religious and non-religious others in pursuit of the common good for the wellbeing of all.[37] An important objective here is not just ensuring that fundamental *rights* (to political participation, free speech, freedom of religion, etc.) be officially acknowledged, but to ensure that people have the *"capabilities"* to actually exercise those rights (mobility, technical help to overcome physical disability, special care for the elderly and the very young, etc.)[38]

The key focus, then, of a local church outreach into a secular society is not to combat secularism but to advance what Luke Bretherton calls a "capacious secularity." This is not just any secularity, because there can be many forms of it, but the kind of secularity that is complexly religious and nonreligious born out of a genuine plurality established and sustained by particular ways of doing democratic politics in pursuit of a common life in which all may flourish.[39] Or as North American theologian Robert Leavitt describes it, "The open public sphere permits and oftentimes encourages indifference, but it also permits religious exploration and rediscovery."[40]

---

36. Taylor, "Foreword: What Is Secularism?" xi–xxii; Taylor, "Why We Need a Radical Redefinition of Secularism," 34–35.

37. Thus Luke Bretherton, for example, argues for the need to maintain the specificity and particularity of Christian witness, and at the same time cooperate with religious and non-religious others in pursuit of goods in common. By "goods in common" he means substantial goods in which the flourishing of all is invested, such as health or education, in which the good of each is conditional upon the good of all. Bretherton, *Christianity and Contemporary Politics*, 18.

38. The language of "capabilities" rather than "rights" has been developed especially by Amartya Sen, and a list of "central human capabilities" that advances the implementation of social justice has been proposed by Martha Nussbaum, "Capabilities as Fundamental Entitlements," 33–59.

39. Bretherton, *Resurrecting Democracy*, 289.

40. Leavitt, *The Truth Will Make You Free*, 297.

Conclusion

The local church's most immediate (though not its only) mission activity is an outreach into the wider society of which the local church is itself a part. Important in this is the attitude the local church and its citizen theologians take towards that society. Local church attitudes towards the wider society no longer include the principles of "Christendom" but do include the theologies of both "inculturation" and "liberation."

The secular society is a common political environment in which many local churches today carry out their mission. Such mission engagement accepts the principle of religious liberty, the moral equality of all citizens, and a distinction between church and state. It accepts too that there are many ways in which this distinction between church and state can be institutionalized and that the church cannot agree to being simply "privatized" away from engagement in society.

While a local church and its citizen theologians do not accept a "secularism" that is anti-religious materialism or a state-imposed ideology, they can be "secularists" in that they work within and for a society that is secular in that human rights, including religious liberty, are maintained there and religion receives no preferential treatment from the state over and above that which is accorded to other organizations and associations within society.

This chapter has grappled with some of the key issues in dealing with "secular society" and "secularism" from the point of view of Christian mission. It has not yet dealt, however, with "secularization" as a *process*. While many local churches are in favor of an open secularism, they remain concerned about the process of secularization. Is "secularization" a counter force to any attempts at Christian mission within a democratic pluralist society?

9

Secularization

In the previous chapter I was concerned with the idea of a "secular society" and the several meanings of "secularism," but I did not deal there with the idea of "secularization" as a process. Yet secularization is a matter of concern for many local churches. The debates in this area are often confusing because of the varied use of terms.

"*Secular*" as an adjective is commonly used to describe a state of affairs or condition of society. Sometimes, however, it is used with an implied evaluation either that it is good or that it is bad. I have suggested that in the context of Christian mission it is best used as a purely descriptive term without any implied evaluation. So, for example, a "secular" state is one in which religious freedom and a separation of some kind between state and religion (or church) is widely accepted. This does not imply that the state is anti-religious in any more general sense. It does not have an implication of commitment to an anti-religious materialism. Religious people may be in favor of such a state as much as anyone else. In that sense, "secular" is a neutral term. We should note too that the term "secular" is a traditional term familiar within theology and religious discourse. We need not abandon it to an irreligious usage. So, we have "secular institutes" and "secular priests," but this does not mean they are anti-religious. They are simply distinguished from other institutes or priests who take specific religious vows.

The noun "*secularity*" is usually a neutral term and refers simply to a state of affairs in which most of the affairs of society can be conducted without explicit reference to religion. It can exist in different degrees; it can be more or less. It is not something specific in itself; it is simply the absence of explicitly religious language or religious justification.

"*Secularism*" commonly refers to an ideology, something one is committed to or believes in, rather than simply a state of affairs. It is a term that has a range of meanings: a) a belief in an anti-religious materialism; b) a political philosophy which is opposed to any appearance of religion in the public sphere, though religion is acceptable as a purely private affair; and c) a political philosophy that advocates the separation of church (or religion) and state though recognizing that these cannot be completely separated and the relationships between them may take different forms in different societies. I have advocated above that religious people can be secularists in this last sense. They can favor a secular society and its democratic processes without any commitment to anti-religious materialism or to the exclusion of religion from the public sphere.

"*Secularization*" is not a state of affairs but refers rather to a social *process* marked by a decline in religious activity over a given period of time. This process may occur differently in different times and places. The implications and evaluations of the process to which this term refers are contested.[1] We should note too that "political" secularization (the process by which the state affirms its independence from any particular religion) should not be confused with "social" secularization (an erosion of the influence of religion in social practices and in the conduct of individual lives).[2]

This chapter explores the idea of "secularization" and what attitude a local church might take towards it.

What Is Secularization?

One succinct and accessible description of "secularization" is North American religious studies writer Barry A. Kosmin's "continuous process whereby religious ideas have been devalued and religious authority has become marginalized."[3] This description is helpful in maintaining our focus in the midst of a rather complicated debate.

---

1. I have drawn for the most part, though not in every detail, on the explanation of these terms in Davie, *Religion in Britain*, 186.
2. Maclure and Taylor, *Secularism and Freedom of Conscience*, 15–16.
3. Kosmin, "Secular Republic or Christian Nation?" 165.

More expansively, British sociologist Steve Bruce's summary of the "secularization paradigm" is that at the level of social structure, religion is marginalized by the differentiation of social life into discrete spheres (such as the polity and the economy) which are increasingly informed by their own values and pay ever less regard to religious concerns. It is also marginalized by the rise of religious liberty consequent on a combination of individualism, egalitarianism, and diversity. The result is a reduction of people's contact with, and socialization into, religious belief and values. Religious identities are increasingly confined to the private sphere of the family and the leisure world as preferences.[4]

Bruce notes, however, that there are circumstances in which religion in liberal industrial democracies retains and even gains political and social salience. These may be grouped under the headings of a) "cultural defense," where a particular culture and religion reinforce each other in minority groups; and b) "cultural transition," where religion helps deal with cultural changes that occur in large-scale migration. He regards these, however, as temporary exceptions rather than long-lasting alternatives to the secularization paradigm.[5]

Not all sociologists of religion regard "secularization" as an accurate description of religious trends or that secularization is tied irreversibly to "modernization."[6] There is quite widespread agreement, nevertheless, that there has been a decline in the influence of Christian churches in European societies in recent decades. Some key indicators of this decline are the level of expressed beliefs and church-related behavior such as attendance at services of worship, adherence to church-dictated codes of personal behavior, and recruitment to the clergy.[7] There has been a decline in doctrinal orthodoxy, a shift in focus from the next world to this one, and a weakening of the ties of obedience.[8] Related indicators are the decline in identification with religion, in membership of congregations, and in attendance at worship services.[9] Also, a growing number of people, notably younger generations, are choosing to live their lives

---

4. Bruce, "History, Sociology, and Secularisation," 192–93.

5. Bruce, "History, Sociology, and Secularisation," 192. See also Bruce, *Secularization*, 49–52.

6. See, for example, Davie, "From Obligation to Consumption," 33–45.

7. Berger, "The Desecularization of the World," 9–10.

8. Bruce, *Secularization*, 14.

9. Kosmin, "Secular Republic or Christian Nation?" 157.

beyond the influence of organized religion.[10] There is, in other words, considerable sociological evidence for a decline in attachment to church loyalties and habits at least in Europe.

While disagreeing with some of the interpretations of "secularization," sociologist David Martin agrees with its standard usage as meaning, in particular, "social differentiation, or the freeing of successive sectors of social life and thought from ecclesiastical oversight and religious concepts. Social differentiation erodes the links between Christian language and emerging secular languages, for example, those of science and politics, and breaks down the comprehensive institutional coverage once provided by the church. The theological mode ceases to provide the overarching frame."[11]

Yet there is still considerable debate about:

- whether "secularization" should be regarded as *geographically widespread* rather than a feature of *just some regions* and nations, such as Europe;
- whether it is *part of a larger process* of "modernization";
- whether it is just *one among several explanations* of the sociological data; and
- whether the whole idea of "secularization" might be a *theoretical construction* of social scientists rather than an objective social reality.

Geographically Widespread or Regional?

Some commentators contest the tendency to attribute features of European religion to the rest of the world. The patterns of religion over time may be different in different parts of the world. Some argue that there are substantial differences in religiosity/secularity between Europe and North America. The relative secularity of Europe, including Britain, may be an exceptional case rather than a global trend.[12] Yet others see Europe not as an exception but as a trend-setter for the rest of the world and for North America in particular.[13]

10. Davie, *Religion in Britain*, 188.
11. Martin, *On Secularization*, 187.
12. Davie, *Religion in Britain*, 11. Berger, "The Desecularization of the World," 10.
13. Kosmin, "Secular Republic or Christian Nation?"

Christian theologians outside of Europe have further pointed out that the particular form of secularism that resulted from the breakup of European Christendom is largely a European and North American affair. While in Europe and North America religion and secularism might seem to be in opposition, in many other regions of the world everything has a spiritual dimension. Asian religions, for example, show great vitality and capacity for renewal rather than decline.[14]

An important factor affecting religious belonging is *transnational migration*, as religions travel from one nation and one continent to another. North American sociologist of religion José Casanova argues that one of the most significant consequences of the new global patterns of transnational migration has been a dramatic growth in religious diversity on both sides of the Atlantic. Moreover, the histories of immigration and modes of immigrant incorporation are different. There are also different patterns of religious pluralism and different types of secularism. In North America, immigrant religiosity is not simply a traditional residue, an Old-World survivor likely to disappear with adaptation to the new context, but rather an adaptive response to the New World. In Europe, by contrast, secularist worldviews and very different institutional patterns of public recognition through different forms of church-state relations make the incorporation of immigrant religions in the public sphere of European civil societies a more contentious issue.[15]

David Martin identifies some of the different "patterns" of secularization. Among these, he sees a major contrast between a) the *revolutionary and violent* tradition of France, Russia, and China, associated with antecedent territorial religious monopolies, and b) the *evolutionary* tradition of Britain associated with the emergence of non-territorial voluntary forms of religion, and most recently the global spread of Pentecostalism.[16]

Yet, to the contrary, other commentators argue that secularization is occurring in North America, even if somewhat later than in Europe, and will continue to occur.[17]

---

14. Putenpurakal, "Catholic Mission in Asia 1910–2010," 24.

15. Casanova, "Immigration and the New Religious Pluralism," 144–63.

16. Martin, *Secularisation, Pentecostalism and Violence*, 119. See also the different, though overlapping, situation regarding secularization in Eastern and Central Europe including Russia, in Fedorov, "Ecumenical Missionary Needs and Perspectives," 66–84.

17. Kosmin, "Secular Republic or Christian Nation?" 169–70. The Europe-North America focus may be put in perspective by global statistics even if we need to be careful about how these statistics are collected and interpreted. Consider, for example,

Tied Irreversibly to Modernization?

It no longer seems adequate to interpret the decline in organized religion as a single-line process leading to secularity or the complete privatization of religion. The persistence of religion into the twenty-first century has led some ("Western") commentators to contest the popular idea that to be "modern" means to be "secular"; that is, they question the idea that the processes of modernization and secularization run together.[18]

Some argue that the world today is characterized by two seemingly contradictory processes: both increasing secularization and also religious resurgence. Alongside continuing secularization there is also increasing attention to religion in public life.[19] While people are becoming more detached from church institutions, many still search for manifestations of the spirit in highly personal therapeutic engagements and small intimate cells or in the ancient forms of the religious impulse, the festival, the pilgrimage, or prayer in the numinous or sacred location.[20] In British society at least, argues sociologist Grace Davie, there appears to be simultaneously a decrease in religious activity and a growing significance of religion in public debate.[21] Similarly paradoxical, argues British theologian Elaine Graham, is "the emergence globally and nationally of revitalized religious activism as a decisive force alongside the continuing trajectory of institutional religious decline accompanied by robust intellectual defense of secularism in Western societies."[22]

The political impact of Islam in many regions of the world in recent decades and the increase in the number of Muslims who are now citizens of many nations in Europe and North America cast further doubt on the idea that secularization is a general trend even if we confine that trend to "modernized" societies. The increasing public articulation and assertiveness of indigenous religions in "modern" societies also runs

---

the global statistics in Johnson et al., "Christianity 2018: More African Christians and Counting Martyrs," 20–28.

18. Martin, *Secularisation, Pentecostalism and Violence*, 170–83.
19. Davie, *Religion in Britain*, 20.
20. Martin, *On Secularization*, 47–55.
21. Grace Davie, among others, uses the term "post-secular" to capture this new development. Davie, *Religion in Britain*, 227–32. See also Bretherton, *Christianity and Contemporary Politics*, 10–16.
22. Elaine Graham similarly uses the term "post-secularity" to refer to this seemingly paradoxical trend. Graham, *Between a Rock and a Hard Place*, 34.

contrary to the idea of secularization and is not easily dismissed as a temporary phenomenon.[23]

Just One of Several Explanations?

The way in which sociological data "fits" into a single evolutionary explanation called "secularization" may be misleading. It misleads us because, among other things, it suggests a single track to a common terminus, yet there are rival trends (such as disillusionment with institutions as such or a search for manifestations of the spirit) and these rival trends are inflected or deflected by the varieties of historical experience.[24] As Luke Bretherton comments, we are "neither falling from a golden age nor are we locked into a historically deterministic process of inevitable change in one direction ... there is a symbiotic relationship between what we might call 'traditional' (e.g., churches), 'modern' (e.g., political parties), and 'emergent' (e.g., Greenpeace) patterns of civic and political association in the contemporary context."[25] The contemporary world is not seeing a linear movement from a religious to a secular age but multiple interrelated movements.

Grace Davie has proposed that a more adequate explanation of the sociological data usually seen as evidence of secularization may be that Europeans are not so much *less* religious than citizens in other parts of the world as *differently* religious.[26] The relation between church and society is an ongoing one, and it is multi-stranded. Davie has proposed three key concepts that help to understand the current status of this evolving relationship, particularly in Europe, but with implications for other societies thought to be undergoing secularization. These are the sociological phenomena of *believing without belonging, vicarious religion*, and the *shift from a religion of obligation to one characterized by choice*.[27]

Believing without belonging, Davie maintains, is a pervasive, not just religious, dimension of modern European societies. If churches as institutions have declined markedly in the post-war period, the same process (decline in membership, financial support, and so on) can be seen in

---

23. Witness the many current journals of indigenous theology and spirituality.
24. Martin, *On Secularization*, 47–55.
25. Bretherton, *Christianity and Contemporary Politics*, 10.
26. Davie, "Europe: The Exception That Proves the Rule?" 65–83.
27. Davie, "From Obligation to Consumption," 33–45.

almost all social activities which require people to "gather" on a regular basis (political parties, trade unions, team sports, etc.).[28] José Casanova adds to this that in the European situation people may also belong to a church even if they don't believe much of what it teaches (*belonging without believing*). In this respect, especially in the case of the historical European churches (Catholic, Lutheran, Anglican, or Calvinist), "secular" and "Christian" cultural identities are intertwined in complex and rarely verbalized modes among most Europeans.[29]

Vicarious religion refers to religion performed by an active minority but on behalf of a much larger number, who (implicitly at least) not only understand but quite clearly approve of what the minority is doing: church leaders perform rituals on behalf of others, believe on behalf of others, embody moral codes on behalf of others, and offer space for the vicarious debate of unresolved issues in modern society.[30]

Most important, however, is what Davie calls the increasingly discernible mutation in the religious lives of Europeans from *a culture of obligation to one of consumption*.[31] This mutation (in Europe) takes the form of a gradual shift away from an understanding of religion as a form of obligation and towards an increasing emphasis on consumption. I go to church (or to another religious organization) because I want to, maybe for a short period or maybe for longer, to fulfil a particular rather than a general need in my life.[32]

Another way of being "differently" religious rather than simply "secular" is involvement in what North American evangelical theologian David Zahl calls "replacement religion." Where some see "secularization" in American society, Zahl sees a marketplace booming with religion. This is because religious observance has "migrated" rather than fading away. The promise of salvation has become attached to more everyday pursuits like busyness, romance, parenting, technology, work, leisure, food, politics, and "Jesusland."[33] The objects of such devotion (food, romance, education, children, technology, and so on) aren't somehow bad, says Zahl.

28. Davie, "From Obligation to Consumption," 34–35.

29. Casanova, "Immigration and the New Religious Pluralism," 143–44.

30. Davie, "From Obligation to Consumption," 36–41. For a fuller discussion of cultural heritage, believing without belonging, and vicarious religion, see Davie, *Religion in Britain*, 71–90.

31. Davie, "From Obligation to Consumption," 41.

32. Davie, "From Obligation to Consumption," 41–44.

33. Zahl, *Seculosity*.

It is when we co-opt them for our self-justification or make them arbiters of salvation that they turn toxic.[34] "Small-r" religion replaces "large-R" religion and promises functional salvation to those who live up to it—they will be accepted, respected, admired, and have a sense of "rightness" (righteousness).[35]

Defendants of the secularization paradigm maintain, nevertheless, that these are relatively small shifts in religious activity or shifts from public to private religion and do not disprove the basic affirmation of the secularization paradigm that the decline of the churches, principally in Europe, is a symptom of a wider loss of interest in the supernatural.[36]

A Theoretical Construction of Social Scientists?

A further critique of "secularization" is that it is driven less by the sociological evidence than by a western academic subculture, found especially in the humanities and social sciences, which is committed to "secularism" (in a "hard" rather than an "open" version) and therefore reads the available evidence in line with this commitment. Sociological data on religion is then seen to be in accord with the idea that religion is in decline and this decline is normal and progressive. It is part of being a modern and enlightened European. The more modern a society is, the more secular it becomes.

On the contrary, argues Casanova, the sociological data in Europe, at least, can be explained better in terms of historical patterns of church-state and church-nation relations, including different paths of secularization among the different branches of Christianity, than in terms of levels of modernization.[37]

David Martin comments that among some social scientists there has been a pervasive idea of "ages and stages" so that the old cannot leak into the new. Allied to this has been the conception of society as composed of structures and superstructures where the latter are causally subject to the

---

34. Zahl, *Seculosity*, ch. 14–16. Zahl proposes the term "seculosity" for religiosity that is directed horizontally rather than vertically, at earthly rather than heavenly objects.

35. Zahl, *Seculosity*, 5–7.

36. Bruce, *Secularization*, 120.

37. Berger, "The Desecularization of the World," 10. Tregenza, "Secularism, Myth, and History," 175–78. Casanova, "Immigration and the New Religious Pluralism," 143–44. But see also Bruce's continuing defense of secularization in Bruce, *Secularization*.

former—they were haunted by the ghost of Marxism. In this case religion can neither have causal efficacy nor leak out of its proper place in the past to affect the future.[38]

Perhaps most importantly, the idea of "secularization" as an interpretation of religion does not account for the strength of Asian religions and, in particular, the public impact of Islam and Muslim citizens in many nations, including now those formerly thought to be "Christian."[39] We may need to call upon more multi-cultural, dialogical, and pluralistic constructs to deal with the future of secularism in contemporary societies.

Local Church Mission and Secularization

What are local churches to make of this debate about secularization? Church reactions to secularization are sometimes reactions of consternation: Are we involved in a dying cause? Is it all heading for failure? Is widespread secularity or even anti-religious secularism inevitable no matter what we do?

At the end of the last century, sociologist of religion Peter Berger noted what he regarded as two unfortunate strategies adopted by religious people (principally in North America) in reaction to the link between modernity and secularity. These were *rejection* (a vigorous upsurge of conservative religion) because modernity was seen as the enemy, and *adaptation* (great efforts to conform to a perceived modernity) because modernity was seen as inevitable. Berger observes that both these strategies can be seen today as having very doubtful results.[40]

What attitudes can local churches adopt today towards "secularization" so that their mission in a secular society is more focused and more strategic than just rejection of an enemy or adaptation to the inevitable?

1) *Geography*. It is clear that the increase or decrease in public religious activity varies between regions of the world and between nations. Religious activity in Europe is different from that in North America and very different from South America, Africa, the Middle East, and Asia. Many proponents of secularization confine its application to industrial democracies. Local churches, in any case, rather than attending to any general theory of secularization, need rather to pay attention (worry

---

38. Martin, *Secularisation, Pentecostalism, and Violence*, 143.
39. Modood, "Muslims, Religious Equality, and Secularism," 164–85.
40. Berger, "The Desecularization of the World," 3–6.

about some and be glad about others) to more specific evidence of a variety of changes such as reduced church attendance, less attention to church teaching, more emphasis on choice than on obligation, and the effects of migration in their own locality or country.

2) *Religion.* The debate about secularization is focused on the public practice of "religion." Yet the definition of what is "religion" and who is "religious" is notoriously arbitrary. What has Buddhism, a religion without God, to do with Greek mythology and its many gods; what has a Reformed Christian church's dedication to "Scripture alone" to do with popular recreations of Celtic rituals; what has Christian liturgy to do with the modern fascination for witches, vampires, and fantastic beasts? Some of these social practices have features in common, and some do not. Yet all of these bits and pieces and many others are commonly assigned to the category of "religion."[41]

Some modern definitions of religion characterize it by its belief in the "supernatural." Yet this requires that we already know what is "natural" (Is sociological data "natural"?) and can state where the boundaries are between what is "natural" and what is "super-natural." "Natural" and "supernatural," "nature" and "grace," and similar binary terms interpenetrate in the real world. My own comments earlier in this book (especially chapters 4 and 5) about "wellbeing" and the "realm of God" are theological, and in that sense also "religious," but are no more "supernatural" than discussions about "democracy," "human rights," "ecological responsibility," and many other common ideas in the public forum. Local church mission is much more focused on the impact of *Christian* beliefs and practices on the wider society than on "religion" in general.

3) *Basic commitments.* The boundaries of what the term "religious" refers to are constantly sliding around. Are Europeans becoming *less* religious (i.e., "secularized") or just "*differently*" religious from what they used to be? Are people who "believe without belonging" still religious? Are people who "belong without believing" still religious? Are Americans becoming more secular or are they simply finding religious "replacements" which do not fit into old classifications of "religion" but have essentially the same functions?

---

41. The debate about what is meant by "religion" or "religious" is still a lively one. Some of this debate is helpfully summarized in Hedges, "Discourse on the Invention of Discourse," 132–48. Similarly enlightening but disconcerting is Hedges, "The Deconstruction of Religion," 385–96.

Secularization

The old categories and demarcations such as "religious" and "secular," "private" and "public," "natural" and "supernatural," may have outlived their usefulness as ways of understanding society and engaging in civil and political negotiations.[42] Democratic societies are populated by many different kinds of basic social and moral commitments, some of which can be called "religious" and some not.

As far as Christian mission's engagement in society is concerned, there is a variety of what we might call "basic commitments," "ultimate concerns,"[43] "spiritualities," or "ideologies" of which some but not all could be called "religious." When a Christian church engages with the wider society it is not just about engagement with "religions" or with "no religion" or with "secularism" but with the many different basic commitments that, in varied ways, drive contemporary society.[44]

Rather than as a process or product of "secularization," the contemporary context may be better understood, as Luke Bretherton proposes, as a period in which, for the first time, multiple "modernities" are overlapping and interacting within the same shared, predominantly urban spaces.[45] These "modern" associations and interrelationships need to be renegotiated in contemporary democracies.

4) *The primary mission objective.* The debates about secularization call us back to the primary objective of Christian mission—service to the realm of God. A Christian mission will want to oppose some instances of "basic commitments" or "modernities," support others, and enter into negotiation with others. Within this decision-making is an awareness too that "religion" is not necessarily good for us just because it goes by the name of "religion." The primary objective of the church's mission is not to promote "religion" but is much more specific: service to the realm of God. This service engages churches in a great number of issues, projects, and dialogues that are not normally classified as "religious" but are about "wellbeing" and, in Christian terms, about participation in the evolving realm of God.

There may be some variation in just how this participation is focused in different places and different times. An important task of the local church is to decide on how their mission activity can be focused.

---

42. As Elaine Graham suggests in Graham, *Between a Rock and a Hard Place*, 18, 65.

43. Hartney, "States of Ultimacy and the Cult of the Dead Soldier," 219–21.

44. Gascoigne, "Building Bridges in a Disconnected World," 424–40.

45. Bretherton, *Christianity and Contemporary Politics*, 15.

Australian theologian Robert Gascoigne, for example, proposes a focus on support for the claims of *human dignity*: to respond to its force, to strengthen and broaden its content, to reinforce commitment, and to inspire hope that this commitment is not in vain.[46]

5) *Freedom of conscience and democracy.* A major refinement in the Christian attitude to society that results from the consideration of "secularization" is a refocus on the local church's commitment to the principles of religious freedom and democracy in society.

Christian mission in service of the realm of God should work to support a movement *away from* an earlier, less tolerant society, with its religion-state or church-state alliance. Christian mission works to support freedom of religion, respect for the dignity of every human person, as well as respect for cultural and religious diversity. If the process (or processes) that we have called "secularization" is bringing about a purification of the dominating power that organized religion once held in some societies, then secularization may be an ally of Christian mission.

Here, though, we should make some important qualifications. Increased secularity takes us away from some serious defects of a previously more "religious" age. Yet this does not mean that a process of secularization will produce the "good" society. A more secular society may rather produce the self-interested egotist, cultural and religious conflict, the collapse of egalitarianism in favor of an increasing gap between rich and poor, and continuing environmental destruction. Secularity is not in itself going to be the savior of society. In itself it is not a substitute for a more positively and carefully articulated commitment to the evolving realm of God.

Religious freedom and democracy do seem to imply that church belonging is becoming more voluntary than obligatory, a matter of choice rather than obligation. This is a process which Christian churches must support even if they do regret any consequent decrease in their own members. In this sense, a degree of secularity in society is part of a Christian mission commitment. It is not something to be lamented but a natural consequence of the principle of religious freedom.

6) *Internal secularization.* Throughout its history, Christianity has negotiated how it might co-exist with different types of political power in society. The results of such negotiations, says David Martin, can be an "internal secularisation." The Renaissance papacy, for example, as a

---

46. Gascoigne, *The Church and Secularity*, 2.

structure of power bidding for pre-eminence with the Holy Roman Empire, successfully secularized the church from within.[47] The Christian church took on the power structures of the wider society.

In the more recent negotiations of Christian churches with secular society, Christianity may have adopted some of the values or structures of its opponents. A "closed" secularism attempted to confine religion to the private sphere and exclude it from the public sphere. While consciously opposing this exclusion, many Christians may have unconsciously accepted that the proper place of Christian belief and action is in the privacy of the individual person and the internal affairs of the church itself. This focuses Christian attention towards a spirituality of personal development and personal devotions. An excessive focus towards the interiority of the person may downplay the mission to the wider society and thus confine itself to the private sphere.

A second form of internal secularization occurs when the church's mission outreach in contemporary democracies accommodates itself to the secular state's requirements. Luke Bretherton outlines three ways in which the local church engaged in contemporary political issues relating to the just and generous ordering of a common life may accept other (that is, non-Christian) ways of framing politics. Effectively, this means the negotiations between the church and other secular entities (state, market, or community) result in an internal secularization of the church. These three ways are: a) the dynamics of *co-option*, where the church is construed as either one more interest groups seeking a share of public money, i.e. a client of state patronage, or just another constituency within civil society which is seen to foster social cohesion and make up the deficiencies of the welfare state, i.e. a new form of establishment under state direction; b) the dynamics of *competition*, where churches construe themselves as part of identity politics, whether as a form of multi-culturalism or as part of the rhetoric of rights; and c) *commodification*, where Christianity is regarded as a product or a commodity, another privatized lifestyle choice.[48]

7) *The secondary mission objective.* Where there is indeed a decline in local Christian belonging, one of the important issues this decline raises for local churches is that of blame attribution: Is it our fault? To blame a decrease in church belonging on "secularization" in society is not a first option for a local church. Christians are used to the call for

---

47. Martin, *Secularisation, Pentecostalism, and Violence*, 40, 119.
48. Bretherton, *Christianity and Contemporary Politics*, 2.

"repentance," a "change of heart," a search for where we ourselves have failed. The first option then is to look to our own actions, not for where we are failing to attract new people into the church (or are losing the old ones), but for where we have failed to engage in authentic mission action or to live authentically ourselves. Are our mission activities indeed a service to the evolving realm of God or not? If they are not, then we should be pleased rather than concerned that other people do not join in this severely faulted mission and this severely faulted church.

It remains, though, that churches whose mission does include support for religious freedom and respect for the beliefs of others will need to make efforts to ensure our own basic commitments are communicated outwards into the wider world so that other people are attracted into membership in the church.[49]

Conclusion

"Secularism" and "secularity" have been important concepts for interpreting the characteristics of many societies from a mission point of view. "Secularization," however, is a troubled concept needing careful definition and applicable in some places rather than others.

In some localities there may be clear evidence for more indifference and less active belonging to Christian churches over recent decades. Where this is the case, it will be of concern to those churches. Nevertheless, the local church mission is focused primarily on service to the realm of God. If such "secularization" means a movement away from an earlier, less tolerant society, then the Christian church would want to support such a movement. Christian mission means engagement with all the variety of basic moral commitments, whether religious or not, within that wider society for the wellbeing of all. This means support for freedom of conscience and for democracy in that society.

An increase in "secularity" implies a decrease in a dominating, perhaps intolerant, power of religion in society. It does not, however, mean an increase in the wellbeing of that society, for it could open the way for deprivation rather than wellbeing (and indeed has done so historically). There is a whole range of beliefs and commitments within that society

---

49. Steve Bruce maintains that the "privatization" of religion removes much of the social support that is vital to reinforcing beliefs, makes the maintenance of distinct lifestyles very difficult, weakens the impetus to evangelize, and encourages a de facto relativism that is fatal to shared beliefs. Bruce, *God Is Dead*, 20, 29–30.

that contribute or are destructive to people's wellbeing. Only some of these are normally called "religious."

It may be that the concept of "secularization" carries the residue of an overly negative and confined assessment of society when other ways of understanding society could be more creatively focused. Are there other key characteristics of contemporary society that are more helpful or more positive for mission action?

Part III
Mission in a Pluralist Society

DISCUSSION OF SECULAR SOCIETY and secularization has often seemed to pit church and secular society against each other. If the primary characteristic of society is its secularism understood in an anti-religious sense, then the mission of the church in that society would be one of opposition (to the norms of that society) and rescue (of people from the power of that society).[1]

Catholics in particular may be affected here by the heritage of the dispute between the papacy and liberal democracy from the late nineteenth century through to the mid-twentieth century and lingering still into the twenty-first century. From the inside, the Catholic Church as represented by the papacy from Leo XIII to Pius XII saw itself as the bastion of truth opposed by and opposed to a secular society, at least in the European world. From the outside, the hierarchical Catholic Church looked like an authoritarian and conservative institution opposed to democracy and freedom.[2] This changed at an official level with the Second Vatican Council (1962–65) especially through its *Declaration on Religious Freedom*[3] and its *Constitution on the Church in the Modern World*.[4]

---

1. This chapter draws on ideas previously published in Darragh, "A Missional Church in Process and Willing to Learn," 73–86.

2. Lacey, "Leo's Church and Our Own," 57–92. See also Zagorin, *How the Idea of Religious Toleration Came to the West*, 305.

3. Second Vatican Council, *Declaration on Religious Freedom*.

4. Second Vatican Council, *Pastoral Constitution on the Church in the Modern World*.

Yet strong remnants of this oppositional attitude to a secular society still remain among church members.

Too much attention to this "secular" dimension of society may have the effect of distracting us from other dimensions of contemporary society more relevant and more important than its secularism and the process of secularization. A more positive attitude towards an open secularism may note that the movement from Christendom to secularity has included a release from authoritarian and conservative church institutions and to that extent may constitute an advance in the evolving realm of God.

Rather than its secularism, the "pluralist" dimension of many contemporary societies deserves the careful attention of local churches focused on their service to the realm of God.

10

Mission in a Pluralist Democracy

LOCAL CHURCH MEMBERS TODAY, seeing themselves as having a stake in the good functioning of their democratic society, will want a more nuanced and more interwoven way of seeing the relationship between church and society than is provided by a focus on secularization. We are members of both the church and society, and we are committed to the good functioning of both. Religious freedom is to be understood as a positive empowerment for participation in social life, not as a negative immunity that relegates religion to the private sphere.[1]

In religiously pluralist and democratic societies, organized religion may have few privileges, but nor is it ignored or automatically disrespected. A religious commitment is one of the choices among many "fundamental" or "ultimate" commitments in a society that is both religiously and culturally pluralist.[2] The relationship between a local church and its society is ongoing and many-stranded. It requires a process of discernment that includes strategies not just of opposition but also of cooperation and negotiation.

---

1. Hollenbach, *The Global Face of Public Faith*, 124–46.

2. Yet no one approaches these choices from a purely objective starting point. Contemporary European societies have deep roots in their Christian history. Guy Liagre, General Secretary of the Conference of European Churches, names not just critical reason, pluralism, and tolerance (here following Karl Popper) but also its Christian roots as the distinguishing feature and destiny of European history. Liagre, *The New CEC*, 12.

The church then is one body of people without special rights or privileges in the midst of the many other public bodies that make up civil and public society: government agencies, sports clubs, associations of various kinds, educational institutions, religious organizations, political parties, etc. Along with state institutions within that public sphere there are many other institutions, including religious ones, working for the wellbeing of citizens. Cooperation among these institutions is usually beneficial for all.

Above all, a missionary church requires a sense of solidarity with "the joys and hopes, griefs and anxieties, of the human beings of this age, especially of those who are poor and afflicted."[3]

It helps to focus the objectives of Christian mission in a pluralist world if we see this contemporary mission as "bookended," so to speak, between the historic principle of *toleration* setting a foundation at one end and, at the other, the more recent *communitarian turn* in pluralist politics providing some immediate objectives.

Tolerance and the Communitarian Turn

The principle of *toleration* is foundational for pluralism. Pluralism can only exist where citizens are prepared to tolerate as a matter of right that other citizens have beliefs and commitments different from their own. American historian Perez Zagorin's definition of religious toleration as it has evolved in the United States and other countries of the Western world is the principle that "society and the state should, as a matter of right, extend complete freedom of religious belief and expression to all their members and citizens and should refrain from imposing any religious tests, doctrines, or form of worship or religious association upon them."[4] Zagorin observes that during the twentieth century, religious freedom and pluralism became largely a reality in Western society and inseparable from political and other freedoms.[5] Yet on the world scene, beyond "Western" societies, religious freedom is increasingly threatened.

---

3. The opening words of Second Vatican Council, *Pastoral Constitution on the Church in the Modern World*, #1.

4. Zagorin, *How the Idea of Religious Toleration Came to the West*, 7.

5. Zagorin, *How the Idea of Religious Toleration Came to the West*, 311.

As far as the democratic state is concerned, tolerance is a necessary political strategy.[6] It is a strategy for maintaining unity and yet avoiding the simple rule of the majority to the exclusion or oppression of minorities in democratic societies. A far as the church is concerned, tolerance is attractive. Yet there remains a caution that tolerance may mask a relativism that does not treat deep commitments of conscience seriously. British theologian Stuart Murray, drawing on Anabaptist traditions, argues that the apparent neutrality of this relativism (all religions are the same and equally valid) masks a secular imperialism and cannot achieve the peaceful plural society it envisages. He suggests that an alternative lies in the "religious liberty" tradition developed within marginal movements like the Anabaptists, Quakers, and English Baptists. These were passionate movements with strong convictions, which they eagerly shared with others, and this sometimes resulted in conflict. But they were deeply committed to religious liberty—not because their own convictions were unimportant, but because they were too important to be imposed.[7]

In recent decades, relations between church and states in pluralist democracies have moved a long way from a simple reliance on the principle of toleration. Negotiation and collaboration between state agencies and churches is common.

I borrow the term *"communitarian turn"* from Luke Bretherton, who calls attention to developments in the "West" in relations between governments and faith communities. In Bretherton's analysis, the communitarian turn in British politics, with parallels in the US and continental Europe, since the early 1990s, emphasizes the need for governments to strengthen participation in civil society and the formation of mediating structures between the state and the individual, devolve power, encourage widespread consultation and participation in decision-making, and foster social inclusion.

In this context there is an increasingly constructive engagement between the state and minority religious groups. Where there is an emphasis on the free market and the retreat of the state from welfare provision, faith communities are seen as obvious partners with the state for the provision of welfare services and education. Governments are also seeking to enlist faith groups in addressing issues like antisocial behaviour, obesity, parenting, and the radicalization of some religious groups. There is now

6. Avis, *A Church Drawing Near*, 69.
7. Murray, *Post-Christendom*, 234–36.

a rhetoric of "active citizenship," "empowering communities," "partnerships," and "building relationships."[8]

Yet churches need to be clear about, and sometimes suspicious about, the motivations of governments for working with churches and other faith-based groups. This includes being alert to the impact of governments on the policy and practice of the churches when those churches enter into negotiations or arrangements with state agencies.[9]

Spheres of Engagement

Societies that are religiously and culturally pluralist, not just as a matter of fact but as a matter of public policy, create new conditions for Christian mission that scarcely existed for most of the history of Christian mission. Local churches engage with their own society not as visitors or foreign evangelists but as citizen theologians committed both to their church and to their society. They do not have to approve of everything within that society nor oppose everything there even though there may be injustices, violence, and death-dealing power structures. They engage at various levels and with various elements within that society as their own contribution to the emerging realm of God.

The bottom line here is that Christian engagement in society does not accept a division between politics and religion in the way often proposed in secularist definitions of society. Mission activity is inherently political. This position, expressed perhaps more clearly than elsewhere in the Catholic Worker Movement, can be clarified by a recognition of "four voices" of theology:[10] a) normative theology, such as that found in Scriptures, creeds, official church teaching, and liturgies; b) formal theology, which includes the work of theologians and dialogue with other disciplines; c) espoused theology, which is the theology that is embedded within a particular group's expression of its beliefs; and d) operant theology, which is the theology that is embedded within actual practice. These four voices of theology are interrelated, but it is the "operant theology" that is most closely aligned with the mission action of a Christian community.

In the eyes of the pluralist and secular state, the church may not be set above other corporate and political bodies within that society, but it

---

8. Bretherton, *Christianity and Contemporary Politics*, 32–37.
9. Bretherton, *Christianity and Contemporary Politics*, 37.
10. Blackman, "Holy Disobedience," 122–41.

may still engage with them both cooperatively and competitively. Social differentiation allows public space for an influential, but not juridical, authoritative exercise of religion.[11] Modern pluralist societies are made up of many different groups, organizations, and social forces, among which are Christian churches. Church communities are *within* that society, rather than outside reaching towards it, and church membership overlaps with that of many other organizations within that society.[12]

Local churches may then consider their mission within society in five different though overlapping "spheres":

a. The mission towards the state and its institutions, where the church has no special privileges, but may still take on the role of influential commentator,[13] sometime co-operator, partner, opponent, or negotiator with the state (and keeping in mind that church members may also be functionaries of the state)—*the public sector.*

b. The mission of engagement, sometimes cooperative, sometimes oppositional, and sometimes in negotiation with the other bodies that operate more or less independently of the state—*civil society.*[14]

c. The mission of engagement with indigenous cultures within the society, especially when these are unique and have been diminished by colonization or large-scale immigration—*indigenous communities.*

11. Hughson, "Missional Churches in Secular Societies, 173–94.

12. For examples of engagement in the Australian context. see Sullivan and Leppert, *Church and Civil Society.*

13. Sociologist David Martin notes the Catholic Church's acceptance of this role in Italy and suggests that it is a role that may increasingly be taken on by the Evangelical movement with its characteristics of participation, pragmatism, competition, and personal discipline. Martin, "The Evangelical Upsurge and Its Political Implications," 48–49.

14. The term "civil society" is used in several different ways. I am influenced particularly here by Indian theologian A. Pushparajan's explanation in which the first (of seven) feature is that "Civil society is thus a location where mediation between individual experience of one's rights and public articulation of them takes place. It includes the processes by which an issue is brought to the forefront of debate and discussion and is made an object of contending theorization, leading to a demand that something should be done about it, or that it should be left alone." A. Pushparajan, "Mission in Civil Society," 269–71. A recent Vatican document on present economic-financial systems recognizes the importance of "civil society" and calls for church engagement "as sentinels, to watch over genuine life and to make ourselves catalysts of a new social behavior, shaping our actions to the search for the common good, and establishing it on the sound principles of solidarity and subsidiarity." Congregation for the Doctrine of the Faith and Dicastery for Promoting Integral Human Development, "Considerations for an Ethical Discernment," #34.

d. The mission to individuals and families where in a secular society the state should not intrude—*the private sector.*

e. The mission with those who do not hold any strong place in society and are therefore disadvantaged, oppressed, afflicted, or isolated—*the excluded.*[15]

The term "civil society," as I use it here, refers to the great number of institutions, corporations, businesses, non-governmental organizations, sports clubs, charitable organizations, and cultural associations that constitute that intermediate zone, so to speak, between the individual and family on the one hand and institutions of the state on the other. These are entities that maintain their own beliefs, values, customs, and protocols, and many have a sense not only of their own identity but also of the common good of society.[16] In some societies relations between church mission and civil society may be more important than the link with the state.[17] In other societies, the churches themselves may play a dynamic role in building civil society.[18]

From a mission viewpoint, it is important that a church's public stance not be just self-protection in the present or nostalgia for the past.

---

15. Wells, *Incarnational Mission*, 216–18. The Vatican document noted above on economic-financial systems also comments on "exclusion": "It is no longer simply the phenomenon of exploitation and oppression, but something new. Exclusion ultimately has to do with what it means to be a part of the society in which we live; those excluded are no longer society's underside, or those on the fringes or its disenfranchised, but rather they are no longer even a part of it. The excluded are not the "exploited" but the outcast, the "leftovers."'" Congregation for the Doctrine and Dicastery for Promoting Integral Human Development, "*Considerations for an Ethical Discernment,*" #34, #15. See also Francis, *Evanglii Gaudium*, #53.

16. Avis, *A Church Drawing Near*, 14–17.

17. In David Hollenbach's view, religious engagement in public life should occur principally through its influence in the broad domain of the social, rather than primarily through direct influence on the legislature or the courts. Thus, institutional separation of church and state is not the same as the removal of religious communities from social influence. Separation of church and state is not the same as the privatization of religion. Hollenbach, *The Global Face of Public Faith*, 147–73. Adolf Ham writes that this at least is something we can learn from the Cuban experience if we understand the kingdom of God to be holistic, i.e., that it includes the material, the ecological, the cultural, and the spiritual. Ham, "Commission Seven in Light of a Century of Experience in Cuba," 228.

18. Coptic theologian Andrea Stephanous advocates an Arab political theology that promotes citizenship and coexistence and will bring the church to the heart of civil society. Stephanous, "Towards an Arabic Political Theology," 218–21.

A missionary church is not just a lobby group seeking its own advantage. It is not just a milder form of the religious fanaticism that excludes all other beliefs in the name of its own version of God. A local church committed to the realm of God has a commitment to finding practical political solutions to the issues of a just and peaceful society when that society is in fact religiously and culturally diverse.

Citizen theologians are members both of society and of church with a commitment to the realm of God that encompasses both. Pluralism, whether religious, ideological, or cultural, may be dangerous to social cohesion as witnessed in so much of the ethnically and religiously aligned violence around the world. Pluralism is in this sense a potential threat to democracy. And in this case, churches and their citizen theologians, already committed to religious and cultural pluralism, have a mission to find a common ground which will have to be in some sense "secular" (not faith-based, yet not anti-religious either) and multi-cultural.

Engagement within a Pluralist Democracy

The church's mission is not simply *outreach into a secular society*, but rather an *engagement within a pluralist society*. The church engages critically with the many other bodies that make up a pluralist society. Its purpose is to play a part in bringing about the realm of God in that society. In this sense, British theologian Joshua T. Searle proposes that Christian mission, in a post-Christendom age, should be re-envisioned in terms of *solidarity* with the world rooted in compassion, yet a voice too that is raised against the trends that obstruct the coming reign of God.[19]

What is hopefully clear in all of this is that a church with a mission in service to the realm of God within a pluralist democracy includes a commitment to the good functioning of that democracy.[20] Some attitudes of Christians to the wider society seem to indicate a suspicion of secular democracy and perhaps a desire to return to former political conditions of church collusion with autocratic regimes. Yet, as Charles Taylor points out, today citizens have to do for themselves what formerly rulers did

19. Searle, *Theology after Christendom*, 87–94, 191–93.
20. I am concerned principally here with societies regarded as liberal democracies, but a mission of cooperation and witness can be carried out in a range of political regimes. Examples of this are contained in the collection of papers from a conference held in Nanjing, China, focusing on how religion can nurture sustainable development. Xinping et al., *Toward a Shared, Sustainable Future*.

for them. The modern democratic state demands a people with a strong collective identity who have answers to the questions: What or whom is this state for? Whose freedom? Whose expression?[21] Christians are then being called to be positive contributors in the public debate about the future of freedom and democracy in the way they present themselves in their liturgy, their intellectual life, their engagement for justice, and their works of mercy.[22] A positive Christian engagement in pluralist democracy requires what North American theologian Jonathon S. Kahn calls, aptly I think, a "democratic faith." The practice of democratic faith includes an ability to articulate and work to bring about what we hold sacred. And we do this with both friends and adversaries. We bring faith-based commitments to each other not in order to defend them or prove that they are right, but in order to see if they open the possibility of doing the risky and improbable work of building trust.[23]

The mission of the Christian church is no longer just a matter of finding a place for religion in a democratic society, but of recognizing that democracy itself is barely developed and even under threat in the contemporary world. If, as philosopher A. C. Grayling argues, democracy is understood as "government *for the people* on terms set, and authority given, *by the people*,"[24] and this implies that the aim of democratic government is to act for the interests and participation of *all*, how can such a society achieve the joint realization of freedom and fairness in society? Democracy entails fair participation and fair opportunity for all. It aims then to ensure equal concern and respect for all, and to enable access to social goods of health, education, and welfare for all. Our democracies have not achieved these aims, and many of our current democracies are inherently flawed and vulnerable or already corroding from within.[25]

The mission of the Christian church is not just for itself but towards the health and reform of democratic systems which have not yet achieved the joint realization of freedom and fairness in society. A church's engagement in a secular pluralist society is measured by its discernment of positive and negative elements in that society and its contribution

---

21. Taylor, "Why We Need a Radical Redefinition of Secularism," 44–45.

22. In his interpretation of the documents and discussions around the Second Vatican Council, Massimo Faggioli presents this as a call to new responsibilities in citizenship for Catholics. Faggioli, *Catholicism and Citizenship*.

23. Kahn, "The Virtue of Democratic Faith," 137–56.

24. Grayling, *The Good State*, 33.

25. Grayling, *The Good State*, 37, 44–46.

to those positive elements. A key characteristic of a liberal democratic society, as Robert Gascoigne describes it, is its ambivalence. It tells *two* stories. The first of these stories is of individual freedom as the source of creativity and diversity. This story proclaims the right of even the most apparently insignificant to make their voices heard in the debates that concern their destiny. The other story is of freedom as a voluntarism that destroys the ethical and cultural substance of tradition, leaving only the emptiness of self-indulgent whim. This ambivalence about freedom suggests a particular role for the Christian church in the context of liberal societies: "to assist those societies in telling their positive story of freedom by illuminating the sources of freedom in human dignity and by acting in solidarity with all those who commit themselves to enhancing our consciousness of this dignity and to giving it practical effect."[26]

Brazilian theologian Leonardo Boff has given local churches some further guidance to democracy in a Christian sense when he describes democracy as based on the co-existence and articulation of five founding forces: participation, solidarity, equality, difference, and communion.

Participation: Rather than seek an egalitarian society directly, today we are seeking a society that is participatory on every possible level. This participation is not reduced to a simple integration into the status quo, but means a share in establishing new relationships and in bringing about situations not yet tried.

Solidarity: the capacity to include others in one's own personal and social interests and to enter into the world of the other in order to uphold it, especially in relation to those most punished by life and history, the most needy.

Equality: societies of the past were characterized by inequality and exclusivity. To the extent that individuals share in and experience solidarity, more symmetrical and therefore humanizing relationships emerge.

Difference: these constitute the riches of every individual and of cultures. Sharing in and valuing singularity ensure that differences do not degenerate into discrimination and inequality.

Communion: the capacity for establishing interpersonal relationships, for nourishing spirituality—an appreciation of ethical, aesthetic,

---

26. Gascoigne, *The Church and Secularity*, 7. Investigative journalist David Crouch provides examples at the national level of efforts for wellbeing in Sweden with its history of both successes and failures in recent years. Churches may need to be alert to such efforts and be prepared to engage with them. Crouch, *Almost Perfekt*.

and religious dimensions, which are all factors that build up human community.²⁷

By way of summary, we can note that a key ingredient in a functioning democracy is the style of government that people accept and trust. This requires that the process of government is deeply *deliberative*, in the sense of working through high-quality democratic discussion; and that it is deeply *participative*, in the sense of handing over more direct influence on decisions to ordinary citizens.²⁸ Churches, along with other organizations of like commitment, can promote public processes that are both deliberative and participative without abandoning or violating the principles of freedom of conscience and the moral equality of all citizens.²⁹

Engagement with a Plurality of Faith Traditions

Engagement in a pluralist democracy is not just engagement with its secular organizations and institutions, but also with its religious ones. A feature of pluralist democracies is that they allow, even require, interaction not just between local Christian communities and other social organizations but also interaction between different faith traditions. We might expect, and historically this has often been the case, that a Christian church's mission to other religions would be simply to convert them to Christianity. The main thrust of the church's mission in the politics of religion today, however, is concerned rather with inter-faith dialogue and cooperation for peace and justice in the world.³⁰

27. Boff, *Ecology and Liberation*, 106–07.

28. New Zealand investigative journalist Max Rashbrooke proposes these as the two key concepts of "liquid government." Liquid government, he proposes, offers a possible path through the twin perils of managerialism and authoritarianism. It can answer the desire for citizen control that the former denies, but without the latter's violence and threats to basic liberties. Rashbrooke, *Government for the Public Good*, 29–30, 266.

29. For ongoing international examples and principles for Open Government Partnerships, including issues such as the right to information, gender and inclusion, digital governance and rights, protection of civic space and natural resources, and corruption, see https://www.opengovpartnership.org.

30. Drawing the World Council of Churches 2012 document "Together towards Life," Nigerian missiologist Ezechiel Lesmore Gibson argues for a pedagogy that prepares Christian missioners and workers to engage in life-affirming dialogue and cooperation with people of other belief systems. He proposes educational principles by which this could be carried out. Gibson, "Missional Formation for Life-Giving Interfaith Encounter," 69–79.

Bevans and Schroeder point to inter-religious dialogue as a clear case of "prophetic dialogue," the model of mission which they advocate for today's world. "As *dialogue*, it demands attentive listening, conversation skills, empathy, study, and respect. As *prophetic*, it demands honesty, conviction, courage, and faith."[31]

The urgency and global importance of inter-faith or inter-religious dialogue is stressed by many commentators who see religion as the most realistic and effective basis on which to build a global ethic for world peace and for values such as respect, love, solidarity, compassion, and forgiveness. For this reason, dialogue must take place between the religions of the world, and in this dialogue, commonalities, not differences, must be stressed.[32] Hence too the multiple research projects relating to the growing religious diversity of Europe and its consequences in relation to key values of tolerance, acceptance, respect, rights, responsibilities, inclusion, and exclusion.[33]

In the context of this discussion of mission in pluralist democracies and at the ground level where members of Christian churches are often in daily contact with followers of other faith traditions, a "pluralist" approach to inter-faith dialogue is the one that interests us most. A "pluralist" approach advocates that all religious traditions have a claim to be bearers of truth and genuine, though different, paths to salvation, and through dialogue they can experience mutual challenge and enrichment.[34]

To those who fear that the pluralist approach makes all religions equal (and therefore erodes commitment to any one of them), Paul Knitter observes that in his experience "pluralists" do not affirm the plurality and *equality* of religions but rather the plurality and the *mutuality* of religions. That is, they seek the possibility of relationships among the religious communities that will further the wellbeing of the religions and of the world.[35] In Knitter's view, the converging point of the mission of

---

31. Bevans and Schroeder, *Constants in Context*, 384.
32. Boff, *Toward an Eco-Spirituality*, 49–50.
33. Davie, *Religion in Britain*, 228.
34. Discussions on inter-religious dialogue commonly take place in reference to the framework of "exclusivist-inclusivist-pluralist" approaches. "Exclusivist": there is only one religion that can claim to have an exclusive hold on truth, and that is Christianity. "Inclusivist": acknowledges the value to be found in other religions and the possibility of salvation there for true followers, but Christianity holds the supreme place and role among the religions of the world.
35. Knitter, "The Transformation of Mission in the Pluralist Paradigm," 93–94.

various religions should be the future shape of the human community and its flourishing.[36]

In a somewhat different, perhaps somewhat "larger-scale," approach than that of "inter-religious dialogue," Felix Wilfred advocates a "religious cosmopolitanism" which maintains that the mystery with which all religions are concerned is not the possession of any particular religion. It belongs to the whole human family, which participates in that mystery and manifests its splendor through its life and its varied expression—including religious ones. No religion can claim to exhaust that mystery, much less possess it.[37] Religious cosmopolitanism is very often practiced most effectively, Wilfred observes, at the grassroots level and in very local circumstances.[38] It is best practiced, in other words, at the level of local churches.

New Dimensions in Missiology

I have suggested above that engagement in culturally and religiously pluralist democracies shifts contemporary missiology into a new phase. The overlap between "mission theology" and "public theology" is an indicator of this new phase.[39] There are dimensions of the contemporary world that were not present in historical missiology. These new dimensions alter our ways of carrying out the mission of the church and they also enter into and alter our mission theology. Many of these new dimensions are positive from the point of view of mission:

   a. The amount of *information on the social, economic, and environmental conditions that affect wellbeing in society* has grown significantly over the last few decades. This information both stimulates and complicates the church's involvement in the wider society. A good deal of this information is publicly accessible through published reports, especially through the internet. In the area of social justice, for example, decisions about priorities (what will really make a difference) can now draw upon recent social, economic, and ecological studies that were not previously available to church missionaries.

---

36. Knitter, "The Transformation of Mission in the Pluralist Paradigm," 114–15.
37. Wilfred, "Christianity and Religious Cosmopolitanism," 113–19.
38. Wilfred, "Christianity and Religious Cosmopolitanism," 120.
39. See chapter 2 of this volume on public theology.

b. Similarly, there is a great deal more information than before about the follow-on *effects of different kinds of human organization and relationships*. Decisions about organizational structures that contribute to good community and mission need not rely just on traditional experience and the personal insights of missionaries but can now draw also on researched sociological and psychological conclusions as well as on recent historical research.

c. Most people in contemporary democratic societies have become used to *"evolutionary" or "process" thinking* which allows Christian church members to maintain continuity with their religious tradition as well as seek innovation that responds to new situations and new generations. We can accept new strategies and new ideas without the confrontational discomfort of having to condemn the theologies of past generations. Such process thinking does nevertheless require intelligent strategies for managing change. Irish theologian Gerard Mannion has argued for the ecclesial virtue of "creative fidelity" or "loyal dissent" that steers between centralizing and legalistic intransigence on the one hand and, at the opposite extreme, a drift toward total disregard for the rich traditions of the church in favor of an out-and-out relativism.[40] The future evolves out of the past. We do not stand on the same ground as our ancestors; we stand on their shoulders. Christian moral tradition in particular, as North American theologian David Hollenbach argues, is dynamic and not given once and for all. Christian ethics should be understood as a pilgrimage that is not yet completed. Such understanding is particularly important when Christianity intersects with the politics of a pluralistic society and requires therefore the virtue of humility and a spirit of genuine solidarity with the people of that society.[41]

d. This process thinking needs to be combined, however, with a *contextual*, rather than uniformly global, thinking—an ecclesial sense of place and time. A church in one contemporary context may evolve styles of leadership somewhat different from a church in another context. It is now relatively common to think about mission and church in a way that is both evolutionary and contextual. The kind of investigation undertaken in this book would be nearly impossible

---

40. Mannion, "A Teaching Church That Learns?" 184.
41. Hollenbach, *The Global Face of Public Faith*, 19–38, 39–53.

in the prevalence of a static and universally uniform view of mission and church.

e. Information technology was not part of traditional missionary communication, but it is today. Along with the widespread use of information technology comes a *digital culture* that alters or at least adds to the style and content of the local church's mission activity. Local churches may find new kinds of "inhabitants of digital culture" in their midst. English theologian Philip R. Meadows identifies the "digital alien," the "digital pioneer," and the "digital native" as all likely to enhance the reach, content, and quality of a church's mission activities, provided the church leadership and its citizen theologians are alert to its opportunities.[42] Christian mission also needs to be aware of the widespread atheist conversations that take place online. Jesse M. Smith, sociologist and frequent commentator on atheism, points out that not only is criticism of religion frequent on many atheist blogs, websites, and other online forums, but there is also discussion and debate about the same social and political issues that many religious groups are concerned with. This creates a space in which the moral dimensions of human behavior and its relationship with the claims of religion and God take the fore.[43] It is notable too that the international mission conference Edinburgh 2010 made extensive use of online technologies. Its organizers saw the use of its website and social networking hubs as a development in both the tools of mission and the character of the ecumenical missionary community.[44]

Conclusion

Many contemporary democracies are not simply "secular" but more importantly are religiously, culturally, and ideologically pluralist, where religion is neither established nor privatized. There the local church can engage with state institutions and non-governmental organizations in a non-privileged but nevertheless legitimate and influential way. Even more

---

42. Meadows, "Mission and Discipleship in a Digital Culture," 163–82.
43. Smith, "Atheism," 41.
44. Hollander, "@Edinburgh2010: Online Ecumenism in an Age of Participation," 329.

importantly, perhaps, from the point of view of a local church, it can engage also with the organizations of civil society, including its indigenous cultures, yet continue to play a role in the private sector of individual and family. It is obliged moreover to exercise a "preferential option" for those excluded from the normal protections and supports of society.

This engagement in the several spheres of a pluralist society is a discerning one that is guided by the church's own understanding of the evolving realm of God. It is an engagement with, not a standing outside of or backing away from, the wider society. The local church recognizes a responsibility to the common good and to the good functioning of democracy in that society.

There are also dimensions of the contemporary world that were unknown to traditional missiology. Noteworthy here are the sheer amount of information now accessible to the local church and its citizen theologian, new knowledge about human organization and relationships, widespread evolutionary or process thinking, contextual thinking, and information technology. All of these can be positive gains for local church mission.

Given a broadly positive and engaged attitude towards the wider pluralist society rather than simply regarding it as "secular," a local church can focus more deliberately on its strategies of engagement within that society, including the faith traditions therein. We can advance this investigation, then, by giving more specific attention to the kind of mission strategies available to the local church.

11

Strategies of Local Church Mission

MANY LOCAL CHURCHES ALONG with their individual members are involved in civil organizations and state agencies whose objectives include the wellbeing of society. Does Christian belief motivate and encourage such involvement, or where does it draw a line and require withdrawal or even opposition?

The previous three chapters of this book looked at the attitudes a local church could or should take towards a wider democratic, secular, and pluralist society in which it exercises its mission. This present chapter seeks to move beyond those broad *attitudes* towards the more specific level of the *strategies* of mission engagement. A mission interest in the realm of God is not just about *understanding* what the realm of God means, but about the ways in which we participate in its *implementation* and evolution. In that sense it can be called a "strategic" approach to the realm of God.

Writing or speaking about the realm of God can be said to be "strategic" when it gives direction and guidance to Christian engagement in contemporary society.[1] A strategic approach is implicit in a dynamic understanding of the realm of God as always-coming-into-being while already-partially-present. Participation in this evolving realm of God

---

1. A national example of such guidance with a call to the exercise of democratic citizenship is contained in the document of the United States Conference of Catholic Bishops, "Forming Consciences for Faithful Citizenship."

takes place within the concrete circumstances of our own particular time and place.[2]

Strategic Engagement in Society

A "strategic" understanding of the realm of God does not then construe the realm of God as an imaginary ideal society in a static and ahistorical way. It is not a utopia in this sense. It is "ideal" only in the sense that it provides principles or goals that direct an activity or movement in the real world that seeks the betterment of society.[3] The realm of God is the opposite of the secular utopian movements of the last three centuries (including the French Revolution, Nazism, Soviet communism, and the Maoist regime) which their proponents attempted to achieve by large-scale violence. In opposition to such utopias, English philosopher John Gray describes them as mutant versions of Christian faith in an end time initiated by God but now thought to be achievable by human action.[4] If the realm of God is to be considered a utopia, then it needs to be understood in a way that avoids such distortions. Rather, it is to be understood in a sense closer to (though not quite identical with) that described by philosopher John Hoffman as an idea that is rooted in history, is sensitive to context, and can never actually be realized.[5]

One of the learnings of recent centuries has been the dangers of large-scale visions, whether religious or secular, of what the perfect society should look like. Christianity is certainly "eschatological" in the sense that it trusts in an eventually positive outcome. It hopes for and works for a better future, but it does not have a concrete plan of what that eventual outcome will be like in political, sociological, or economic terms. A "strategic" understanding of the realm of God does not pretend to have a large-scale, long-term plan. It seeks the next steps in the betterment of society and holds that those steps must be just, peaceful, and

---

2. In contemporary missiology, this kind of reflection sometimes goes under the name of "social innovation." See Tongoi, "Bridging the Divide:," 170–77. See also Bickley, "Treasures Old and New," 178–91.

3. Mary Ann Beavis uses the distinction between *"utopia"* generally referring to imaginary ideal societies and *"eutopia"* referring to efforts or movements with the goal of improving society. Beavis, *Jesus & Utopia*, 2. The realm of God as I understand it here should be seen as "eutopia" rather than "utopia."

4. Gray, *Black Mass*, 2–3.

5. Hoffman, *John Gray and the Problem of Utopia*, 193.

compassionate. It seeks then to discover what these next steps might be in the concrete, contemporary world.

Levels of Engagement

With a strategic perspective on the realm of God, local churches can usefully think of their engagement in society as operating at four overlapping levels:

a. local,

b. regional (diocesan),

c. national, and

d. international

We could no doubt add more levels, but restricting them to four allows us to manage them together without over-complicating our strategies.

a) Local Church and Its Neighborhood

This book is in fact concerned more with the local rather than the regional, national, and international level since this is the level that is most accessible and most actionable (and, I think, most neglected theologically) for the majority of local churches. At this level, the local church and many of its members are relating to their surrounding neighborhood where they themselves live and perhaps work, where their children go to school, and where many of them shop and access health and other community services. Here also church membership overlaps with that of other local organizations—church members will often themselves belong to several of these local organizations. The latter part of this chapter focuses particularly on this level of local church and local engagement.

b) Local Church and Region

A local church does not, however, relate *only* to its own immediate neighborhood. Effective engagement will often require collaboration at a wider level. There are often identifiable "regions" (larger than local neighborhoods and parishes) such as cities with many local churches or rural areas with some common identity and several small local churches. In many churches, including local parishes, this regional cooperation may coincide with a diocese and its already established organization. Common facilities and central offices provide means of collaborative action across parishes and need support from parishes. Collaboration with diocesan mission offices, peace and justice organizations, support for indigenous peoples where threatened, support for migrants and refugees, inter-faith activities, and cross-cultural relations are also part of the local church's mission. This second level of cooperation also helps the local church avoid "parochialism," where its concerns become selfishly confined to itself.[6] Local churches can also learn here from the experience and studies of local government where community-based organizations can sometimes pursue parochial interests at the expense of broader regional goals.[7]

c) Local Church and Nation

Beyond the neighborhood and region (diocese), a local church will also be alert to issues at a larger national level. This might include, for example, issues requiring nation-wide legislation and the work of national agencies such as those working with refugees and with other vulnerable and disenfranchised people.[8] At this wider level, a local church may well be concerned also with "capacity-building," that is, with developing *people* with the capacity to advance the realm of God through their own professions or roles in society.[9] A local church may further play a mission role in relation to business corporations with national and international interests.[10]

d) Local Church and International Mission

Traditionally, mission has often been understood primarily as a mission overseas and often also as cross-cultural. The emphasis in this book on

---

6. One of the criticisms of the Anglican Church's important 2004 report "Mission-shaped Church" was that it did not give sufficient weight to the historic, representative, and active role of bishops. In this sense it lacked that larger regional viewpoint. Riem, "Mission-Shaped Church: An Emerging Critique," 137–39.

7. A good example of how this can happen is discussed in Jun, "Escaping the Local Trap?" 343–63.

8. See, for example, Langmead, "Refugees as Guests and Hosts," 29–47.

9. Cole and Helfer, *Church Transfusion*, 196–98.

10. Bretsen, "The Creation, the Kingdom of God, and a Theory of the Faithful Corporation," 115–54.

the local mission of the local church is intended as a timely, and therefore "strategic," focus on the local mission in which all are missionaries and mission activity is close to hand.[11] Nevertheless, international and cross-cultural mission activity still remains an important dimension of the mission of the local church and is not replaced by local mission activity.

Can Local Churches Contribute to Community Wellbeing?

Churches can overrate their capacity to contribute to the realm of God. Church missions can go wrong, and criticism of church mission by people outside the church has often turned out to be valid.

At a deeper level than this discussion of community engagement lies a more fundamental question about whether local churches *can actually* contribute to the wellbeing of the wider local community. Good mission intentions are not enough here. There are people in the wider society who think that churches can do little good, or that in fact they haven't done any good, in the wider society. They would rather see churches keep out of attempts at influencing or "helping" the wider community and focus just on caring for their own adherents.

Local (non-church) welfare and community development agencies may be negative towards church involvement because of an unfortunate past history in the local area or because of prejudice derived from public media, or because there is a suspicion of proselytizing, or simply because those agencies are themselves defending their own territory against any intruders. Some of this negative attitude to churches may be justified. Probably the worst, and certainly the scariest, are the proven complaints of the abuse of children by church personnel. Some churches are mission-driven but insensitive to other people and to existing services. Attempts at community wellbeing may derive from an internal need of the local church to "do good" or to be "missionary" rather than from any real known need in the local community. Such attempts are quite reasonably treated with suspicion in the wider local community.

The key point here is that local churches cannot simply assume that because they are Christians they are good at working for community wellbeing. We need to be alert to situations where church missionary

---

11. Daniel G. Groody, for example, argues that migration is fundamental to our identity as human beings, and it is also at the core of Christian mission. Groody, "The Church on the Move," 27–42.

activity may do more harm than good. Good intentions are not enough to produce good outcomes, nor is there any guarantee that missionary activity done in the name of God is actually the work of God.[12] The mission of the local church takes place in "dialogue" with the wider local community about contributions to wellbeing.

Is There a Role for Faith-Based Communities in Urban Regeneration?

With an eye towards the issue of a local church's *actual* mission capacity, rather than simply its good intentions, I propose here to discuss a particular example of church engagement in the wider neighborhood. The purpose of this example is to illustrate two strands of local mission: a) learning from the views of people "outside" the local church but within the same neighborhood, and b) learning from the already active mission of local churches. I hope that this example makes more concrete what can be involved in local church mission within its own neighborhood. I hope too that it will stimulate other local churches to give deliberate attention to their own particular times and places.

This example concerns a case of "urban regeneration"—one aspect of "wellbeing." The neighborhood concerned was an urban area with a high percentage of low-income households and a high level of health and welfare intervention by government and philanthropic organizations with a high level of failure. It was not a case of extreme poverty but of relative poverty with clear signs of deprivation, especially in children. Nearly everybody inside and outside that locality recognized that it needed some "regeneration." It also had a high number of faith communities,[13]

---

12. Some church leaders, by contrast, argue against the need for missionary selection and training. Oduro, for example, proposes that the training of missionaries is the responsibility of the Holy Spirit, and this practice has contributed to the success of the African Independent Church missions. Oduro, "Arise, Walk through the Length and Breadth of the Land," 86–89. Perhaps this strategy is specific to a more charismatic style of worship and to the transitional situation of migrants. See also Asamoah-Gyadu, "Prayer and Power from the South," 327–37.

13. The term "faith community" (along with "faith-based community," "faith-based organization," "faith-designated-group") are all problematic because they tend to homogenize associations that are in fact quite varied, and the variations can be quite crucial in the exercise of democratic politics. Yet it is difficult to avoid them in a brief discussion. Luke Bretherton discusses some of the issues here in Bretherton, *Christianity and Contemporary Politics*, 37–45.

most of which were Christian churches. How could or should local faith communities contribute to wellbeing in this suburban area?

This question was addressed in an inquiry sponsored by one of the social service agencies in a suburban area.[14] The inquiry asked social service and community development agencies (not faith-based organizations) in the area their views on the ways that faith communities in the area could contribute to the wellbeing of the people of that area.

Part of this project was a series of interviews with representatives of thirteen local agencies, all concerned in one way or another with community wellbeing. These social agencies all recognized faith communities as a legitimate component of civil society but did not always welcome their involvement in social services in the area. The interviews produced the following list of what faith-based communities *could* do in service to the suburban area. We should note that, in this example, *non-faith-based* service organizations are here giving their views on what they see as the *potential* role of *faith-based* communities.

Address critical issues in the community along with or in support of other agencies, for example, youth suicide and other youth issues, gambling, alcohol and drug abuse and availability, violence (especially domestic violence), debt, no provision for savings, loan sharking, housing shortages, unhealthy houses, issues with rental housing, displacement of families in state rental houses, immigration problems.

Enhance health and wellbeing in the community (preventive action before critical issues arise), again in cooperation with other agencies, for example, recognition of indigenous dignity and the rights that flow from it, financial literacy and budgeting, community-based and affordable housing, socially responsible lending, encourage realistic family and cultural policies on how to deal with pressure to donate money, continuing education such as parenting skills and budgeting, "drop-in" center, support for school attendance, services for the elderly.

Communication between faith communities and service agencies, such as awareness among faith community leaders of resources to address the kind of issues noted above, more formal and equal communication between faith communities and service agencies on a mutually accessible basis.

---

14. The social service agency was the Langafonua Community Centre in Glen Innes, Auckland, David Tolich was the main field researcher, and I was responsible for the planning and reporting of the research.

Voice of the people and advocacy, such as advocacy to government and through public media for the benefit of the local people, advocate for individual cases to government agencies, address the issue of poverty.

Encourage to attend/participate. Faith community leaders could encourage their own people to participate in agencies as volunteers or as local support, encourage participation in community events and community engagement forums, encourage parents to make more use of early childhood education opportunities.

This list includes activities that can be designated "social services" in the sense that they are about dealing with immediate "needs," but it also includes activities that are better designated "community development" in that, rather than needs, they are about recognizing and developing strengths within the community, enhancing self-reliance, capacity-building, and coordination. Many of these agencies have this double focus.

The purpose of this first strand of the project sought to find out what local service agencies that were *not* faith-based thought about potential contributions to community wellbeing from faith-based organizations. The list of examples is a collection of views from all the service organizations put together: some said a lot, and some said little. Some service agencies in fact have little familiarity with how faith communities actually operate or what service work they already do in the area. Some of this may be because of that agency's desire to be "secular" and not be seen to be privileging churches. On the other hand, many of the people active in these non-faith agencies are themselves also members of faith communities and well familiar with their service activities.

This strand of the survey named a solid list (above) of services to community wellbeing that could be undertaken helpfully by faith-based organizations.

What Churches Actually Do

Non-Christian faith communities in the area surveyed (Buddhist, Muslim, and Baha'i) were quite small and not sufficiently involved at that time to allow generalizations to apply with any validity outside of Christian churches. The rest of this report applied specifically to Christian churches rather than faith-communities in general.

A second strand in this project was a series of interviews with local churches themselves to discover what they are actually doing currently towards the wellbeing of people in the area. Activities for community wellbeing were understood here to be activities *in addition to* the more obviously "religious" activities of prayer, preaching, church community-building, and religious education.

Examples of such activities include youth work, dealing with grief and loss, providing venues for other community groups, advocacy with government departments, health care programs, food banks, political activism, housing assistance, working with schools, family support, programs to combat violence, early childhood education, emergency relief, breakfast and homework programs, language services, and housing assistance. In addition, many local churches network with, or have their own community members involved in, other community development or service organizations in the area.

This quite localized research revealed that people with a good deal of experience in local community services and development do see opportunities for churches to engage in action for community wellbeing. Some, however, remain cautious about church motivation, and some probably see church engagement as competitive with their own (non-church) activities. It also showed that churches are already engaged in many of these activities anyway, although some other service agencies are not always aware of it. Churches are often unaware themselves of the activities of other churches. A number of churches are engaged in community wellbeing to the extent that they take care of their own members.

Perhaps most importantly, the project's results served to alert local faith communities to a range of activities that contribute to wellbeing in the local community. It further alerted them to a lack of coordination among churches themselves as well as a lack of awareness of non-faith social service agencies in the area about church activities. In addition, and less positively, it alerted them to the existence of competition in the provision of social services and the suspicions that exist out there about the motivations of faith-based communities in the area.

This kind of research helps local churches to answer the question of what kind of benefits its mission activities can bring to the wellbeing of their local community and identifies some of the harmful side effects they need to avoid. It further helps to identify the qualities they need to look for or develop in their own members as missionaries.

The Strategic Position of Local Churches

The position of local churches precisely as *local* is an important ingredient of that church's missionary strategy. Government agencies and NGOs (non-governmental organizations) normally employ salaried professionals who begin with an acknowledgement of responsibility for (some of) the conditions in the local area. Where these agencies are not local community trusts, their direct accountabilities are to a governance structure (often national or city government) rather than to those who live or work in this suburban area. Most of them neither live nor work there, though some of those at the lowest level of the public service hierarchy do have offices in the area. Their activity in the suburban area is inherently an intervention from the outside. The intentional language of the public service does often indicate nevertheless a belief in the principle that client participation in decision-making leads to better decisions. In effect this means they believe officially in "consultation" of the people affected by agency planning, but they are not themselves members of that local community and they will not have to live with the results of their actions in their daily lives.

Most local churches begin from a different standpoint. They begin with already existing organized relationships and a common bond. Their outreach in the local area is not primarily an "intervention" there. Most of them live, and some work, in the local area anyway. Insofar as there are existing deficiencies or deprivation in the local community, they are themselves part of, or victims of, those deficiencies. Conversely, insofar as there are strengths in the local community, they are themselves part of those strengths. Many churches do also have loyalties to a larger hierarchical organization, particularly to the bishop of a diocese or to a central church committee. This larger church organization may either support or inhibit mission activity. Nevertheless, the local parishioners are commonly the drivers of local mission activity where it exists, and as such their actions are from inside the area rather than interventions from outside.

In the project I have described above, almost all local church leaders in the area approved of church outreach for the wellbeing of the whole local community rather than just their own church members. Many of these leaders, however, including full-time pastors, made it clear they already had too many internal church calls on their time—worship, prayer, preaching, church community-building, personal and family support, counselling, and religious education. Outreach for wellbeing into the wider local community, in other words, while a noble and valid objective, was not a *priority*. Their church's theology of mission was not sufficiently articulated or sufficiently strong to attract a major expenditure of time, energy, and funding.

Relationships of Local Churches with Other Service Agencies

In their mission activity, local churches commonly interact with other agencies, both religious and secular, who also work for a common well-being though they may differ in their objectives and methods. Some of these are "secular" agencies not in the sense that they are opposed to faith communities, but more objectively in the sense that they do not claim for themselves any faith or religious basis. They all, nevertheless, have beliefs and policies that in practice may turn out to be very similar to, though not expressed in theological terms, those of the local churches.

Surrounding any work for social wellbeing is the possibility of *alliances* between local churches and other agencies such as NGOs or state services that have the same objectives. This does not mean that the objectives will be exactly the same, but that there is sufficient agreement for partnerships to become valuable. Sometimes Christian churches are unwilling to engage in partnerships with non-Christian agencies on the basis that their Christian theology will be watered down or compromised. Yet if local churches see themselves as agents of transformation, they are not the *only* agents. The "mission of God" is not just a mission of the churches. It includes other agencies. Local churches need to be actively looking for who those other partner agencies might be. One of the central alerts of any citizen theologian is to look for where the Holy Spirit is already active outside of the church itself. It is important for local churches that they recognize where these similarities lie since this will provide a basis for cooperation, opposition, or negotiation with them for the common good.[15]

At the same time, local churches cannot afford to enter into such negotiations or alliances with naivety. As well as differences in intention,

---

15. In his argument for a "holistic" mission (combining evangelism with social responsibility) especially in Africa, James Nkansah-Obrempong advocates relationships which include partnerships with non-governmental organizations, educational and social amenities, relief work, advocacy, and policy formulation. Nkansah-Obrempong, "The Mission of the Church and Holistic Redemption," 196–211.

there are also power differences and power abuse which may lead the churches, like the apostle Peter, to places they "do not wish to go" (John 21:18). If, for example, a church enters into public debates, it must do so with careful attention to the imbalances of power already existing there and the already existing complicity of churches with powerful public agencies.[16] A local church enters into engagement with other organizations and agencies with discernment, not with naivety. It is engaged in *prophetic* dialogue, not just *friendly* dialogue. It is making choices for cooperation, opposition, and negotiation. And it is doing so with "civility" understood not as deception or just "niceness" but as "the part of justice that disposes citizens to confront unjust relationships in ways that leave open the possibility of relational repair."[17]

By way of practical warnings against friendly naivety, let me record here some instances from my own experience of "alerts" worth taking note of in on-the-ground engagement of local churches with other local agencies.

Some of these other agencies are best considered as "foreign" missions in that they operate in a location where their policy makers and planners do not live and only a few work, and where there is a large cultural gap between the agency personnel and the local community residents.

What these other agencies regard as "wrong" with the recipients of their actions is a key element of their services. Do they identify these recipients as deprived and needing help? Or are they focused more on strengths and opportunities?

Both churches and secular social service agencies may suffer from promotional language, that is, language which exaggerates successes and slides over deficiencies. Here there is a potential language of deceit, where language such as "strength-based" and "challenge" is thought to be proper ("appropriate") rather than the language of deprivation, need, mistakes, and problems. Language such as "transformation into a vibrant community" (used by an agency in which I took part) may not in fact be anything more than a social service handout to the poor.

Civil and public agencies are likely to use the language of "deprivation" and "perverse outcomes" to describe situations that are wrong or go

---

16. An instructive example on this point is the debate within the Church of England between Rod Garner and Andrew Davey. Garner, *Facing the City*, 152–54; Davey, "Facing the City," 152–54.

17. Ward, "Democratic Civility and the Dangers of Niceness," 115.

wrong. Churches may need to note when and how this language synchronizes with theological language of social or structural "sin."

Other agencies, often more than churches, may be well aware of the qualities required for their agents, such as personal integrity, professionalism, and political expertise, as well as cross-cultural and communication skills. Churches are more likely to be deficient in this if they rely too much on good will or "God's grace."

Local churches are interested in communicating explicitly their own Christian values. Other "secular" agencies may deny such intention but nevertheless operate from an assumed, but not publicly stated, value-base or rely on what is considered "publicly acceptable"!

Other agencies, especially government agencies, may be much more explicitly "risk averse" than churches. Since "risk" is commonly related to civil service or political careers, rather than to the potential dangers for the intended beneficiaries of the project (as discussed in chapter 7, "Dangerous Missions") church personnel can be perplexed that a promising project in fact goes nowhere.

Conclusion

A strategic approach to local church mission recognizes the dynamic and evolving nature of the realm of God and the different levels of its engagement in society.

By way of example, I have included here a survey of the views of non-church organizations about how churches could contribute to their common neighborhood. Combined with a survey of how local churches were in fact already doing this themselves, this information illustrates how strategic engagement at the local level can work. Important to note here is the strategic position held by local churches as insiders to the neighborhood rather than interventionists from outside.

In the course of this survey and the discussion among churches that followed, it became apparent that many church leaders, while in agreement with the idea of mission in principle, did not, or could not, see that mission as a priority among their other regular commitments. A critical question that remains here for local churches is whether their local mission theology is sufficiently motivating and well enough articulated to establish priorities for the church's vision and action. If it is not, then the local church may remain focused on itself rather than on its mission within the larger mission of God, or, worse, remain impotent within its own good but inactive intentions. It may have fallen back into "maintenance" rather than "mission."[18]

---

18. Cf. Rivers, *From Maintenance to Mission*.

12

A Local Theology of Mission

WHETHER AND HOW A local church engages in the wider society depends upon its mission theology. What theological emphases serve to motivate and guide local church action for the wellbeing of the wider society? What, in other words, are the key features of a local theology of mission?

Drawing upon and focusing the previous chapters (chapters 6–11) of this book, I propose five main features of a mission theology of a local church. A local mission theology would be

- transformational for wellbeing,
- place-based,
- strength-based,
- alert to different kinds of agency, and
- self-critical.

A Theology of Transformation

An understanding of the realm of God as a transformed continuity of the present encourages a church mission that is concerned with the present time moving into the future. It is concerned with transforming the present reality of people and planet into something better, something closer to the realm of God. It means we approach the Bible not just looking for true doctrine or how people can be saved or become holier, but in a more

A Local Theology of Mission

dynamic way in which "the reading, praying, studying, and teaching of the New Testament transform communities into missional bodies." This, says Scripture scholar N. T. Wright, is what the New Testament texts themselves were doing, and what the authors wanted their hearers to be doing.[1]

A contemporary theology of mission cannot remain expressed simply in biblical language and biblical descriptions of the realm of God. A theology of mission is abstract and perhaps delusory, even if biblically based, if it is unable to say what the realm of God would look like now in our own current circumstances. It needs to articulate some specific local and contemporary objectives for those who participate in bringing about this evolving realm of God.

"Transformation" is a contemporary term for this idea of change for the better. It also captures the sense of a realm of God that is already-but-not-yet and of wanting something better for people, especially those living in relative deprivation or vulnerability. "Transformation" is an idea that is familiar both in theology and in public discourse.

In theology, the idea of "transformation" is a central one. British theologian Oliver Davies argues expressly for a "transformation theology" where the function of transformation is integral to the theological enterprise. He notes that all Christian theologies in fact operate with transformational principles—as salvation, deification, or liberation, for instance.[2] In missiology in particular,[3] Charles van Engen argues for a theology of transformation which builds on classical concepts of mission developed over the last one hundred years, overcomes the dichotomies between evangelism and social action that arose fifty years ago, and re-creates itself in a trinitarian praxis of mission appropriate to the contemporary world. This theology of transformation builds on the apostle Paul's use of "transformation" or "metamorphosis" (Rom 12:2).[4]

---

1. Wright, "Paul and Missional Hermeneutics," 181.
2. Davies, *Theology of Transformation*, 58.
3. The Conference on World Mission and Evangelism in its 2018 conference used the term "transforming discipleship" to describe the call of Christians to mission. Conference on World Mission and Evangelism, "Moving in the Spirit," 542–46. "The church's mission is not just about translation and transmission of the gospel, but also about the transformation of the world," Simon, "Mission and Its Three Pillars," 399–412.
4. Van Engen, "Conclusion," 289–96. See also Michael Barram's interpretation, from a missional economics points of view, of Paul's idea of "transformation" in Romans 12:1–2. Barram, "Missional Economics," 5–18.

In public discourse, the term "transformation," like the term "well-being," is also familiar and allows a conversation between citizen theologians and non-Christian activists in a pluralist society. The term is a broad one and can have a variety of interpretations, implications, and practical outcomes. Nevertheless, it provides a common ground on which the practical outcomes can be discussed. This is rarely the case with other theological terms like "salvation," "redemption," "atonement," "deification," and often even "liberation." Peter Pavlovic from the Conference of European Churches provides an example of this in the Christian engagement with other parties in dealing with climate change. While arguing for the use of the concept of "transformation," he notes that this term was edited out of the final text of the Paris Agreement on climate change in favor of a more concrete commitment expressed in terms of mobilizing financial commitments. Yet the concept of transformation is still implicit in the text.[5]

The idea of transformation also has a time component. The realm of God is an already-but-not-yet reality in the world. The objectives of transformation are carried out over time in the knowledge that some outcomes of transformational action will need to be in place before others can be attempted. It is a transformed continuity from the past, through present action, towards future long-term results. Mission theology understood as transformation also has common ground with the discipline of "practical theology"[6] where reflection follows action and in turn leads to further action.[7] Some steps need to be in place before another step can be taken. A second step is made possible by the direction, size, and momentum of an earlier step. North American urban missionary Jude Tiersma Watson gives an example of transformation in a city context when she describes a mission action (based on a spirituality of accompaniment) that has three dimensions over time: missionary (we walk and share with those at the margins), then prophetic (we work towards the transformation of system injustice), then contemplative (the transformation of our own lives and families as we walk humbly with our God).[8]

---

5. Pavlovic, "Christian Hope in Reflecting the Challenge of Climate Change," 278.

6. Bonnie, *The Wiley-Blackwell Companion to Practical Theology*. Going further, Brian Macallan argues for the benefits of a "missional practical theology" in Macallan, "Trinitarian Mission and Practical Theology," 389–400.

7. Darragh, "The Practice of Practical Theology," 1–13.

8. Watson, "Engaging the Nations in Los Angeles," 263–70.

Nevertheless, I am not advocating here that it is the term "transformation" itself that is important. Like many such terms, it can outlive its usefulness if it acquires too many different meanings to suit different agendas or if it becomes too abstract without clear practical implications as indicated in Pavlovic's example above, or if, as David Zahl suggests, it occupies center stage in a person's spiritual life that turns Christianity into a vehicle of anxiety and exhaustion.[9] It is not the term itself that is important but the mission commitment to participation in the evolving realm of God.

A Place-Based Theology

A local church that puts emphasis on the realm of God as located in the wider society (of which the church itself is a part) rather than as internal to the individual or as internal to the church community itself will have strong motivation to work for the wellbeing of that society. It motivates the community to prioritize its organization in that direction rather than just towards personal, pastoral, administrative, and community-building roles within the church community itself.

Historically, mission has often been seen as primarily an activity in *another* place, geographically or culturally distant from the local church. Only a few local church members can engage in this kind of "foreign" mission. By contrast, the mission that enables all local church members to be missionaries is the mission conducted within their own local area even though not confined there. The "missionaries" are also "locals"; they are (hopefully) citizen theologians.

A place-based approach to wellbeing recognizes the value of *neighborhoods*. The local area in which people live and work is important to their welfare. This is as well as, not instead of, maintaining links with the organizations, networks, movements, and state agencies that also contribute to (or diminish) human wellbeing. The focus on neighborhood also directs our attention to the natural and built environments which are part of our neighborhoods and whose own wellbeing has effects on human wellbeing.

In Luke Bretherton's terms, "faithful political action" is in the first instance place-based, envisaging the local and regional as the primary arenas of faithful Christian action, and it involves the church as a legal,

---

9. Zahl, *Seculosity*, 11–12, 20.

physical, and social institution within which worship is constitutive of its public life.[10]

Within the neighborhood there are always a large number of issues in wellbeing. What a place-based theology recognizes is that local issues may need to be addressed *together* and solutions to these issues may often be found *within* that neighborhood itself. Local solutions do not have to wait for regional or national solutions. One can, for example, develop local protocols for dealing with destructive tenants from social housing or for dealing with law-and-order issues or with environmental degradation without those protocols necessarily becoming generalized to the whole nation.

A key ingredient in a place-based approach is that the "agents," the people who can best bring about a transformation of current living conditions, are the residents and workers of that place itself. The local community (residents and workers) often have the local knowledge, local sensitivities, and local networks to make any program or action effective. Outside agents, government, NGOs, and philanthropy are important for their funding, their expertise in certain areas, and for their contacts with the wider society, but they often lack local knowledge of how things can actually work, and they lack the particular knowledge of those most affected by any action.

Some of the action for wellbeing is the liberating of people from the damaging actions of government agents, some of which is systemic to those agencies. Neighborhood networks and neighborhood organizations can often provide that counterforce to dysfunctional public agencies.

The local churches for the most part recruit their members from local residents. In most cases, they live in the local neighborhood, they use the local shops, the local schools, the local health professionals, and they work close by if they can. They are strategically positioned, then, to engage in a place-based theology of mission that is built on a foundation of familiarity with the local neighborhood. They are part of the build-up of trust among people which is foundational in the good functioning of society. By way of contrast, we can note the difference between this local mission activity and that more common in overseas missions where the missionary is unfamiliar and unskilled in local protocols and sensitivities. Geography matters in the real world, although it is often not acknowledged in the worlds of economic theory and public policy.

---

10. Bretherton, *Christianity and Contemporary Politics*, 221–22.

Location matters in the kinds of opportunities available to people and the quality of life that they might expect.[11]

To focus on the neighborhood is not to ignore the wider dimensions of society. A local church needs also to be alert to the mass migration of people into and through some neighborhoods. Today more than ever before, "diaspora" mission has become important and interacts with place-based mission.[12] The local church attracts, negotiates with, resists, contributes to, and adapts to these migrations. It may be radically changed by them. Its own membership may undergo large cultural or political change as a result. Yet that church is "local" precisely because it responds to whatever happens in its locality. And everything that happens there is part of its mission.

But is this theology? Isn't it just practical community development or community engagement? Our response to this question may note that there is little else that reveals a person's or a church's theology more clearly than how they live it out. A place-based theology reveals clearly *where* they believe God is or *where* they believe the Holy Spirit is active or *where* the realm of God is most immediately and intensely alive. A mission theology is "place-based" when it directs community awareness and action to *where* God's realm is most active and to where the divine initiative is calling them. This is "espoused" and "operant" theology.[13] In this sense, local action is an expression of faith and a statement of that person's and that community's theology.

A Strength-Based Theology

A *strength*-based approach to community transformation stands in contrast to a deprivation-based approach. The *deprivation*-based approach notes and analyzes a state of deprivation, then looks for resources from elsewhere to push or pull people out of that bad situation. Local churches strongly influenced by a "redemption-oriented" or "salvation-oriented" theology, reliant on the idea of "rescue," may feel a sense of kinship with

---

11. A position argued strongly for by Salvation Army social policy researcher Alan Johnson, "Mixed Fortunes," 7.

12. Tira and Yamamori, *Scattered and Gathered*.

13. Rather than "normative" or "formal" theology. See, in this volume, chapter 10, "Mission in a Pluralist Democracy: Spheres of Engagement."

this deprivation-based approach to wellbeing and, even unconsciously, adopt it in their mission strategies.

A strength-based program, on the other hand, while acknowledging deprivation in a local community, looks for the strengths of the local community that can contribute directly to local community wellbeing. Programs or actions for transformation aim then to be local community-led or at least to be co-designed and co-led by members of the local community along with outside agencies. In this it contrasts with programs and actions fully designed and led by outside agencies whose accountability is to their governing bodies outside this local community.

Public agencies are often required to show they have "consulted" the people affected by their actions. Yet nearly any citizen theologian working in or engaged with public agencies will have experienced "consultations" that have been reduced to seeking the views of some selected people from the community followed by a later agency decision on what, if anything, can be done with this collection of varied and scattered opinions. In theological terms, this is a theology of "rescue" though it does at least attempt some show of respect for the local people. Nevertheless, this kind of "show" leads quite quickly to loss of trust and, to that extent, a diminishment of local energy.

A strength-based theology is grounded in belief in the creative presence of God in society and the basic goodness of people who make up society. It recognizes the activity of the Spirit already present there and seeks to empower and enhance that goodness and those gifts. To avoid simple romanticism, it needs also to include a realistic acknowledgement of evil and wrongdoing. And indeed, the state of deprivation is itself at least in part the result of evil. The state of deprivation itself causes evil, disability, and diminishment in the lives of the people who live in it. Hence a strength-based theology needs to include "capacity-building" of the local community in order to counter the already existing effects of diminishment in the local people, their environment, their networks, their family relationships, and their community groups. Local community groups, including churches, are in a good strategic position to use their own strengths, but with a willingness to call on outsiders where needed, to engage in this capacity-building.

A theology that believes in the radical corruption of human beings would be skeptical about such a strength-based theology of mission. Similarly, a theology that makes a strong distinction between the "saved" and the "unsaved" by some obvious criteria, such as a profession of Jesus as personal savior or membership in a Christian church, also has difficulty with a strength-based theology of mission. The "unsaved" masses would need to be "saved" before they could be encouraged or funded into leadership. Such theologies are more akin to deprivation-based approaches to community development and imply a missiology of rescue rather than of transformation.

A Theology of Agency

Who are the agents of this mission? That is, who are the people who bring about this intended transformation? Are some people better as agents of mission than others? Can some people bring it about for others? Who are partners in mission?

Christian theology understands mission as the action of God in the world. But the question asked here is about the sense in which *human beings may participate* in this action of God and so, in that sense, become agents of this mission. We can helpfully distinguish three *levels* of agency.

a. The "citizen theologian" may operate simply as a *private citizen* or may also occupy a position of influence in an NGO, a government agency, or private company. Rather than ignoring them, a local church can provide encouragement, learning opportunities, and critique for such citizen theologians among its own members

b. The *local church* itself, as missionary, operates at a different level of agency from that of the individual citizen theologian because it is an identified and named community with public objectives and mission priorities. As a publicly organized group rather than as an individual it may have greater (or sometimes less) civil and public influence.

c. At another level again, an ecumenical or inter-faith *association* of churches or faith communities in a particular area has a capacity for stronger action and more widespread communication but requires more complex processes (requiring more time and skill) for representation, decision-making, and public identity

A citizen theologian, a local church, or an association of churches may go it alone in their mission activities, but the practice of *partnerships* in mission with other agents is particularly important in mission as social engagement in contemporary democratic societies. Samuel Wells has distinguished four models of mission as social engagement:

a. *Working for* (I do things that make your life better).

b. *Working with* (we create coalitions of interest where it is possible for all the stakeholders to win). Both these models assume that problems can be fixed.

c. *Being with* (the most significant moments of life are not problems requiring a solution, rather we accompany people while they find their own methods, answers, and approaches and enjoy the rest of their identity—we start with people's assets, not their deficits).

d. *Being for* (we need to get the ideas and attitude right, ensure products are sustainably resourced, investments are ethically funded, people are described in positive ways, and accountable public action is firmly distinguished from private consumer choice).

Wells opts for model (c) *being with* as fundamentally the Jesus model, an *incarnational* model of mission.[14] If we accept the model of "being with" as a primary model of local church mission but supported also by a "working with" model in many situations, there are two kinds of agency that claim most attention from the point of view of a local church. I shall call these "agency partnerships" in mission, and "companionship" missions.

"*Agency partnerships*" are those where the agents of mission are partnerships between two or several groups such as local churches, local service agencies, or government agencies. One kind of these is the public-private partnership, where a government agency works with a private agency (such as a church or philanthropic trust) to meet some social objectives. Elaine Graham notes that, in the United Kingdom at least, religious organizations are seen as rich in what is known as "social capital" (human resources, the ability to forge networks, to mobilize resources, and to espouse the values that foster altruism and community).[15] Chapter 11, "Strategies of Local Church Mission," of this book gave examples of actual and potential partnerships between local service organizations and churches for wellbeing in the neighborhood.

"*Companionship*" mission is another notable "being with" model of mission. Michael Moynagh contrasts the "companionship" model of mission with previous models of mission, particularly in the evangelical tradition. The one-sided "herald" model stressed proclaiming Jesus in word and action rather than listening to the audience. This can be seen in the

---

14. Wells, *Incarnational Mission*, 10–15.
15. Graham, *Between a Rock and a Hard Place*, 21.

"crusade" approach (mainly in the 1960s–80s) which sought to bring people to a point of conversion. This was followed (1980s–90s) by the evangelistic *course*, especially "Alpha," which softened the one-way communication but was still weighted towards instruction by an "expert" rather than being the free-flow of conversation between equals. Today, Moynagh advocates the "companionship" model in which the stress is less on bringing people to a point of conversion, or on leading people to faith, and more on Christians accompanying their friends and contacts on their spiritual paths. These quests may become journeys to Christ, or they may not. Whatever the outcome, Christians remain faithful to their companions.[16]

Local communities often assume that the agents and models of mission they have been used to are the only ones they need to consider. A local mission theology needs, however, to be aware of the different kinds of agency by which their mission can be conducted. It can then make deliberate choices about encouraging a range of agents and of models of mission (as indicated above) suitable for its own mission.

Further than that, any local church with a mission into the wider society must be concerned with the *qualities* of missionaries so that their activities are beneficial rather than harmful to the recipients of their mission (Chapter 7, "Dangerous Missions," was concerned with missions that are harmful). Along with benefits, the missionaries may bring to the recipients of their mission a package of harmful side effects. In the case of place-based mission, good and bad qualities of church personnel are more easily monitored than in overseas or cross-cultural missions, but they still require an established process for doing this.

A Self-Critical Theology

The consideration of agency already indicates a need for a theology that is self-critical, attentive to its own weaknesses, and prepared to deal with its own failures.

A good deal of this self-criticism can be derived from within theology itself, particularly the church's traditional theology of sin and conversion. This has been shown to be particularly important in contemporary ecotheology where our belated attempts to reverse the effects of human abuse and destruction of the environment could perhaps have been

---

16. Moynagh, "A Conversational Approach to New Forms of Church," 117–46.

avoided if we had paid more attention to traditional concepts of frugality and asceticism.[17]

Self-criticism can also be derived from the experience of interaction and dialogue with secular agencies. When isolated from secular encounter, theology can develop an exalted view of its own importance. It is often self-promotional when it regards itself as working from divine revelation and somehow superior to other knowledge disciplines. The amount of time, energy, and professionalism secular agencies often put into clarifying their objectives and strategies challenge theology on the adequacy of its own views on missionary organization. Secular projects often illustrate the complexities that need to be dealt with to achieve the intended objectives rather than result in perverse outcomes. These projects challenge a tendency in missiology to rely on the personal faith and commitment of the missionaries with less attention to planning and professionalism. The idea in theology that the mission is *God's* mission may indicate rather an expectation of divine intervention to compensate for the inadequacies of missionary organization and sensitivity. Local churches need to be aware of this interpretation of the concept of "God's mission" that allows and perhaps even encourages irresponsible mission activity.

Secular agencies are also capable of making direct criticisms towards local churrches which are often, even if not always, valid. Churches can gain from awareness of the negative way in which they are being perceived by other local agencies which have a similar commitment to wellbeing in their neighborhood. From my own listening to the criticisms of church activities by secular agencies, I suggest the following as examples of secular agency critique that local churches may want to apply to themselves:

- Some churches appear to have a "control-at-all-costs" attitude rather than a "with-and-for" approach to other organizations and communities.

- Some church leaders appear to be authoritarian in their relationships with their own communities. Church leaders then may need to take steps to be more clearly accountable to their own congregations before dialogue with non-church community organizations can take place in a climate of mutual cooperation and learning.

---

17. Bartholomew, *On Earth as in Heaven*, 201. See also Darragh, "An Ascetic Theology, Spirituality, and Praxis," 76–85.

- Churches should make more use of the expertise and knowledge of local service organizations, including resourcing and programs for the good of their own people, rather than try to go it alone with their own congregations.
- Some local non-church organizations have approached church leaders with a view to mutual cooperation but met with little success.
- Some churches are themselves the cause of deprivation in the local neighborhood in, for example, their fundraising activities, their excessive demands for money, or their excessive calls on time and energy from their own members.
- Although church members often have need of the skills and services of local community organizations, church leaders are often not alert to directing them towards these resources. Many church leaders, in other words, appear not to be aware that these resources are available in their own neighborhood.

A self-critical mission theology is one that pays attention to religious dysfunction, particularly to religious fundamentalism, authoritarianism, and issues of power and control within the churches themselves. Conversely, while attending to their own dysfunction, local churches may also need to be respectfully alert to defects within non-church agencies. Such defects are, for example, problems in the public service, where careerism rather than altruism being rewarded, government agencies working in silos, policies or attitudes that are not place-based, commitments that are short- rather than long-term, reliance on inaccurate outsider viewpoints on the local community, and a tendency to be risk averse ("mistakes ruin careers") rather than courageous.

Churches (in a way parallel to secular service agencies) can operate within a self-deception that over-estimates the nobility of their religious cause and claims too much of divine favor. A self-critical theology takes note of the differences between intention and practice; it is ready to acknowledge failure and it is prepared to change. If it is sufficiently self-critical, it can contribute to a realistic building of trust between churches and other agencies that work within the local community. Ultimately such self-criticism is part of the church's own accountability before God.

Conclusion

A local mission theology that could provide the motivation for engagement within society that is carried out in service to the realm of God would contain the following features: transformational for wellbeing, place-based, strength-based, alert to different kinds of agency, and self-critical.

The difference between *implementing* a mission-focused theology and merely talking about it depends upon the last feature noted above, that is, the ability to be self-critical. The next step in this investigation into the mission of the church is then to find a way in which the local church can undertake a process of self-criticism.

13

Self-Critique

SELF-CRITIQUE IS AN ELEMENT in all theological reflection. It seeks to take into account our capacity for self-delusion or self-aggrandizement. It is especially needed when we associate ourselves with the mission of God.

A "performance review" is a way of assessing in a transparent way how a person who acts in a particular role has met the objectives of that role. In this chapter, I propose to use some of the basic elements of a performance review as a way of doing a theological *self*-review or *self*-critique. The review proposed here is not something someone else does to us; it is something we do to and for ourselves, either collegially as members or leaders of a church or individually as citizen theologians. It is a way of looking honestly at whether our mission theology and our mission actions are aligned.[1]

I do not propose to follow closely here the common methods of a performance review used in institutions and business organizations. People's experience of such performance reviews varies and has been both positive and negative depending a good deal on what it is being used for and who is using it. Rather, here I have drawn upon two important elements of a performance review that help us to construct a schedule for our own mission self-review:

---

1. Readers may also find helpful the readily accessible though more complex "Community Justice Assessment Tool for Churches" developed by Christa Hayden Sharpe. This tool is concerned specifically with social justice rather than the broader ecological objectives of mission.

- Transparency: our mission objectives are articulated as clearly as possible and agreed upon by those doing the self-review.
- Priorities: the review is not broad ranging but very focused on the most *basic questions* and the *priorities* that follow from them.

The assumption foundational to this review is that the church is in service to the realm of God and that the wellbeing of all is a way of characterizing that evolving realm of God in our time and place. Mission objectives have traditionally been concerned with our responsibility to *society*, that is, towards other human beings. Today we have been alerted to a wider understanding of mission that extends beyond a concern just with other human beings to one that includes larger considerations of the planet Earth, which may then call for a specifically *ecological* review of the church's mission.[2] There is a long Christian tradition of positive and appreciative attitude towards God's creation.[3] This long tradition could be considered "innocent," however, in the sense that creation was not then under any large-scale threat from human activity. That tradition could regard human beings as the "apex" or "crown" of creation without any suspicion that human beings were also irresponsible destroyers of creation. Such innocence was no longer possible after the mid-twentieth century, when the evidence of destruction became apparent. Hence, the planet Earth, that part of God's creation of which we are most intimately a part becomes a focus of mission.[4]

The *basic questions* in our mission self-review should then include both mission in society and mission in the Earth:

- Mission in society: In our local church, what engagement is there for the wellbeing of society?
- Mission in the Earth: In our local church, what evidence is there of belief in a Creator God?

---

2. Such as Pope Francis's call for an ecological conversion in Francis, *Laudato Si'*, #216–21. Or, similarly, the ecological reformation called for in Conradie, "Manifesto on Ecological Reformation of Christianity," ch. 5.

3. This positive and appreciative attitude towards all of creation is documented in Meconi, *On Earth as It Is in Heaven*.

4. Zambian theologian Kapya Kaoma proposes that instead of speaking of "*Missio Dei*: the mission of God" as a basic missiological concept, we should speak of "*Missio Creatoris Dei*: the mission of the Creator God," so as to put creation at the heart of this mission. Kaoma, "From *Missio Dei* to *Missio Creatoris Dei*," 159–77.

In this second question we could ask simply, "What engagement is there in care of the Earth?" or some similar direct question. I have proposed rather the theologically-referenced question about evidence of belief in a Creator God because it forces us back to the first article of the Creed ("I believe in God, the Father almighty, Creator of heaven and earth") and asks not just for ideas or argument but for "evidence" of this belief lived out in practice. My own experience in using this schedule indicates that people find this way of putting it makes an interesting and engaging question, but especially that it helps avoid the vague generalities about the universe or the cosmos which questions about "creation" often fall into.

These two questions are inherent in all mission activity of every church. As in all useful reviews, however, there is no point in looking at everything. We need to be specific about *priorities*—how we are doing this at *this* time in actual engagement rather than just ideas or broad policies. These priorities will be different between one local church and another. I suggest my own priorities below and invite readers to substitute their own as necessary.

As we seek to answer the questions in this self-review, we will need also to be alert to the "levels" of engagement (local, regional, national, and international) described in chapter 11, "Strategies of Local Church Mission." The way we engage in the politics of culture at the local level, for example, is most likely different from how we engage at an international level.

No church is responsible for the whole of the realm of God or its evolving, but hopefully it has some part in it. We can expect that our particular part will be different from others according to the characteristics of the local church and to the conditions of the wider society. It will also change over time for the same local church. A mission review is something a local church needs to do from time to time rather than just once. Each review is a stage in a process and each one will be a little different from the previous one.

So far, then, in our review schedule we have two basic questions:

Mission Review

Basic Questions	Priorities
Mission in Society: In our church, what engagement is there for the wellbeing of the wider society?	
Mission in the Earth: In our church, what evidence is there of belief in a Creator God?	

Mission in Society

There is no universal way of stating the mission priorities of all churches. Each local, regional, or national church doing this review will want to articulate its own objectives. By way of an example, the Federation of Asian Bishops Conferences begins its vision for a church in Asia that is "truly Asian, in triple dialogue with the religions, cultures, and peoples of Asia, especially the poor."[5]

An important part of this review lies in achieving an agreement on our own church's priorities. Local Catholic churches may be guided in this by official Catholic teaching on social justice.[6] Other such guides can be found in recent ecumenical documentation.[7] Churches may also be guided by United Nations objectives such as those of the Sustainable Development Agenda, which calls on national governments to spell out their contributions towards the big five P's (People, Planet, Prosperity, Peace, Partnership).[8]

My own proposal here, which I hope may also serve others as an illustration of how to proceed with this review, is for three areas of focus:

---

5. Federation of Asian Bishops Conferences, "FABC at Forty Years."

6. Pontifical Council for Justice and Peace, "Compendium of the Social Doctrine of the Church."

7. Such as the World Council of Churches' "Together towards Life." And for Orthodox reflection on this document, see Kariatlis, "Together towards Life," ix–xix.

8. United Nations, "The 17 Goals." See also Conradie, Tsalampouni, and Werner, "Manifesto on Ecological Reformation of Christianity," esp. ch. 5.

- the politics of culture (or ethnicity),
- the politics of wealth, and
- the politics of religion.

I use the term "politics" here (the politics of culture, the politics of wealth, the politics of religion) because the term "politics" implies that a) we are concerned with the wider *society* not just the church, b) the church's mission is not usually to go it alone but rather to *negotiate* with other social institutions for a hoped-for consensus—in that sense it is an engagement in politics, and c) there is *power* involved here, not just conversation, i.e., it is about influence and the political skill to negotiate a peaceful and just society. This engagement in society is, in a fundamental way, about the ethical use of power.

The Politics of Culture

By "culture" I intend here a social identity with a relatively coherent way of living based on ethnicity. This is thus an ethnicity-based understanding of culture, rather than other understandings of culture such as the culture of a business organization, the culture of a school, or the culture of a sports body. Cultural identity carries values and beliefs about the ways things should be. Throughout the world it is sometimes associated with horrendous ethnic violence and hence is vitally important in the pursuit of international and intra-national peace.[9] Within nations today this often requires negotiating a new national consensus on the basis of respect for a variety of cultural identities. Contemporary cultures are not static but constantly changing in interaction with other local cultures, and with changes in technology, economy, information media, and physical environment. A peaceful and respectful future may depend on our capacity to change the culturally defined ways we are used to doing

---

9. A recent overview of Christian attitudes to peacebuilding in situations of armed conflict, helpful to local churches unsure of their own stance (Pacifism? Just war? Humanitarian intervention? Punishment? Realist compromise?) is Cahill, "Just War, Pacifism, Just Peace, and Peacebuilding," 169–85.

things.¹⁰ Especially important for local churches is their relationship with local indigenous cultures.¹¹

The Christian church is inherently multi-cultural in its theology. It is not always so in its practice. The story of Pentecost (Acts 2:1–13) where people of different languages and cultures understood the message of the apostles is the iconic story that illustrates the multi-cultural nature of the new Christian church even as it acknowledges its Jewish origins. Since the realm of God is understood in Christianity to be a peaceful and just society that respects the cultural identity of all peoples, the church has a vital interest in ensuring that different cultures within the same neighborhood and nation can live together in mutual respect and cooperation.

The review question we can ask ourselves in this aspect of our mission engagement is:

How much does our local church contribute to the search for a consensus among cultures? Or is it largely monocultural?

The Politics of Wealth

By the "politics of wealth" I mean the negotiations and strategies to do with how much we want, how much we need, what resources are available within the regenerative capacity of the Earth, and how these can be distributed equitably.

One of the concluding affirmations of the World Council of Churches 2012 mission document "Together towards Life: Mission and Evangelism in Changing Landscapes" states:

"We affirm that the economy of God is based on values of love and justice for all and that transformative mission resists idolatry in the free-market economy . . . Mission, then, is to denounce the economy of greed and to participate in and practice the divine economy of love, sharing, and justice."¹²

---

10. Good illustrations of cultural/religious differences at a personal level through Australian eyes can be found in Adeney, "Making Friends with People of Other Religions," 18–23.

11. For up-to-date information on their own indigenous cultures, local churches may wish to consult the International Work Group for Indigenous Affairs (IWGIA), https://www.iwgia.org/en/.

12. World Council of Churches, "Together towards Life," #108.

Social justice is a central quality of the realm of God and therefore part of the church's mission.[13] A good deal of this is about access to public services—especially health, employment, security, housing, and education. Particularly important today is the plight of migrants, refugees, and asylum seekers.[14] The widespread effect of the politics of economic rationalism that was so prominent in the 1980s and 1990s now seems to be enjoying a resurgence. Even where faith in market forces, privatization, and globalization is no longer as prominent as it was, its ideology of self-promotion and freedom to pursue self-interest may still be vigorous. Most disturbing is the increase in *inequality* in the world today.[15]

The review question we can ask ourselves in this aspect of our mission policy is:

How does our local church contribute towards justice and equality in society? Is our local church a living witness to the Christian ideal of living simply?

The Politics of Religion

Religious politics is particularly important and problematic in the contemporary world because it invites commitment that can fall into fundamentalism—a one-eyed and intolerant version of religion. It is also vulnerable to violent political campaigns in the sense that it can be used to support such campaigns, as we have witnessed throughout the world in recent decades. Religious freedom, like the right to one's own culture, is usually regarded as a basic human right in liberal democracies, but religions can be in conflict with one another and with the search for a broader national consensus.

Inter-faith relations need to be both "appreciative" and "critical" in the sense that we look for where we agree but are honest too about where we disagree.[16] Other faith traditions, just by being religions, are not auto-

---

13. F. Albert Tizon proposes an evaluative tool through which missionaries may challenge classism and align their personal lifestyles and organizational practices with an image of Christ among the classes. Tizon, "Lifestyles of the Rich and Faithful," 6–28.

14. Tan, "Pope Francis's Preferential Option for Migrants, Refugees, and Asylum Seekers," 58–66.

15. Churches may profitably consult the World Inequality Database: https://wid.world/wid-world/.

16. This approach builds on the principle articulated many years ago by Hans Küng: "Nothing of value in the other religions is to be denied, but neither is anything

matically good for us in all aspects. Like Christianity, there are elements of the practices of other religions that are simply bad for us. In the politics of religion, rather than just naive well-wishing, we need processes for conducting inter-religious dialogue that results not just in good relations among the religions concerned but also contributes to social cohesion in multi-religious and multi-cultural societies.[17]

A "pluralist" approach to inter-faith dialogue maintains that the differences between faith traditions are real and should not be minimized, yet there is a great deal in common and the path ahead is through mutual and honest evaluation. Following a pluralist approach, Australian theologian David Pitman gives some key markers that churches can use to check their own approaches to other faiths. These are:

a. recognize the essential interaction of religion and culture and recognize the profound impact that each has on the other,

b. perceive the significance that one's place of birth tends to have on religious identity and allegiance,

c. affirm the uniqueness and salvific efficacy of the individual traditions,

d. understand that there are no easy solutions to the problems that have developed over many centuries,

e. affirm the profound differences that exist,

f. respect the identity and tradition of each religion, and

g. understand that any significant relationship will incorporate a process of mutual evaluation and criticism.[18]

---

of no value to be uncritically accepted." Küng, *Christianity and the World Religions*, xvi.

17. An example of such a process, called a "deliberative democratic" process, is that proposed by Adams, "Mission and Inter-religious Dialogue," 309–10. A deliberative democratic process is here understood as "an unconstrained exchange of arguments that involves practical reasoning and always potentially leads to a transformation of preferences." With somewhat similar intent, Guli E. Francis-Dehqani proposes a "sympathetically critical" approach to Christian-Muslim dialogue. This requires both self-criticism but also a vigorous yet courteous criticism of the other. And he warns that it is too easy to move from a position whereby Islam is demonized to a typically post-colonial, guilt-induced, appreciation of all it stands for. Francis-Dehqani, "Adventures in Christian-Muslim Encounters since 1910," 134. For an example of an intentional co-location of a synagogue, mosque, and church for the purpose of being intentional neighbors, see Alexander, "The Tri-Faith Initiative," 24–28.

18. The three-fold paradigm of the "exclusivist-inclusivist-pluralist" approaches

At the grassroots, "agency partnerships" in mission and "companionship" mission undertaken by local churches is particularly important. Cross-cultural and cross-religious friendship is an essential component of mission, especially in a world in which migration and human mobility play a central role.[19]

The review question we could ask ourselves in this aspect of our mission policy is:

In our local church, are we engaged in appreciative and critical relations with other religions?

Our review schedule now has two basic questions with a set of priorities attached to the first of those questions:

Mission Review

Basic Questions	Priorities
Mission in Society: In our church, what engagement is there for the wellbeing of the wider society?	Politics of culture: consensus in pluralist society? Politics of wealth: justice—reducing inequality? Politics of religion: relations with other religions?
Mission in the Earth: In our church, what evidence is there of belief in a Creator God?	

I have suggested that the politics of culture, wealth, and religion are priorities for our mission in society, but this depends upon the context in which a local church exercises its mission. In other contexts, other kinds of politics, such as the politics of gender or of reconciliation or of health or of peace or of democratic process, may be particularly important and,

---

to inter-faith dialogue has quite a long history now as a framework for describing the variety of approaches. David Pitman provides a summary of this discussion and concludes with an option for what he calls the "classical *pluralists*" (mainly Hans Küng and Raimundo Panikkar). Pitman, *Twentieth-Century Christian Responses to Religious Pluralism*, 217. We should note though the differences in approach to inter-faith dialogue between the World Council of Churches (an inclusivism with a wider opening towards pluralist aspects) and the "evangelical" churches (emphasis on proclamation, truth, and uniqueness of Christ). Kjøde, "Convergence or Divergence in Theology of Religions?" 92–115.

19. Campese, "Mission and Migration," 260.

in that case, substituted for one or other of the priorities I have proposed above. With this understanding, we can turn our attention to the second of the basic questions: mission in the Earth.

Mission in the Earth

A review of the kind we are attempting here acknowledges that we need a "conversion," a change of heart. Today, for many of us, the most neglected part of that change of heart lies in our attitudes and actions towards the beings and processes of Earth. The problem here does not lie in the environment itself but in the human heart, individually and collectively. One of the earliest Christian advocates of a Christian ecological ethics is Ecumenical Patriarch Bartholomew, who reminds us that the world is not ours to use for our own convenience. It is God's gift of love.[20]

The church's mission as participant in the mission of God cannot be restricted to just human beings. One of the concluding affirmations in the World Council of Churches 2012 mission document "Together towards Life: Mission and Evangelism in Changing Landscapes" states:

> We affirm that the mission of God's Spirit is to renew the whole creation... The God of life protects, loves, and cares for nature. Humanity is not the master of the earth but is responsible to care for the integrity of creation. Excessive greed and unlimited consumption which lead to continuous destruction of nature must end. God's love does not proclaim a human salvation separate from the renewal of the whole creation. We are called to participate in God's mission beyond our human-centered goals. God's mission is to all life, and we have to both acknowledge it and serve it in new ways of mission. We pray for repentance and forgiveness, but we also call for action now. Mission has creation at its heart.[21]

While it may be fanciful to think the church could have a mission to the whole of creation, it is realistic that the mission of the church includes the planet Earth, especially those beings and processes of Earth with which we are most intimately connected.

In his 2015 encyclical *Laudato Si': On Care for our Common Home*, Pope Francis called for an "ecological conversion." This is a call to an

---

20. Bartholomew, *On Earth as in Heaven*, 172.
21. World Council of Churches, "Together towards Life," #105.

"integral ecology" which respects all the environmental, human, and social dimensions of the planet. An integral ecology is one in which we recognize one complex crisis which is both *social* and *environmental* and which requires an *economics* in service of a more integrating vision. It is one in which we respect not just the natural but also the *historic, artistic, and cultural patrimony* which has shaped our cultural identity and sense of meaning; in which the quality of *daily life* is influenced by an ordered and beautiful environment; in which human ecology is inseparable from the *principle of the common good*; where the notion of the common good also extends to *future generations*.[22]

While mission in the Earth is a latecomer in missiology, there is now an abundance of literature which not only discusses the theology of Christian concern for the planet Earth but also recreates theology's relationships with science and the practical ways in which Christians may engage in ethical action in this Earth-related mission.[23]

A way of entering into this discussion on the ways in which the church may be engaged in God's mission towards the wellbeing of planet Earth and its constituent beings and processes is to ask the basic question:

In our local church, what evidence is there of belief in a Creator God?

This basic question needs to be spelled out in terms of some more specific priorities. There are many questions we could ask in attempting to be more specific about the church's mission in the Earth. I propose here to deal with two of these that will hopefully serve our purpose:

How do we prioritize environmental issues? and

What is our basic moral position in regard to environmental ethics?

---

22. Francis, *Laudato Si'*, #137–62. Local churches may be helped here by Stan Chu Ilo's summary of Pope Francis's teaching under three emphases: (1) a compassionate church, moved by the suffering and injustice in the world; (2) a church whose mission is to accompany humanity with the leaven of the gospel in order to bring about a radical conversion of hearts and worldly systems and institutions; and (3) a transformative missional praxis that brings about integral salvation through solidarity with the poor and marginalized, and a prophetic commitment to human and cosmic flourishing. Ilo, "Poverty and Economic Justice in Pope Francis," 38–56.

23. See, for example, Miller, *The Theological and Ecological Vision of Laudato Si'*; Kim and Draper, *Christianity and the Renewal of Nature*; Clifford, "From Ecological Lament to a Sustainable *Oikos*," 247–52.

Prioritizing Environmental Issues

There have been many official reports recently on the state of the environment, global, national, regional, and local. The order of the priorities we make here may depend on where we live.

In his encyclical *Laudato Si': On Care for our Common Home*, Pope Francis names the most troubling ecological issues of the day as pollution and climate change, the depletion of natural resources (especially water), the loss of biodiversity, the decline in the quality of human life and the breakdown of society, and global inequality.[24] Some environmental issues are global while others affect people in one location rather than others. Climate change, for example, is global, but is more devastating in some areas of the globe than others and some people's lifestyles contribute more to it than others. Churches located in a large city, for example, might be more immediately concerned about air pollution than a rural or seaside church where other issues are more obvious.

The central point here though is that any local or regional church will have a strategy and priority towards current environmental issues if it does actually believe in a Creator God as it proclaims. An example of a non-religious statement of priorities was proposed by the president of the New Zealand Forest and Bird Society, one of the largest and most effective environmental societies in my own country, in the lead-up to the 2017 parliamentary elections: "If each and every member keeps these issues—clean water, clean air, sustainable oceans, the impacts of climate change—to the forefront . . . then we will have achieved a real impact."[25] This was a deliberate effort to prioritize environmental issues at a national level by an environmental society. Local church leaders might aim to compose a similar list of priorities and actions for their own members, include these in the church's current mission or policy statements, then ask what combined actions are being undertaken, and take note of current individual actions of its citizen theologians.

Environmentally responsible actions are not just practical ways of conserving life in the planet; they are also theological actions and statements of faith which invite commitment. British theologian and ethicist Michael S. Northcott notes that acts of "love and sacrifice," such as solar panels on church roofs, bicycles outside Sunday services, Christians who refuse to fly and drive, wind farms commissioned by Christian climate

---

24. Francis, *Laudato Si'*, #17–61.

25. Hanger, "Editorial: Vote for the Planet," 2.

activists, are not just examples of ecclesiastical footprint shrinking but the publicity of love in a time of climate change.[26] And in more general terms, there already exists an expanding literature that outlines strategies which churches can adopt to go about an ecological conversion.[27]

A question that can prioritize our current engagement in the Earth is:

In our local church, what are the top two or three priorities in environmental concerns?

Our Basic Moral Position in Environmental Ethics

A second question that renders this section of our review more specific is related not so much to the *objectives* of our environmental actions, but our moral *position* within a range of moral attitudes towards the Earth. The following list of seven positions allows us to place ourselves and our own local church in reference to a "moral positions" chart that includes both religious and non-religious moral positions.

Seven competing models:[28]

1. Ruthless pioneer: takes from nature whatever is of benefit to humans.

2. Enlightened ruler: limits use of natural world so as to safeguard one's own future needs.

3. Secular steward: recognizes the need for sustainability for the sake of future generations.[29]

4. Participant in nature: human beings are part of the natural world, all beings are interdependent.

---

26. Northcott, "The Concealments of Carbon Markets and the Publicity of Love in a Time of Climate Change," 84.

27. Such as that proposed by Kaoma, "From *Missio Dei* to *Missio Creatoris Dei*," 135–46. This is a large-scale plan. Local churches will need to be much more specific, and this assumes that the local church has already done its own self-critique. Or the educational strategy developed in South Korea: Hwang, "Introduction into the *Oikos* Theology Movement in South Korea," 263–73.

28. I have adapted these from an original proposition by Klop, "Equal Respect and the Holy Spirit," 95–106.

29. At the very least the position of the "secular steward" is necessary for sustainability—the position of the United Nations, as seen in the Bruntland Report of 1985 and in the Declaration of Rio de Janeiro in 1992. This image is still commonly used in environmental ethics to refer to situations where human intervention is required to remedy earlier destructive activities by human beings, such as the introduction of exotic pests into new environments. Darragh, "Ecology and Politics for Peace," 128–42.

5. Religious steward: humans are stewards under God who both use and are responsible for other beings.[30]

6. Partner of nature: all beings have intrinsic value of their own regardless of their use to humans.

7. Mystical union with nature: ultimately all beings are one in mystical union with their Creator.

A question that focuses our missionary strategy here is:
Which of these basic moral positions is demonstrated in the activities of our local church?

---

30. The notion of "religious steward" is particularly problematic today. R. J. Berry retains this idea of stewardship as rooted in the idea of "relationships." Relationships are not always positive but that need not be a reason to discount the idea altogether. But he notes that for some people the notion is wholly negative, conjuring up undesirable traits of subservience and hierarchy, absentee landlords and exploitation; as alternatives they propose such images as trustee, agent, companion, and priest. Berry, "Introduction. Stewardship: A Default Position?" 1–31. Ecumenical Patriarch Bartholomew retains the belief that God has designated the human person as a steward (also governor, provider, priest), but not a destroyer of creation. Bartholomew, *On Earth as in Heaven*, esp. 35, 74, 184. Orthodox theologian John D. Zizioulas opts for the model of "priest": "Thus the Eucharist ceases to be a "religious experience" or a means to individual salvation and becomes a mode of being, a way of life, illumined by the vision and the expectation of the future, by that which the world will be when it is finally transfigured into the Kingdom of God." Zizioulas, *The Eucharistic Communion and the World*, 82, 140–41. In his 2015 encyclical on ecology, Pope Francis, while not rejecting the image of "steward," the image commonly used by Pope John Paul II, strongly favours the alternative image of "care for our common home." Francis, *Laudato Si'*.

Conclusion

Our mission review schedule now looks like this:

Mission Review

Basic Questions	Priorities
Mission in Society: In our church, what engagement is there for the wellbeing of the wider society?	Politics of culture: consensus in pluralist society? Politics of wealth: justice—reducing inequality? Politics of religion: relations with other religions?
Mission in the Earth In our church, what evidence is there of belief in a Creator God?	Our priorities in environmental ethics? Our basic moral position in environmental ethics?

This chapter is an attempt to provide the building blocks for a review of a local church's mission performance. The "priorities" for any particular local church may well differ from place to place and should then replace the priorities I have proposed here. The important point is that, although there already exists a literature on the attitudes and actions that could constitute a local church's mission strategy, local churches and citizen theologians still need to do their own review and decide on their own mission strategies. The review schedule proposed here sets out in simple visual form the pattern for such a review. I hope it may serve as a template which local churches can adapt for their own needs.

14

The Next Step

THIS BOOK HAS BEEN an investigation into what the church is *for*. If we cannot answer this question for our own local church, then we are a self-focused community looking after ourselves. In chapter 6, "Mission Theologies," I proposed that we identify the mission of the local church as *the activity of a local church and its members directed outwards to the wider world in response to the Holy Spirit, with a primary objective of service to the realm of God, and a secondary objective of attracting new people into its community life and action.*

When our local church is situated in a religiously and culturally pluralist society, this mission requires of us, both as a local church and as citizen theologians, that we engage in service to the realm of God in the society in which we live and work—it involves more than this of course, but at least this. To do this requires a local theology of mission that directs and supports a strategic engagement in that society (including the further ramifications and relationships implicit in being a member of society).

I have proposed that we could expect a local mission theology to be transformational for wellbeing, place-based, strength-based, alert to different kinds of agency, and self-critical.

I concluded this overview of mission with a structure for self-critique by means of which a local church could move beyond broad intentions towards articulating more strategic priorities and to an examination of its actual mission activities. Once it has done this, a local church is in a strong position to make the move, if necessary, from a merely self-focused church to a mission-focused church.

The Next Step

The purpose of this investigation into the mission of the local church and its impact in society is transformational. It is intended as an aid to both our mission theology and our mission practice so that we become better at both.

I suspect, however, that one of the outcomes of such an investigation in nearly every local church (and affecting all the larger church structures and institutions interrelated with local churches) will be a question mark over the church itself. Is the church, as it stands with its current theology and its current styles of relating, adequate to this mission task?

This book has been an investigation in missiology—the *purpose* of the church. Yet it leads immediately into a study of ecclesiology—the *nature* of the church. A review of our "actual" mission, as distinct from just our broad good intentions, will probably find that our church is not itself well designed to implement these good intentions.

Mission and church are interwoven, not independent, social and spiritual realities. One of our inherited problems in theology is that the study of Christian mission (missiology) and the study of the Christian church (ecclesiology) have often been carried out independently of each another. Members of missionary orders and missionary societies in the mainstream churches, for example, have been expected to study missiology, but priests and ministers destined for local pastoral work were usually thought to need ecclesiology rather than missiology.[1] The more evangelical churches normally began with a strong mission agenda, but mission has been more commonly understood as "evangelism" in the sense of an "attractional" mission rather than a mission in service to the larger realm of God.

One of the principal drivers of this book has been the principle that mission comes before church. Yet the study of ecclesiology, reflection on the nature of the church, has often begun by looking at the church in the New Testament with its origins in the Old Testament, then the way the church and its organization have developed in history with changing times and changing places. Scripture and tradition, including reforms and counter-reforms, have been the foundations for our ecclesiology. But this is doing things back to front. Today, we begin by asking what the mission of God is in the world and how we might participate in that

---

1. Stuart Murray comments, accurately I think, that in the age of Christendom "questions about church involved neither culture nor mission. Engaging in mission and interacting with culture were secondary concerns that did not affect how churches were understood, governed, or organised." Murray, *Post-Christendom*, 251.

larger mission. If we know what the mission of the church is, then that is the first foundation for how we arrange and organize our relationships within the church as disciples of Christ—so that we are capable of carrying out that mission. We do not first have a church, then see what we can do about its mission. We first have a mission and then we see how we can best arrange ourselves to carry out that mission faithfully and effectively. Our ecclesiology should match our missiology, not the other way round.

This brings me to the conclusion of this book. If we can get our missiology right, then our next step will be to work on our ecclesiology to see if we can get that right too: a church in process and willing to learn so that it is in fact able to contribute to the ongoing mission of God. This book, however, finishes here. The first step is missiology. It is only after this that we can take the next step into ecclesiology.

Bibliography

Adams, Brian J. "Mission and Inter-religious Dialogue: A Deliberative Democratic Framework." In *World Religions and Their Missions*, edited by Aaron J. Ghiloni, 307–42. New York: Peter Lang, 2015.
Adeney, Frances S. "Making Friends with People of Other Religions: Pitfalls of Giftive Mission." *Missiology* 47.1 (2019) 18–23.
Alexander, Christopher. "The Tri-Faith Initiative." *Missiology* 47.1 (2019) 24–28.
Asamoah-Gyadu, J. Kwabena. "Prayer and Power from the South: African Diaspora Churches on Mission." In *Scattered and Gathered: A Global Compendium of Diaspora Missiology*, edited by Sadiri Joy Tira and Tetsunao Yamamori, 327–37. Eugene, Oregon: Wipf and Stock, 2016.
Avis, Paul. *A Church Drawing Near: Spirituality and Mission in a Post-Christian Culture*. London: T. & T. Clark International, 2003.
Badcock, Gary D. *The House Where God Lives: Renewing the Doctrine of the Church for Today*. Grand Rapids, Michigan: Eerdmans, 2009.
Barram, Michael. *Missional Economics: Biblical Justice and Christian Formation*. Grand Rapids, Michigan: Eerdmans, 2018.
Bartholomew, Ecumenical Patriarch. *On Earth as in Heaven: Ecological Vision and Initiatives of Ecumenical Patriarch Bartholomew*. New York: Fordham University Press, 2012.
Beavis, Mary Ann. *Jesus & Utopia: Looking for the Kingdom of God in the Roman World*. Minneapolis: Fortress, 2006.
Benedict XV, Pope. *Maximum Illud: On the Propagation of the Faith Throughout the World*. https://www.vatican.va/content/benedict-xv/en/apost_letters/documents/hf_ben-xv_apl_19191130_maximum-illud.html.
Bennett, Zoe, et al. *Invitation to Research in Practical Theology*. London: Routledge, 2018.
Berger, Peter L. "The Desecularization of the World: A Global Overview." In *The Desecularization of the World: Resurgent Religion and World Politics*, edited by Peter L. Berger, 1–18. Grand Rapids, Michigan: Eerdmans, 1999.
Berry, R. J. "Introduction. Stewardship: A Default Position?" In *Environmental Stewardship: Critical Perspectives—Past and Present*, edited by R. J. Berry, 1–31. London: T. & T. Clark, 2006.
Bevans, Stephen, ed. *A Century of Catholic Mission*. Oxford: Regnum Books International, 2013.
———, ed. *Essays in Contextual Theology*. Boston: Brill, 2018.

———, ed. "God Inside Out: Toward a Missionary Theology of the Holy Spirit." *International Bulletin of Missionary Research* 22.3 (1998) 102–09.

———. "Mission as the Nature of the Church: Developments in Catholic Ecclesiology." *Australian eJournal of Theology* 21.3 (2014) 184–96.

———. "Pope Francis's Missiology of Attraction." *International Bulletin of Mission Research* 43.1 (2019) 20–28.

———, ed. "Revisiting Mission at Vatican II: Theology and Practice for Today's Missionary Church." *Theological Studies* 74.2 (2013) 261–83.

Bevans, Stephen, and Roger P. Schroeder. *Constants in Context: A Theology of Mission for Today*. Maryknoll, New York: Orbis, 2004.

———. *Prophetic Dialogue: Reflections on Christian Mission Today*. Maryknoll, New York: Orbis, 2011.

Bickley, Paul. "Treasures Old and New: Social Innovation and the Renewal of Mission." In *Missional Conversations: Dialogue between Theory and Praxis in World Mission*, edited by Cathy Ross and Colin Smith, 178–91. London: SCM, 2018.

Bielskis, Andrius, and Egidijus Mardosas. "Human Flourishing in the Philosophical Work of Alasdair Macintyre." *International Journal of Philosophy and Theology* 2 (2014) 185–201.

Blackman, Anna. "Holy Disobedience: Political Resistance in the London Catholic Worker Community." *Implicit Religion* 21.2 (2018) 122–41.

Boff, Clodovis. "Methodology of the Theology of Liberation." In *Systematic Theology: Perspectives from Liberation Theology*, edited by John Sobrino and Ignacio Ellacuria, 1–22. Maryknoll, New York: Orbis, 1996.

Boff, Leonardo. *Ecology and Liberation: A New Paradigm*. Maryknoll, New York: Orbis, 1995.

———. *Good News to the Poor: A New Evangelization*. Maryknoll, New York: Orbis, 1992.

———. *Toward an Eco-Spirituality*. Crossroad, 2015.

Boff, Leonardo, and Virgil Elizondo. "Editorial: Ecology and Poverty: Cry of the Earth, Cry of the Poor." *Concilium* 5 (1995) ix–xii.

Boff, Leonardo, and Clodovis Boff. *Introducing Liberation Theology*. Maryknoll, New York: Orbis, 1986.

Bonk, Jonathan. *Missions and Money: Affluence as a Western Missionary Problem*. Maryknoll, New York: Orbis, 1991.

———. "Mission and the Problem of Affluence." In *Toward the Twenty-First Century in Christian Mission*, edited by James M. Phillips and Robert T. Coote, 295–309. Grand Rapids, Michigan: Eerdmans, 1993.

Bonnie, J. Miller-McLemore. *The Wiley-Blackwell Companion to Practical Theology*. Wiley-Blackwell Companions to Religion. Chichester, UK: Wiley-Blackwell, 2012.

Bosch, David J. *Believing in the Future: Toward a Missiology of Western Culture*. Valley Forge, Pennsylvania: Trinity Press International, 1995.

———. *Transforming Mission: Paradigm Shifts in Theology of Mission*. New York: Orbis, 1991.

Boyd, David R. *The Optimistic Environmentalist: Progressing toward a Greener Future*. Toronto: ECW, 2015.

Bretherton, Luke. *Christianity and Contemporary Politics: The Conditions and Possibilities of Faithful Witness*. Chichester, UK: Wiley-Blackwell, 2010.

———. *Resurrecting Democracy: Faith, Citizenship, and the Politics of a Common Life*. New York: Cambridge University Press, 2015.
Bretsen, Stephen N. "The Creation, the Kingdom of God, and a Theory of the Faithful Corporation." *Christian Scholar's Review* 38.1 (2008) 115–54.
Brown, L. E. "Missional Ecclesiology in the Book of Acts." *Journal of the Grace Evangelical Society* 24.47 (Autumn 2011) 65–88.
Bruce, Steve. *God Is Dead: Secularization in the West*. Oxford: Blackwell, 2002.
———. "History, Sociology, and Secularisation." In *Secularisation: New Historical Perspectives*, edited by Christopher Hartney, 190–213. Newcastle upon Tyne, UK: Cambridge Scholars, 2014.
———. *Secularization: In Defence of an Unfashionable Theory*. Oxford: Oxford University Press, 2011.
Burnside, Jonathan. "Words of Wisdom, Words of Prophecy: Why and How Biblical Law Speaks in the Public Square." *Political Theology* 18.7 (2017) 560–76.
Buxton, Graham, and Norman Habel, eds. *The Nature of Things: Rediscovering the Spiritual in God's Creation*. Eugene, Oregon: Pickwick, 2016.
Cahill, Lisa Sowle. "Just War, Pacifism, Just Peace, and Peacebuilding." *Theological Studies* 80.1 (2019) 169–85.
Calhoun, Craig. "Afterword: Religion's Many Powers." In *The Power of Religion in the Public Sphere*, edited by Eduardo Mendieta and Jonathan VanAntwerpen, 118–35. New York: Columbia University Press, 2011.
Campese, Gioacchino. "Mission and Migration." In *A Century of Catholic Mission*, edited by Stephen B. Bevans, 247–68. Oxford: Regnum Books International, 2013.
Casanova, José. "Immigration and the New Religious Pluralism: A European Union-United States Comparison." In *Secularism, Religion, and Multicultural Citizenship*, edited by Geoffrey Brahm Levey, Tariq Modood, and Charles Taylor, 139–63. Cambridge, UK: Cambridge University Press, 2009.
Church of England's Mission and Public Affairs Council. "Mission-Shaped Church: Church Planting and Fresh Expressions of Church in a Changing Context." London: Church Publishing House, 2004.
Clifford, Anne M. "From Ecological Lament to a Sustainable *Oikos*." In *Environmental Stewardship: Critical Perspectives—Past and Present*, edited by R. J. Berry, 247–52. New York: T. & T. Clark, 2006.
Cobb, John B., Jr. "Commonwealth and Empire." In *The American Empire and the Commonwealth of God: A Political, Economic, and Religious Statement*, edited by David Ray Griffin et al., 137–50. Louisville, Kentucky: Westminster John Knox, 2006.
Cole, Neil, and Phil Helfer. *Church Transfusion: Changing Your Church Organically—from the Inside Out*. San Francisco: Jossey-Bass, 2012.
Conference on World Mission and Evangelism. "Conference on World Mission and Evangelism Report: 'Moving in the Spirit: Called to Transforming Discipleship.' Arusha, Tanzania, 8–13 March 2018." *International Review of Mission* 107.2 (2018) 547–60.
Congregation for the Doctrine of the Faith. "Doctrinal Note 'On Some Aspects of Evangelization.'" Vatican City, 2007. https://www.vatican.va/roman_curia/congregations/cfaith/documents/rc_con_cfaith_doc_20071203_nota-evangelizzazione_en.html.
Congregation for the Doctrine of the Faith and Dicastery For Promoting Integral Human Development. "Considerations for an Ethical Discernment Regarding

Some Aspects of the Present Economic-Financial System: *Oeconomicae Et Pecuniariae Quaestiones.*" Vatican City, 2018. https://press.vatican.va/content/salastampa/en/bollettino/pubblico/2018/05/17/180517a.html.

Connolly, Noel, and Brian Lucas. "A Theological Reflection on the *Missio Ad Gentes.*" *The Australasian Catholic Record* 9.4 (2019) 411–20.

Conrad, Richard. "Moments and Themes in the History of Apologetics." In *Imaginative Apologetics*, edited by Andrew Davidson, 126–41. Grands Rapids, Michigan: Baker Academic, 2012.

Conradie, Ernst, Ekaterini Tsalampouni, and Dietrich Werner. "Manifesto on Ecological Reformation of Christianity—the Volos Call." In *Eco-Theology, Climate Justice, and Food Security: Theological Education and Christian Leadership Development*, edited by Dietrich Werner and Elisabeth Jeglitzka, 99–106. Geneva: Globethics.net, 2015.

Conradie, Ernst. "Climate Justice, Food Security . . . and God: Some Reflections from the Perspective of Eco-Theology." In *Eco-Theology, Climate Justice, and Food Security: Theological Education and Christian Leadership Development*, edited by Dietrich Werner and Elisabeth Jeglitzka, 110–34. Geneva: Globethics.net, 2015.

Cronshaw, Darren, and Steve Taylor. "The Congregation in a Pluralist Society: Rereading Newbigin for Missional Churches Today." *Pacifica* 27.2 (2014) 206–28.

Crossan, John Dominic. *God and Empire: Jesus against Rome, Then and Now.* New York: HarperCollins, 2007.

Crouch, David. *Almost Perfekt: How Sweden Works and What We Can Learn from It.* London: Blink, 2019.

Curtis, Steve. "Missiological Missteps and the Need for Theological Education in Myanmar." *International Bulletin of Mission Research* 42.1 (2018) 56–66.

D'Orsa, Jim, and Therese D'Orsa. "Mission and Catholic Education." In *A Century of Catholic Mission*, edited by Stephen Bevans, 239–46. Oxford: Regnum Books International, 2013.

Darragh, Neil. "An Ascetic Theology, Spirituality, and Praxis." *Concilium* 3 (2009) 76–85.

———. *At Home in the Earth: A Christian Earth Spirituality.* Auckland, NZ: Accent, 2000.

———. "Ecology and Politics for Peace: How Does Ecology Deal with Violence?" *The Australian and New Zealand Theological Review* 50.2 (2018) 128–42.

———. "Hazardous Missions and Shifting Frameworks." *Missiology* 38.3 (2010) 271–80.

———, ed. *Living in the Planet Earth: Faith Communities and Ecology.* Auckland, NZ: Accent, 2016.

———. "A Missional Church in Process and Willing to Learn." In *Bridging the Divide between Faith, Theology, and Life*, edited by Anthony Maher, 73–86. Adelaide, Australia: ATF, 2015.

———. "Pacific Island Theology." In *Global Dictionary of Theology*, edited by William A. Dyrness and Veli-Mati Karkkainen, 624–26. Downers Grove, Illinois: InterVarsity, 2008.

———. "The Practice of Practical Theology: Key Decisions and Abiding Hazards in Doing Practical Theology." *Australian eJournal of Theology* 9 (2007) 1–13.

Davey, Andrew. "Facing the City: Urban Mission in the 21st Century." *Ecclesiology* 3.1 (2006) 152–54.

Davie, Grace. "Europe: The Exception That Proves the Rule?" In *The Desecularization of the World: Resurgent Religion and World Politics*, edited by Peter L. Berger, 65–83. Grand Rapids, Michigan: Eerdmans 1999.

———. "From Obligation to Consumption: Understanding the Patterns of Religion in Northern Europe." In *The Future of the Parish System: Shaping the Church of England for the Twenty-First Century*, edited by Steven Croft, 33–45. London: Church Publishing House, 2006.

———. *Religion in Britain: A Persistent Paradox*. 2nd ed. Chichester, UK: Wiley-Blackwell, 2015.

Davies, Oliver. *Theology of Transformation: Faith, Freedom, and the Christian Act*. Oxford: Oxford University Press, 2013.

De La Torre, Miguel A., ed. *Introducing Liberative Theologies*. Maryknoll, New York: Orbis, 2015.

Dunn, James D. G. "Is There Evidence for Fresh Expressions of Church in the New Testament?" In *Mission-Shaped Questions: Defining Issues for Today's Church*, edited by Steven Croft, 54–56. London: Church Publishing House, 2008.

Duraisingh, Christopher. "From Church-Shaped Mission to Mission-Shaped Church." *Anglican Theological Review* 92 (Winter 2010) 7–28.

Effa, Allan. "Celtic and Aboriginal Pathways toward a Contemporary Ecospirituality." *International Bulletin of Mission Research* 41.1 (2017) 54–62.

———. "Spiritual Renewal and the Healing of Creation." *Missiology* 47.4 (2019) 360–71.

Ehrman, Bart D. *The Triumph of Christianity: How a Forbidden Religion Swept the World*. New York: Simon & Schuster, 2018.

Elbasani, Arolda. "Governing Islam in Plural Societies: Religious Freedom, State Neutrality, and Traditional Heritage." *Journal of Balkan & Near Eastern Studies* 19.1 (2017) 4–18.

Faggioli, Massimo. *Catholicism and Citizenship: Political Cultures of the Church in the Twenty-First Century*. Collegeville, Minnesota: Liturgical, 2017.

Farrell, B. Hunter. "Re-Membering Missiology: An Invitation to an Activist Agenda." *Missiology* 46.1 (2018) 37–49.

Federation of Asian Bishops' Conferences. "FABC at Forty Years: Responding to the Challenges of Asia. A New Evangelization." 2012. http://www.fabc.org/10th%20plenary%20assembly/Documents/FABC%20-%20X%20PA%20Final%20Document.pdf.

Fedorov, Vladimir. "Ecumenical Missionary Needs and Perspectives in Eastern and Central Europe Today: Theological Education with an Accent on Mission as a First Priority in Our Religious Rebirth." *International Review of Mission* 92.364 (2003) 66–84.

Folke, C., et al. "Resilience Thinking: Integrating Resilience, Adaptability, and Transformability." *Ecology and Society* 15.4 (2010) art 20.

Forrester, Duncan B. "Speak Truth to Power: Theology and Public Policy." In *Developing a Public Faith: New Directions in Practical Theology. Essays in Honor of James W. Fowler*, edited by Richard R. Osmer and Friedrich L. Schweitzer, 175–88. St. Louis, Missouri: Chalice, 2003.

Fourie, Willem, and Hendrik Meyer-Magister. "Contextuality and Intercontextuality in Public Theology: On the Structure of Churches' Public Engagement in South Africa and Germany." *International Journal of Public Theology* 11.1 (2017) 36–63.

Francis-Dehqani, Guli E. "Adventures in Christian-Muslim Encounters since 1910." In *Edinburgh 2010: Mission Then and Now*, edited by David A. Kerr and Kenneth R. Ross, 125–38. Eugene, Oregon: Wipf and Stock, 2009.

Francis, Pope. *Evanglii Gaudium: The Joy of the Gospel*. http://w2.vatican.va/content/francesco/en/apost_exhortations/documents/papa-francesco_esortazione-ap_20131124_evangelii-gaudium.html.

———. *Laudato Si': On Care for Our Common Home*. http://w2.vatican.va/content/francesco/en/encyclicals/documents/papa-francesco_20150524_enciclica-laudato-si.pdf.

Gaillardetz, Richard R. *Ecclesiology for a Global Church: A People Called and Sent*. Maryknoll, New York: Orbis, 2008.

Garner, Rod. *Facing the City: Urban Mission in the 21st Century*. Peterborough, UK: Epworth, 2004.

Gascoigne, Robert. "Building Bridges in a Disconnected World: A Christological Perspective." *The Australasian Catholic Record* 95.4 (2018) 424–40.

———. *The Church and Secularity: Two Stories of Liberal Society*. Washington, DC: Georgetown University Press, 2009.

Gibson, Ezekiel Lesmore. "Missional Formation for Life-Giving Interfaith Encounter." *International Review of Mission* 106.1 (2017) 69–79.

Gittins, Anthony. *Ministry at the Margins: Strategy and Spirituality for Mission*. Maryknoll, New York: Orbis, 2002.

Goldman, Gerard M. "Church: Seeking First the Kingdom of God." *Compass* 44.2 (2010) 3–9.

Gorski, John F. "From 'Mission' to 'Evangelization': The Latin American Origins of a Challenging Concept." In *The New Evangelization: Faith, People, Context, and Practice*, edited by Kirsteen Kim and Paul Grogan, 31–44. London: Bloomsbury, 2015.

Graham, Elaine. *Between a Rock and a Hard Place: Public Theology in a Post-Secular Age*. London: SCM, 2013.

Gray, John. *Black Mass: Apocalyptic Religion and the Death of Utopia*. New York: Farrar, Straus, and Giroux, 2007.

Grayling, A. C. *The Good State: On the Principles of Democracy*. London: Oneworld, 2020.

Gregory, William P. "Pope Francis's Effort to Revitalize Catholic Mission." *International Bulletin of Mission Research* 43.1 (2019) 7–19.

Griffin, David Ray, et al., eds. *The American Empire and the Commonwealth of God: A Political Economic and Religious Statement*. London: John Knox, 2006.

Groody, Daniel G. "The Church on the Move: Mission in an Age of Migration." *Mission Studies* 30.1 (2013) 27–42.

Haasl, Michael. "Catholic Parish Mission Partnerships: Faith Basis, Practice, and Ethical Considerations." *Missiology* 46.4 (2018) 407–27.

Ham, Adolf. "Commission Seven in Light of a Century of Experience in Cuba." In *Edinburgh 2010: Mission Then and Now*, edited by David A. Kerr and Kenneth R. Ross, 217–29. Eugene, Oregon: Wipf & Stock, 2009.

Hanger, Mark. "Editorial: Vote for the Planet." *Forest and Bird Magazine* 365 (2017) 2.

Harris, R. Geoffrey. *Mission in the Gospels*. London: Epworth, 2004.

Hartney, Christopher. "States of Ultimacy and the Cult of the Dead Soldier: The Anzac Tradition, the Secularisation Paradigm, the Charisma of Materiality, and Civil Religion as It Is Embodied in the Australian War Memorial, Canberra." In

Secularisation: New Historical Perspectives, edited by Christopher Hartney, 214–70. Newcastle upon Tyne, UK: Cambridge Scholars, 2014.

Hatmaker, Brandon. *Barefoot Church: Serving the Least in a Consumer Culture*. Grand Rapids, Michigan: Zondervan, 2011.

Haug, Kari Storstein. "Migration in Missiological Research." *International Review of Mission* 107.1 (2018) 279–93.

Hedges, Paul M. "The Deconstruction of Religion: So What Next in the Debate?" *Implicit Religion* 20.4 (2017) 385–96.

———. "Discourse on the Invention of Discourse: Why We Need the Terminology of 'Religion' and 'Religions.'" *The Journal of Religious History* 38.1 (2014) 132–48.

Heikkilä, Ida. "The World Council of Churches' Mission Statement 'Together towards Life': Mission, Evangelism, and *Missio Dei*." *European Journal of Theology* 27.1 (2018) 78–88.

Hertig, Paul. "Introduction." In *Contemporary Mission Theology: Engaging the Nations: Essays in Honor of Charles E. Van Engen*, edited by Robert L. Gallagher and Paul Hertig, xxvii–xxxi. Maryknoll, New York: Orbis, 2017.

Hibbert, Richard Yates, and Evelyn Hibbert. "Defining Culturally Appropriate Leadership." *Missiology* 47.3 (2019) 240–51.

Hoffman, John. *John Gray and the Problem of Utopia*. Cardiff, UK: University of Wales Press, 2008.

Hoffmeyer, John F. "The Missional Trinity." *Dialog: A Journal of Theology* 40.2 (2001) 108–11.

Hollander, Aaron T. "@Edinburgh2010: Online Ecumenism in an Age of Participation." In *Edinburgh 2010: Mission Today and Tomorrow*, edited by Kirsteen Kim and Andrew Anderson, 321–29. Eugene, Oregon: Wipf & Stock, 2011.

Hollenbach, David. *The Global Face of Public Faith: Politics, Human Rights, and Christian Ethics*. Washington, DC: Georgetown University Press, 2003.

Holy and Great Council of the Orthodox Church. "The Mission of the Orthodox Church in Today's World." 2016. https://www.holycouncil.org/-/mission-orthodox-church-todays-world.

Horsley, Richard A. *Jesus and Empire: The Kingdom of God and the New World Disorder*. Minneapolis: Fortress, 2003.

Hovdelien, Olav. "In Favour of Secularism, Correctly Understood." *Australian eJournal of Theology* 21.3 (2014) 234–47.

Howell, Robert. *Investing in People and the Planet*. Auckland, NZ: Robert Howell, 2017.

Hughson, Thomas. "Missional Churches in Secular Societies: Theology Consults Sociology." *Ecclesiology* 7 (2011) 173–94.

Hwang, Hong-Eyul. "Introduction into the *Oikos* Theology Movement in South Korea." In *Eco-Theology, Climate Justice, and Food Security: Theological Education and Christian Leadership Development*, edited by Dietrich Werner and Elisabeth Jeglitzka, 263–73. Geneva: Globethics.net, 2015.

Ilo, Stan Chu. "Poverty and Economic Justice in Pope Francis." *International Bulletin of Mission Research* 43.1 (2019) 38–56.

International Institute for Democracy and Electoral Assistance. "The Global State of Democracy 2019: Addressing the Ills, Reviving the Promise." International IDEA, 2019. https://www.idea.int/sites/default/files/publications/the-global-state-of-democracy-2019-summary.pdf.

John Paul II, Pope. *Redemptoris Missio: On the Permanent Validity of the Church's Missionary Mandate*. http://w2.vatican.va/content/john-paul-ii/en/encyclicals/documents/hf_jp-ii_enc_07121990_redemptoris-missio.html.

Johnson, Alan. "Mixed Fortunes: The Geography of Advantage and Disadvantage in New Zealand." Auckland: The Salvation Army Social Policy and Parliamentary Unit, 2015.

Johnson, Elizabeth A. *Women, Earth, and Creator Spirit*. The 1993 Madeleva Lecture in Spirituality. Mahwah, New Jersey: Paulist Press, 1993.

Johnson, Todd M., et al. "Christianity 2018: More African Christians and Counting Martyrs." *International Bulletin of Mission Research* 42.1 (2018) 20–28.

Jun, Kyu-Nahm. "Escaping the Local Trap? The Role of Community-Representing Organizations in Urban Governance." *Journal of Urban Affairs* 35.3 (2013) 343–63.

Kahn, Jonathon S. "The Virtue of Democratic Faith: A Recovery for Difficult Times." *Political Theology* 18.2 (2017) 137–56.

Kaoma, Kapya. "From *Missio Dei* to *Missio Creatoris Dei*: Toward an African Missional Christology of Jesus as the Ecological Ancestor." In *Eco-Theology, Climate Justice, and Food Security: Theological Education and Christian Leadership Development*, edited by Dietrich Werner and Elisabeth Jeglitzka, 159–77. Geneva: Globethics.net, 2015.

Kariatlis, Philip. "'Together towards Life': A New World Council of Churches Affirmation on Mission and Evangelism: An Orthodox Reflection." *Phronema* 34.1 (2019) ix–xix.

Kasper, Walter. *The Catholic Church: Nature, Reality, and Mission*. London: Bloomsbury, 2015.

Kaveny, Cathleen. *Prophecy without Contempt: Religious Discourse in the Public Square*. Cambridge, Massachusetts: Harvard University Press, 2016.

Kerr, David A., and Kenneth R. Ross, eds. *Edinburgh 2010: Mission Then and Now*. Regnum Studies in Mission. Eugene, Oregon: Wipf & Stock, 2009.

Kim, Kirsteen. *Joining in with the Spirit: Connecting World Church and Local Mission*. London: Epworth, 2009.

———. "Mission in the Twenty-First Century." In *Edinburgh 2010: Mission Today and Tomorrow*, edited by Kirsteen Kim and Andrew Anderson, 351–64. Eugene, Oregon: Wipf & Stock, 2011.

Kim, Kirsteen, and Andrew Anderson, eds. *Edinburgh 2010: Mission Today and Tomorrow*. Regnum Edinburgh 2010. Eugene, Oregon: Wipf & Stock, 2011.

Kim, Sebastian, and Jonathan Draper, eds. *Christianity and the Renewal of Nature: Creation, Climate Change, and Human Responsibility*. London: SPCK, 2011.

Kitanovic, Elizabeta, and Aimilianos Bogiannou, eds. *Advancing Freedom of Religion or Belief for All: Contributions from the Conference 6–9 September 2015, Halki, Istanbul, Turkey*. Geneva: Globethics.net, 2015.

Kjøde, Rolf. "Convergence or Divergence in Theology of Religions?" *Mission Studies* 34.1 (2017) 92–115.

Klop, Kees J. "Equal Respect and the Holy Spirit: The Liberal Demand for Moral Neutrality in the Political Sphere and Christian Respect for the Creation." In *Public Theology for the 21st Century: Essays in Honour of Duncan B. Forrester*, edited by William F. Storrar and Andrew R. Morton, 95–106. London: T. & T. Clark, 2004.

Knitter, Paul F. "Mission and Dialogue." *Missiology* 33.2 (2005) 200–210.

———. "The Transformation of Mission in the Pluralist Paradigm." In *Pluralist Theology: The Emerging Paradigm*, edited by Andres Torres Queiruga, Luiz Carlos Susin, and Jose Maria Vigil, 93–101. London: SCM, 2007.

Kosmin, Barry A. "Secular Republic or Christian Nation?: The Battlefields of the American Culture War." In *Secularisation: New Historical Perspectives*, edited by Christopher Hartney, 151–72. Newcastle upon Tyne, UK: Cambridge Scholars, 2014.

Krom, Michael P. "Secularism and Freedom of Conscience." *American Catholic Philosophical Quarterly* 86.2 (2012) 387–90.

Küng, Hans. *Christianity and the World Religions: Paths of Dialogue with Islam, Hinduism, and Buddhism*. London: Collins, 1987.

Lacey, Michael J. "Leo's Church and Our Own." In *The Crisis of Authority in Catholic Modernity*, edited by Michael J. Lacey and Francis Oakley, 57–92. New York: Oxford University Press, 2011.

Lakeland, Paul. "Ecclesiology and the Use of Demography: Three Models of Apostolicity." In *A Church with Open Doors: Catholic Ecclesiology for the Third Millennium*, edited by Richard R. Gaillardetz and Edward P. Hahnenberg, 23–42. Collegeville, Minnesota: Liturgical, 2015.

———. *The Liberation of the Laity: In Search of an Accountable Church*. New York: Continuum, 2003.

Langmead, Ross. "Ecomissiology." *Missiology* 30.4 (2002) 505–18.

———. "Refugees as Guests and Hosts: Towards a Theology of Mission among Refugees and Asylum Seekers." *Exchange* 43.1 (2014) 29–47.

Leavitt, Robert F. *The Truth Will Make You Free: The New Evangelization for a Secular Age: A Study in Development*. Collegeville, Minnesota: Liturgical, 2019.

Lee, David Tai-Woong. "Training Cross-Cultural Missionaries from the Asian Context: Global Missionary Training Center." *Missiology* 36.1 (2008) 111–30.

Levey, Geoffrey Brahm. "Secularism and Religion in a Multicultural Age." In *Secularism, Religion, and Multicultural Citizenship*, edited by Geoffrey Brahm Levey, Tariq Modood, and Charles Taylor, 1–24. Cambridge, UK: Cambridge University Press, 2009.

Lewis, Bonnie Sue. "The Dynamics and Dismantling of White Missionary Privilege." *Missiology* 32.1 (2004) 37–45.

Liagre, Guy, ed. *The New CEC: The Churches' Engagement with a Changing Europe*. Geneva: Globethics.net, 2015.

Lord, Andy. "Spirit-Driven Gospel Communities of Transformation: Towards a Renewalist Missiology." *Mission Studies* 34.2 (2017) 168–92.

Luciani, Rafael. "Medellín Fifty Years Later: From Development to Liberation." *Theological Studies* 79.3 (2018) 566–89.

Macallan, Brian. "Trinitarian Mission and Practical Theology: Conversations in Service of the Local." *International Review of Mission* 108.2 (2019) 389–400.

Maclure, Jocelyn, and Charles Taylor. *Secularism and Freedom of Conscience*. Cambridge, Massachusetts: Harvard University Press, 2011.

Maddox, Marion. "Religion, Secularism, and the Promise of Public Theology." *International Journal of Public Theology* 1.1 (2007) 82–100.

Maloney, Elliott C. *Jesus' Urgent Message for Today: The Kingdom of God in Mark's Gospel*. New York: Continuum, 2004.

Mannion, Gerard. "A Teaching Church That Learns?" In *Church and Religious "Other,"* edited by Gerard Mannion, 161–91. Edinburgh: T. & T. Clark, 2008.

Marsden, Maori. *The Woven Universe: Selected Writings of Rev. Maori Marsden*. Edited by Te Ahukaramu Charles Royal. Otaki, NZ: The Estate of Rev. Maori Marsden, 2003.

Marshall, Glen. "A Missional Ecclesiology for the 21st Century." *Journal of European Baptist Studies* 13.2 (2013) 5–21.

Martin, David. "The Evangelical Upsurge and Its Political Implications." In *The Desecularization of the World: Resurgent Religion and World Politics*, edited by Peter L. Berger, 37–49. Grand Rapids, Michigan: Eerdmans, 1999.

———. *On Secularization: Towards a Revised General Theory*. Aldershot, UK: Ashgate, 2005.

———. *Secularisation, Pentecostalism, and Violence: Receptions, Rediscoveries, and Rebuttals in the Sociology of Religion*. London: Routledge, 2017.

McKnight, Scot. *Kingdom Conspiracy: Returning to the Radical Mission of the Local Church*. Grand Rapids, Michigan: Brazos, 2014.

Meadows, Philip R. "Mission and Discipleship in a Digital Culture." *Mission Studies* 29.2 (2012) 163–82.

Meconi, David Vincent, ed. *On Earth as It Is in Heaven: Cultivating a Contemporary Theology of Creation*. Grand Rapids, Michigan: Eerdmans, 2016.

Meireis, Torsten, and Rold Schieder, eds. *Religion and Democracy: Studies in Public Theology*. Baden-Baden, Germany: Nomos Verlagsgesellschaft, 2017.

Mesa, José M. de. "Mission and Inculturation." In *A Century of Catholic Mission*, edited by Stephen B. Bevans, 224–31. Oxford: Regnum Books International, 2013.

Miller, Vincent J., ed. *The Theological and Ecological Vision of Laudato Si': Everything Is Connected*. New York: Bloomsbury, 2017.

Missional Church Network. "History of Missional Church." http://missionalchurchnetwork.com/history-of-missional-church.

Modood, Tariq. "Muslims, Religious Equality, and Secularism." In *Secularism, Religion, and Multicultural Citizenship*, edited by Geoffrey Brahm Levey, Tariq Modood, and Charles Taylor, 164–85. Cambridge, UK: Cambridge University Press, 2009.

Moloney, Francis J. "Mission in the Acts of the Apostles: 'The Protagonist Is the Holy Spirit.'" *The Australasian Catholic Record* 96.4 (2019) 400–410.

Moltmann, Jurgen. *God in Creation: A New Theology of Creation and the Spirit of God*. San Francisco: Harper & Row, 1985.

Morgan, Alison. "What Does the Gift of the Spirit Mean for the Shape of the Church?" In *Mission-Shaped Questions: Defining Issues for Today's Church*, edited by Steven Croft, 146–60. London: Church Publishing House, 2008.

Motte, Mary. "Signs of a Future Transformation in Mission." *International Bulletin of Mission Research* 43.1 (2019) 30–37.

Moynagh, Michael. *Church in Life: Innovation, Mission and Ecclesiology*. London: SCM, 2017.

———. "A Conversational Approach to New Forms of Church." In *Missional Conversations: Dialogue between Theory and Praxis in World Mission*, edited by Cathy Ross and Colin Smith, 137–46. London: SCM, 2018.

Murray, Stuart. *Post-Christendom: Church and Mission in a Strange New World*. Milton Keynes, UK: Paternoster, 2004.

Nacpil, Marian. "The Church in the Twenty-First-Century Diaspora: The Local Church on Mission." *International Bulletin of Mission Research* 42.1 (2018) 68–75.

Nazir-Ali, Michael. *From Everywhere to Everywhere*. Eugene, Oregon: Wipf and Stock, 2009.

Newbigin, Lesslie. *The Gospel in a Pluralist Society*. London: SPCK, 1989.

Nguyen, vanThanh. "Missionary Churches in Acts: A Model of Intercultural Engagement with the Nations." In *Contemporary Mission Theology: Engaging the Nations: Essays in Honor of Charles E. Van Engen*, edited by Robert L. Gallagher and Paul Hertig, 135–45. Maryknoll, New York: Orbis, 2017.

Niemandt, Nelus. "Missiology and Deep Incarnation." *Mission Studies* 34.2 (2017) 246–61.

Nkansah-Obrempong, James. "Africa's Contextual Realities: Foundation for the Church's Holistic Mission." *International Review of Mission* 106.2 (2017) 280–94.

———. "The Mission of the Church and Holistic Redemption." *Evangelical Review of Theology* 42.3 (2018) 196–211.

Northcott, Michael S. "The Concealments of Carbon Markets and the Publicity of Love in a Time of Climate Change." In *Christianity and the Renewal of Nature: Creation, Climate Change, and Human Responsibility*, edited by Sebastian Kim and Jonathan Draper, 70–84. London: SPCK, 2011.

Nothwehr, Dawn M. "For the Salvation of the Cosmos: The Church's Mission of Ecojustice." *International Bulletin of Mission Research* 43.1 (2019) 68–81.

Nussbaum, Martha. "Capabilities as Fundamental Entitlements: Sen and Social Justice." *Feminist Economics* 9.2/3 (2003) 33–59.

Oduro, Thomas A. "'Arise, Walk through the Length and Breadth of the Land': Missionary Concepts and Strategies of African Independent Churches." *International Bulletin of Missionary Research* 38.2 (2014) 86–89.

OECD. "How's Life? 2015: Measuring Wellbeing." OECD, 2015. https://www.oecd.org/statistics/How-s-life-2015-60-seconde-guide.pdf.

Ormerod, Neil. *Re-Visioning the Church: An Experiment in Systematic-Historical Ecclesiology*. Minneapolis, MN: Fortress, 2014.

Ott, Craig, ed. *The Mission of the Church: Five Views in Conversation*. Grand Rapids, Michigan: Baker Academic, 2016.

Patterson, Colin. "What Has Eschatology to Do with the Gospel?: An Analysis of Papal Documents on Mission Ad Gentes." *Missiology* 47.3 (2019) 285–99.

Paul VI, Pope. *Evangelii Nuntiandi: Evangelization in the Modern World*. http://w2.vatican.va/content/paul-vi/en/apostexhortations/documents/hf_p-vi_exh_19751208_evangelii-nuntiandi.html.

Pavlovic, Peter. "Christian Hope in Reflecting the Challenge of Climate Change: Perspectives from ECEN." In *Eco-Theology, Climate Justice, and Food Security: Theological Education and Christian Leadership Development*, edited by Dietrich Werner and Elisabeth Jeglitzka, 275–82. Geneva: Globethics.net, 2015.

Phan, Peter C. "A New Christianity, but What Kind?" In *Landmark Essays in Mission and World Christianity*, edited by Robert L. Gallagher and Paul Hertig, 201–18. Maryknoll, New York: Orbis, 2009.

Pitman, David. *Twentieth-Century Christian Responses to Religious Pluralism: Difference Is Everything*. Farnham, UK: Ashgate, 2014.

Pius X, Pope. *Vehementer Nos: Encyclical of Pope Pius X on the French Law of Separation*. http://w2.vatican.va/content/pius-x/en/encyclicals/documents/hf_p-x_enc_11021906_vehementer-nos.html.

Pontifical Council for Justice and Peace. "Compendium of the Social Doctrine of the Church." http://www.vatican.va/roman_curia/pontifical_councils/justpeace/documents/rc_pc_justpeace_doc_20060526_compendio-dott-soc_en.html.

Price, J. Matthew. "Popular Notions of the Missionary Task in the Post-Missionary Era: A Hopeful Response to the Images of Missionaries Depicted in Twentieth-Century Novels." *Missiology* 36.2 (2008) 245–57.

Pushparajan, A. "Mission in Civil Society." In *The Church in Mission: Universal Mandate and Local Concerns*, edited by Thomas Malipurathu and L. Stanislaus, 265–80. Gujarat, India: Gujarat Sahitya Prakash, 2002.

Putenpurakal, Joseph. "Catholic Mission in Asia 1910–2010." In *A Century of Catholic Mission*, edited by Stephen B. Bevans, 24–33. Oxford: Regnum Books International, 2013.

Rashbrooke, Max. *Government for the Public Good: The Surprising Science of Large-Scale Collective Action*. Wellington, NZ: Bridget Williams, 2018.

Richardson, Rick. "Emerging Missional Movements: An Overview and Assessment of Some Implications for Mission(s)." *International Bulletin of Missionary Research* 37.3 (2013) 131–36.

Rieger, Joerg. "Empire, Deep Solidarity, and the Future of Liberation Theology." *Political Theology* 18.4 (2017) 354–64.

Riem, Roland. "Mission-Shaped Church: An Emerging Critique." *Ecclesiology* 3.1 (2006) 125–39.

Rivers, Robert S. *From Maintenance to Mission: Evangelization and the Revitalization of the Parish*. New York: Paulist, 2005.

Robinson, Eric. "Witness, the Church, and Faithful Cultural Engagement." *Missiology* 47.2 (2019) 140–52.

Ross, Andrew C. *A Vision Betrayed: The Jesuits in Japan and China 1542–1742*. Maryknoll, New York: Orbis, 1994.

Rynkiewich, Michael A. "The World in My Parish: Rethinking the Standard Missiological Model." *Missiology* XXX.3 (2002) 301–21.

Sayyid, S. "Contemporary Politics of Secularism." In *Secularism, Religion, and Multicultural Citizenship*, edited by Geoffrey Brahm Levey, Tariq Modood, and Charles Taylor, 186–99. Cambridge, UK: Cambridge University Press, 2009.

Scott, Jamie S. "Missions and Film." *International Bulletin of Missionary Research* 32.3 (2008) 115–20.

———. "Missions in Fiction." *International Bulletin of Missionary Research* 32.3 (2008) 121–25.

Searle, Joshua T. *Theology after Christendom: Forming Prophets for a Post-Christian World*. Eugene, Oregon: Cascade, 2018.

Second Vatican Council. *Declaration on Religious Freedom: Dignitatis Humanae*. Vatican: Vatican City, 1965.

———. *Decree on the Missionary Activity of the Church: Ad Gentes*. Vatican: Vatican City, 1965.

———. *Dogmatic Constitution on the Church: Lumen Gentium*. Vatican: Vatican City, 1964.

———. *Pastoral Constitution on the Church in the Modern World: Gaudium et Spes*. Vatican: Vatican City, 1965.

Sharpe, Christa Hayden. "Community Justice Assessment Tool for Churches: Discovering Issues of Injustice and Opportunities for Justice Ministry in Your

Community." International Justice Mission. https://www.ijm.org/sites/default/files/download/resources/Community-Justice-Assessment-Tool.pdf.

Silberman, Tim. "Imitation in Cross-Cultural Leadership Development." *Missiology* 46.3 (2018) 240–50.

———. "Un-Missional Church?: Knox-Robinson Ecclesiology and the Mission of the Local Church." *Colloquium* 51.2 (2019) 61–76.

Simon, Benjamin. "Mission and Its Three Pillars: Translation, Transmission, and Transformation." *International Review of Mission* 107.2 (2018) 399–412.

Sintado, Carlos Alberto. *Social Ecology, Ecojustice, and the New Testament: Liberating Readings*. Geneva: Globethics.net, 2015.

Skreslet, Stanley H. *Comprehending Mission: The Questions, Methods, Themes, Problems, and Prospects of Missiology*. Mayknoll, New York: Orbis, 2012.

Smith, Jesse M. "Atheism." In *World Religions and Their Missions*, edited by Aaron J. Ghiloni, 17–45. New York: Peter Lang, 2015.

Sobrino, John, and Ignacio Ellacuria, eds. *Systematic Theology: Perspectives from Liberation Theology*. Maryknoll, New York: Orbis, 1996.

Spencer, Stephen. "Missional Identity of a Parish Church: A Case Study from the Church of England." *Journal of Anglican Studies* 11 (2013) 84–99.

Stephanous, Andrea Z. "Towards an Arabic Political Theology: A Contextual Approach to Co-Existence and Pluralism." In *Edinburgh 2010: Mission Today and Tomorrow*, edited by Kirsteen Kim and Andrew Anderson, 216–21. Regnum Edinburgh 2010. Eugene, Oregon: Wipf & Stock, 2011.

Storrar, William F., and Andrew R. Morton, eds. *Public Theology for the 21st Century: Essays in Honour of Duncan B. Forrester*. London: T. & T. Clark, 2004.

Sullivan, Francis, and Sue Leppert, eds. *Church and Civil Society: A Theology of Engagement*. Adelaide, Australia: ATF, 2004.

Tan, Jonathan Y. "Pope Francis's Preferential Option for Migrants, Refugees, and Asylum Seekers." *International Bulletin of Mission Research* 43.1 (2019) 58–66.

Tate, Henare. *He Puna Iti I Te Ao Marama = a Little Spring in the World of Light*. Auckland, NZ: Libro International, 2012.

Taylor, Charles. "Foreword: What Is Secularism?" In *Secularism, Religion, and Multicultural Citizenship*, edited by Geoffrey Brahm Levey, Tariq Modood, and Charles Taylor, xi–xxii. Cambridge, UK: Cambridge University Press, 2009.

———. "Why We Need a Radical Redefinition of Secularism." In *The Power of Religion in the Public Sphere*, edited by Eduardo Mendieta and Jonathan VanAntwerpen, 34–59. New York: Columbia University Press, 2011.

Tira, Sadiri Joy, and Tetsunao Yamamori, eds. *Scattered and Gathered: A Global Compendium of Diaspora Missiology*. Eugene, Oregon: Wipf and Stock, 2016.

Tizon, F. Albert. "Lifestyles of the Rich and Faithful: Confronting Classism in Christian Mission." *Missiology* 48.1 (2020) 6–28.

Tongoi, Dennis. "Bridging the Divide: Mission and Social Innovation in East Africa." In *Missional Conversations: Dialogue between Theory and Praxis in World Mission*, edited by Cathy Ross and Colin Smith, 170–77. London: SCM, 2018.

Tregenza, Ian. "Secularism, Myth, and History." In *Secularisation: New Historical Perspectives*, edited by Christopher Hartney, 173–89. Newcastle upon Tyne, UK: Cambridge Scholars, 2014.

Trigg, Roger. *Religion in Public Life: Must Faith Be Privatized?* Oxford: Oxford University Press, 2007.

Twelftree, Graham H. *People of the Spirit: Exploring Luke's View of the Church*. Grand Rapids, Michigan: Baker Academic, 2009.

United Nations. "The 17 Goals." https://sustainabledevelopment.un.org/?menu=1300.

United States Conference of Catholic Bishops. "Forming Consciences for Faithful Citizenship: A Call to Political Responsibility from the Catholic Bishops of the United States with Introductory Note." 2015. https://www.usccb.org/issues-and-action/faithful-citizenship/forming-consciences-for-faithful-citizenship-title.

Van Eck, Ernest. "Interpreting the Parables of the Galilean Jesus: A Social-Scientific Approach." *Hervormde Teologiese Studies* 65.1 (2009) 310–21.

———. "Mission, Identity, and Ethics in Mark: Jesus, the Patron for Outsiders." *Hervormde Teologiese Studies* 69.1 (2013) 1–13.

———. "A Prophet of Old: Jesus the 'Public Theologian.'" *Hervormde Teologiese Studies* 66.1 (2010) 1–10.

Van Engen, Charles. "Conclusion: Seeking Ways Forward." In *Contemporary Mission Theology: Engaging the Nations: Essays in Honor of Charles E. Van Engen*, edited by Robert L. Gallagher and Paul Hertig, 289–96. Maryknoll, New York: Orbis, 2017.

———. "Towards a Missiology of Transformation." *Global Missiology* 3 (October 2005) 18. www.globalmissiology.org/english/archive/vanengen_missiology_transformation_4_2005.html.

Van Gelder, Craig. "The Future of the Discipline of Missiology: A Brief Overview of Current Realities and Future Possibilities." *International Bulletin of Missionary Research* 38 (2014) 10–16.

Voulgaraki-Pissina, Evi. "Reading the Document on Mission of the Holy and Great Council from a Missiological Point of View." *International Review of Mission* 106.1 (2017) 136–50.

Wallace, Mark I. *Fragments of the Spirit: Nature, Violence, and the Renewal of Creation*. New York: Continuum, 1996.

Ward, Ian. "Democratic Civility and the Dangers of Niceness." *Political Theology* 18.2 (2017) 115–36.

Watson, Jude Tiersma. "Engaging the Nations in Los Angeles: A Spirituality of Accompaniment." In *Contemporary Mission Theology: Engaging the Nations: Essays in Honor of Charles E. Van Engen*, edited by Robert L. Gallagher and Paul Hertig, 263–70. Maryknoll, New York: Orbis, 2017.

Weigel, George. *Evangelical Catholicism: Deep Reform in the 21st-Century Church*. New York: Basic Books, 2013.

Wells, Samuel. *Incarnational Mission: Being with the World*. Grand Rapids, Michigan: Eerdmans, 2018.

Whiteman, Darrell L. "Integral Training Today for Cross-Cultural Mission." *Missiology* 36.1 (2008) 5–16.

Wild-Wood, Emma, and Peniel Rajkumar, eds. *Foundations for Mission*. Eugene, Oregon: Wipf and Stock, 2013.

Wilfred, Felix. "Christianity and Religious Cosmopolitanism: Towards Reverse Universality." In *Pluralist Theology: The Emerging Paradigm*, edited by Andres Torres Queiruga, Luiz Carlos Susin, and Jose Maria Vigil, 112–22. London: SCM, 2007.

———. "A Vision for the New Century Role of Religions and Approaches to Christian Mission." In *A Vision of Mission in the New Millennium*, edited by Thomas Malipurathu and L. Stanislaus, 83–114. Mumbai, India: St. Pauls, 2000.

But What Is the Church *For*?

Williams, Jane. *The Holy Spirit in the World Today*. London: Alpha International, 2011.
Woods, Philip. "CWM Perspective on Missional Congregations as Life-Affirming Communities." *International Review of Mission* 103.1 (2014) 77–81.
World Council of Churches. "Together towards Life: Mission and Evangelism in Changing Landscapes." https://www.oikoumene.org/resources/documents/together-towards-life-mission-and-evangelism-in-changing-landscapes.
World Inequality Database. "Home." https://wid.world/wid-world/.
Worsley, Howard. "Mission as Public Theology: Bridging the Worlds of Mission and Religious Education (Re) in Church of England Schools." *Missiology* 46.2 (2018) 171–82.
Wright, N. T. "Paul and Missional Hermeneutics." In *The Apostle Paul and the Christian Life: Ethical and Missional Implications of the New Perspective*, edited by Scot McKnight and Joseph B. Modica, 179–92. Gand Rapids, Michigan: Baker Academic, 2016.
Wrogemann, Henning. *Intercultural Theology: Theologies of Mission*. Downers Grove, Illinois: IVP Academic, 2018.
Xinping, Zhuo, et al., eds. *Toward a Shared, Sustainable Future: The Role of Religion, Values, and Ethics*. Hong Kong: The Amity Foundation, 2018.
Yazell, W. James. "Radical Orthodoxy, Political Ecclesiologies, and the Secular State." *International Journal of Philosophy and Theology* 2.2 (2014) 155–64.
Yong, Amos. "The *Missio Spiritus*: Towards a Pneumatological Missiology of Creation." In *Creation Care in Christian Mission*, edited by Kapya J. Kaoma, 121–33. Oxford: Regnum Books International, 2015.
Yun, Chul Ho. "*Missio Dei Trinitatis* and *Missio Ecclesiae*: A Public Theological Perspective." *International Review of Mission* 107.1 (2018) 225–39.
———. "The Points and Tasks of Public Theology." *International Journal of Public Theology* 11.1 (2017) 64–87.
Zabatiero, Júlio Paulo Tavares. "From the Sacristy to the Public Square: the Public Character of Theology." *International Journal of Public Theology* 6.1 (2012) 56–69.
Zagorin, Perez. *How the Idea of Religious Toleration Came to the West*. Princeton, New Jersey: Princeton Univrsity Press, 2003.
Zahl, David. *Seculosity: How Career, Parenting, Technology, Food, Politics, and Romance Became Our New Religion and What to Do About It*. Minneapolis: Fortress, 2019.
Zizioulas, John D. *The Eucharistic Communion and the World*. Edited by Luke Ben Tallon. Edinburgh: T. & T. Clark, 2011.

www.ingramcontent.com/pod-product-compliance
Lightning Source LLC
Chambersburg PA
CBHW062040220426
43662CB00010B/1579